HEGEL'S SOCIAL ETHICS

Hegel's Social Ethics

RELIGION, CONFLICT, AND RITUALS OF RECONCILIATION

Molly Farneth

PRINCETON UNIVERSITY PRESS

PRINCETON & OXFORD

Published by Princeton University Press,
41 William Street, Princeton, New Jersey 08540

In the United Kingdom: Princeton University Press,
6 Oxford Street, Woodstock, Oxfordshire OX20 1TR

press.princeton.edu

ISBN 978-0-691-17190-6

Library of Congress Control Number: 2017936618

British Library Cataloging-in-Publication Data is available

This book has been composed in Miller

Printed on acid-free paper. ∞

Printed in the United States of America

10 9 8 7 6 5 4 3 2 1

To Ethan

CONTENTS

PREFACE

THIS IS A BOOK for people who care about Hegel and people who don't.

For those who care about Hegel, it draws on important recent work on his epistemology and shows how his account of how we know is linked to his account of how we ought to live. The latter is what I call Hegel's social ethics. Social ethics, on this account, is not primarily about what we ought to do in the face of particular moral quandaries; rather, it is about the relationships, practices, and institutions that a community ought to cultivate. It is about *Sittlichkeit*. A modern *Sittlichkeit*, according to Hegel, involves contestation as well as rituals of reconciliation. Without both of these—practices of conflict and reconciliation—neither his epistemology nor his ethics can be realized. This book shows what those practices are and how they can be sustained in religiously diverse communities.

For those who don't care about Hegel, the book offers something else. It develops a distinct approach to social ethics that attends to conflict and reconciliation in contemporary life. It details how this approach emerged in one significant strand of modern Western philosophy, and it shows what this approach might teach the members of religiously diverse communities about how to talk and listen to one another across difference, build relationships of reciprocal recognition, and forge solidarity in the struggle for justice. While the book includes close readings of passages of Hegel's *Phenomenology of Spirit*, my hope is that readers unfamiliar with the details of Hegel's philosophy will be able to see what is worth seeing in those passages.

This book is itself the result of countless conversations, some contestations, and many relationships of reciprocal recognition. Thomas A. Lewis suggested to me, before I counted myself among those who care about Hegel, that Hegel might have something to add to conversations about religious diversity and democracy. I am grateful to him for that suggestion and for our many conversations about Hegel in the years since. At Princeton University, I was fortunate to work with an extraordinary group of faculty. I owe a particular debt of gratitude to Jeffrey Stout. He has offered sage advice, generous encouragement, and profound criticism, in the right measure and at the right moments. More than that, his example as a teacher and scholar has helped me to imagine a place for myself in this work. Far-ranging conversations about religion, ethics, and democracy with Leora Batnitzky, Eddie Glaude, Eric Gregory, and Cornel West encouraged me, on many occasions, to see the forest and not only the trees.

The book benefited from the generosity of many colleagues who read and commented on portions of the manuscript over the years that I was working on it, including Danielle Allen, Lawrie Balfour, Anna F. Bialek, John Bowlin, David Decosimo, Eric Gregory, Amy Hollywood, Bonnie Honig, Thomas A. Lewis, Louis Ruprecht, Jeffrey Stout, Ronald F. Thiemann, Cille Varslev, James Wetzel, Derek Woodard-Lehman, Kathleen Wright, and the members of the Religion and Critical Thought workshop at Princeton University. The book is much better for their questions, comments, and criticisms. Conversations with Joseph Winters and Kevin Wolfe challenged me to think more deeply about the promises and perils of Hegel's thought and modeled the best of collegiality and friendship. Special thanks to Terrance Wiley, for countless conversations about the ideas at the heart of this book, and to Joel Schlosser, for helping me think about how to bridge the gap between religious studies and democratic theory. Thanks, too, to Michael Lamb and Elias Sacks for their camaraderie and insight. Alda Balthrop-Lewis, Anna F. Bialek, Shira Billet, Emily Dumler-Winckler, and Sarah Stewart-Kroeker have been steadfast companions through the writing and revising process, and they have infused it with their wisdom and good humor.

The book was written with the support of several institutions and organizations. During my years at Princeton University, I received research fellowships from the Center for the Study of Religion, the University Center for Human Values, and the Charlotte W. Newcombe Foundation. The book would barely have been begun, let alone completed, without that support. At Haverford College, the generosity of the Provost's Office made the final stages of research and revision possible. I am grateful to my colleagues in Haverford's Department of Religion—Ken Koltun-Fromm, Naomi Koltun-Fromm, Anne McGuire, and Terrance Wiley—for their support and wise counsel.

It has been a pleasure to work with Princeton University Press. I am particularly indebted to Fred Appel for his guidance through the process. Thanks as well to Jenn Backer, Thalia Leaf, and Jenny Wolkowicki for their assistance and advice. Two anonymous reviewers for the press provided exceedingly thoughtful and insightful feedback on the manuscript that helped me see the project in new ways.

I presented portions of this book at a number of conferences and workshops, and I am grateful to the audiences on those occasions for their feedback. Portions of chapter 2 appeared in Farneth, M. (2013), "Gender and the Ethical Given: Human and Divine Law in Hegel's Reading of the *Antigone*," *J Relig Ethics*, 41, no. 4, 2013, © Journal of Religious Ethics, Inc. and Wiley-Blackwell. Portions of chapters 1 and 4 appeared in Farneth, M. (2015), "Hegel's Sacramental Politics: Confession, Forgiveness, and Absolute Spirit," *Journal of Religion* 95, no. 2, © 2015, Journal of Religion, University of Chicago Press Journals. In both cases, modifications have been made to the originally published text. I am grateful to the publishers for their permission to use that material here.

The epigraph for Chapter 7 is an excerpt from the Preface of *When I Was a Child I Read Books* by Marilynne Robinson. © 2012 by Marilynne Robinson. Reprinted by permission of Farrar, Straus & Giroux; HarperCollins Canada; and Little, Brown and Company, UK. All rights reserved.

I am grateful to Terry Pinkard for permission to use his unpublished translation of the *Phenomenology of Spirit* throughout this book: G. W. F. Hegel, *Phenomenology of Spirit*, facing-page translation, trans. Terry Pinkard, https://www.academia.edu/16699140/Translation_of_Phenomenology_of_Spirit. Where I have altered Pinkard's translation, I note the alteration in the endnotes.

Finally, my parents' goodness and generosity have made everything possible, this book included. I am grateful for their help and that of my in-laws in keeping things afloat over the past year. My daughter, Natalie, has tolerated my work, but, more important, she has offered the best of reasons to set it aside. Ethan has been a source of boundless enthusiasm, support, and good humor, as well as much-needed perspective. For that, and for so much else, I owe him more than I can say.

A NOTE ON PRIMARY TEXTS

IN-TEXT CITATIONS of the *Phenomenology of Spirit* include the paragraph number in Terry Pinkard's translation, followed by the page number in Hegel, *Phänomenologie des Geistes*, Werke 3, edited by Eva Moldenhauer and Karl Markus Michel (Frankfurt am Main: Suhrkamp Verlag, 1970).

For Hegel's "Tübingen Essay," in-text citations include the page number of the English translation in Hegel, *Three Essays, 1793–1795*, edited and translated by Peter Fuss and John Dobbins (Notre Dame, IN: University of Notre Dame Press, 1984), 30–58, followed by the page number in Hegel, *Frühe Schriften*, Werke 1, edited by Eva Moldenhauer and Karl Markus Michel (Frankfurt am Main: Suhrkamp Verlag, 1971). In-text citations of the *Philosophy of Right* include the paragraph number followed by the page number in Hegel, *Grundlinien der Philosophie des Rechts*, Werke 7, edited by Eva Moldenhauer and Karl Markus Michel (Frankfurt am Main: Suhrkamp Verlag, 1970).

Hegel often italicizes words and phrases for emphasis. Any emphasis in quotations of Hegel's text is in the original, unless otherwise stated.

CHAPTER ONE

Social Ethics in Hegel's
Phenomenology of Spirit

ON OCTOBER 14, 1806, Napoleon faced off with Prussian troops outside the city of Jena. It was the middle of the Napoleonic Wars, and this battle was the latest in a series of confrontations between the French and the Prussians. The Holy Roman Empire was collapsing. The Battle of Jena only lasted one afternoon, but the Prussians suffered a devastating defeat.

At the time, G. W. F. Hegel was struggling to make ends meet as an unsalaried lecturer at the University of Jena. He was also working on a long-promised, book-length exposition of his philosophical system. That autumn, he had almost completed it. That book would be the *Phenomenology of Spirit*. In a letter to Friedrich Schelling, Hegel claimed to have finished the book in the middle of the night before the Battle of Jena.[1] He entrusted the final pages of the book to a courier who traveled through French lines to deliver them to Hegel's publisher in Bamburg. Hegel's student Eduard Gans would later write that "under the thunder of the battle of Jena [Hegel] completed the *Phenomenology of Spirit*."[2]

Hegel's *Phenomenology of Spirit* was conceived and written amid great political and social upheaval. Hegel was hopeful about the latent possibilities of his changing society but concerned about the collapse of old communities and ways of life. He watched as political and military alliances shifted, and he wondered what would hold the emerging society together. He anticipated the tensions between individuals and the political entities that would demand their allegiance and sacrifice. At the same time, Hegel noticed and began to theorize the way that traditional roles and duties, including gender roles, were constructed and performed within these local and national communities. He tried to make sense of the apparent authority of these socially constructed norms as well as their capacity to change. What emerged from Hegel's efforts to grapple with these issues was the brilliant and often maddening *Phenomenology of Spirit*—at once a highly abstract treatise on epistemology and an account of ethics rooted in communities.

This book holds these two aspects of Hegel's project together—epistemology and ethics, knowing and living well. In doing so, it gives an account of the relationships and practices that a community ought to cultivate, and of what happens when those relationships and practices are absent or deformed. In the *Phenomenology of Spirit*, Hegel shows what domination looks like and suggests that there is an alternative to it, a way of coping with conflict and forging solidarity. And, while Hegel was no democrat, he describes how conflicts can be confronted and hope for reconciliation sustained through just means in diverse communities. Read in this way, the *Phenomenology of Spirit* has much to teach the denizens of contemporary societies about what democracy ought to be.

The Structure and Movement of Hegel's Phenomenology of Spirit

The abstraction of the *Phenomenology of Spirit*, particularly in its early chapters, may not seem to bode well for social ethics. It is a notoriously difficult text. Hegel uses his own philosophical vocabulary throughout the text, and he warns his readers that the meaning of the terms he uses will only become clear as the book goes on. Their meaning will be specified by their use over the course of the text. Readers, therefore, ought not to import the familiar sense of words like "spirit," "God," "essence," and "absolute" into Hegel's use of them; readers are left in the dark for a long time about how to read and understand these words. This is also true of the argument of the text as a whole. In the preface, Hegel insists that he cannot provide a summary of his argument in advance. Light will dawn gradually. But it is nearly impossible to read or to consider the *Phenomenology of Spirit* without at least having a sense of what kind of text Hegel intends it to be, what his aims are, and what his method is.

In the introduction to the *Phenomenology of Spirit*, Hegel writes that the book is an epistemological project. It is concerned with our knowledge about the world and, in particular, with what "standard" (*der Maßstab*) we might use to assess our claims to such knowledge. An adequate standard would be a yardstick against which our claims could be judged as true, right, or good. Hegel believes that there *is* such a standard, and he promises that we (his readers) will understand what it is by the end of the book. But Hegel also believes that the standard cannot be assumed or specified in advance. We must *arrive* at it through a dialectical process of assessing the strengths and weaknesses of the various standards that one *could* posit.

Hegel refers to the *Phenomenology of Spirit* as a "voyage of discovery"—a voyage undertaken by his protagonist, whom he calls consciousness, in its search for an adequate theory of knowledge. Hegel and his readers only arrive at the destination by undertaking this voyage along with consciousness. The point of departure is the most straightforward account of the standard that consciousness could claim to rely on in assessing the truth or falsity of its judgments. Hegel calls this account "sense-certainty." The voyage leads, through experiences that reveal that initial account's internal conflicts and contradictions, to increasingly complex accounts. Along the way, Hegel and his readers themselves learn from consciousness's experiences.

Hegel characterizes his phenomenological investigation as "the path of *doubt*, or, more properly, as the path of despair" (§78/72). This doubt or despair must be distinguished from Cartesian doubt and Kantian skepticism; it is more like immanent critique. Hegel and his readers track consciousness as it gives an account of itself and its object, finds its account wanting, and reassesses it. Hegel calls this a "self-consummating skepticism" (ibid.), in which he shows what consciousness posits as its standard for assessing its knowledge claims, how it tries to apply this standard in practice, and what its experience of doing so reveals about the inadequacies of the standard that it has set for itself. Hegel shows his readers what the logical consequences of this failure are by way of a subsequent account of the standard that attempts to overcome the problems plaguing the previous one. The goal of the phenomenology, Hegel writes, "lies at that point where knowledge no longer has the need to go beyond itself, that is, where knowledge comes around to itself, and where the concept corresponds to the object and the object to the concept" (§80/74). Through this dialectic, consciousness eventually arrives at an adequate theory of knowledge. Hegel calls this "absolute knowing."

Initially, this story about consciousness's voyage from sense-certainty to absolute knowing may appear irrelevant to what I am calling Hegel's social ethics. By Hegel's own description, the *Phenomenology of Spirit* is concerned with finding the standard against which knowledge claims are judged and conflicts are adjudicated. On this level, it is an epistemological project. But as the story of the *Phenomenology of Spirit* unfolds, it becomes clear that any adequate account of that standard would have to address the social and historical context in which people make knowledge claims. Hegel's account of *spirit*—the collection of norms and norm-generating practices of a form of life—highlights the ways that individuals' knowledge is mediated and judged in a community through its social practices. When Hegel begins to consider spirit, the *Phenomenology of Spirit* becomes a story about *authority*—the authority of norms (whether and why they count as good, right, or true) and the authority of the people who uphold and contest those norms. The ground of authority claimed by consciousness or by a community is, in Hegel's words, its *essence*.[3]

The epistemological project, therefore, is inseparable from the ethical project. Hegel considers what relationships and social practices ought to be cultivated in order to overcome domination and to build solidarity among the members of a community. The relationships and practices that are capable of doing this are characterized by what Hegel calls reciprocal recognition. His discussion of reciprocal recognition comes toward the end of the *Phenomenology of Spirit*. Hegel describes two individuals who have come into conflict but who manage to reconcile with one another through practices of confession and forgiveness. These practices are important because they express and embody each person's recognition of the authority of the other. Each person is a locus of authority—and of accountability—with respect to the other.

Without relationships and practices of the right kind, communities and societies can only be held together by violence, manipulation, or deceit. In what is perhaps the most famous section of the *Phenomenology of Spirit*, Hegel describes the emergence of a relationship between two individuals who find themselves locked in a conflict that results in a life-and-death struggle. Their conflict is overcome, and their struggle comes to an end, only when one of the two gives up the fight, submits to the other, and becomes his bondsman. This is the episode known as the master-slave dialectic or the lordship and bondage section of the *Phenomenology of Spirit* (§178–89/145–50).[4] The lord forces the bondsman to acknowledge his power. Therefore, their relationship is drastically asymmetrical in its distribution of power and accountability. The lord claims power over the bondsman but no accountability for his treatment of him. The bondsman, meanwhile, is accountable to the lord but is not himself recognized as having power or authority. Because of this asymmetrical distribution of power and accountability, the coerced recognition that the bondsman offers the lord cannot possibly satisfy the lord's desire to be recognized as rightfully authoritative.

The lord dominates the bondsman, standing in a position to interfere arbitrarily with his desires, plans, and choices.[5] The master-slave relationship may be the paradigm case of domination, but Hegel shows how the specter of domination hovers over every shape of consciousness or shape of spirit that does not achieve relationships of reciprocal recognition. By the end of the book, Hegel has not only considered domination in its abstract form; he has also discussed practical matters such as slavery, tragedy, the sacrifices of young men in war, burial rites, gender roles, religion, the culture war standoff between religious faith and secular rationalism, and political revolution.

Although Hegel identifies various accounts of the standard of knowledge with other philosophical positions, works of literature, and historical events, the *Phenomenology of Spirit* is not strictly a historical narrative. It does not describe the unfolding of actual historical events, let alone the progressive articulation and actualization of God in history. Instead, it is a conceptual narrative that uses a dialectical method to gradually specify what standard of knowledge a person in Hegel's social and historical context would be entitled to uphold. In the *Phenomenology of Spirit*, the collapse of one position leads to the development of the next in a *conceptual*, rather than historical, sense.

This development unfolds at the level of thought. Hegel does not claim—in the *Phenomenology of Spirit*, at least—that historical events track, in any straightforward way, the conceptual progression presented here. It is not the case, for example, that slavery or bondage was left behind, historically, with the lord and bondsman. Among other problems, that reading would make no sense of Hegel's later invocation of ancient Greek life. Rather, the account of the standard of knowledge that he describes with reference to lordship and bondage is left behind, conceptually, owing to its inadequacies. The account of the standard of knowledge that Hegel describes with reference to Greek *Sittlichkeit*, or ethical life, overcomes those inadequacies (while introducing new problems of its own). On my reading of Hegel, the necessity of the conceptual development does not imply the necessity of historical development. There is nothing inevitable about the practical achievement of nondomination, reconciliation, or solidarity under actual social and historical circumstances.

The *Phenomenology of Spirit* tells its conceptual narrative in three sections, which are divided into eight chapters. Following the preface and introduction, Section A ("Consciousness") comprises three chapters: "Sense-Certainty," "Perception," and "Force and the Understanding"; Section B ("Self-Consciousness") includes only one chapter: "The Truth of Self-Certainty"; and Section C comprises four chapters: "Reason," "Spirit," "Religion," and "Absolute Knowing." The transition from Chapter V ("Reason") to Chapter VI ("Spirit") is particularly pivotal for understanding the book's social and ethical import because it begins with the moment in which consciousness's account of the standard of knowledge acquires its social and historical context. Unlike the first five chapters, which discuss what Hegel calls "shapes of consciousness," Chapter VI focuses on "shapes of spirit." This is a significant shift.[6] Whereas a shape of consciousness is an abstract conceptual scheme—the way a particular person or group characterizes itself, the ground of authority for its beliefs or norms, and its relationship to the world in which it finds itself—a shape of spirit is an embodied form of social life, including its norms and laws, social practices, and language. As Terry Pinkard notes, "A 'shape of spirit' is thus more fundamental than a 'shape of consciousness,'" for it provides the social and historical context in which particular conceptual schemes can even appear as live options.[7] In Hegel's words, "Spirit is thereby the self-supporting, absolute, real essence. All the previous shapes of consciousness are abstractions from it" (§439/325).

In Chapter VI, Hegel discusses a succession of shapes of spirit, considering not only the accounts that individuals and communities within these shapes of spirit give of themselves but also the norms and social practices that appear in them. Hegel presents a progression of people and communities who, for reasons that will become clear, cannot give an adequate account of why their norms, laws, institutions, and practices ought to be binding on them. He describes the ways that these people come into conflict with one another and the ways that their own understanding of the authority of their norms fails to help them confront and overcome these conflicts. Some of these communities and conflicts are familiar to readers. The conflict between Antigone and Creon, which Hegel draws from Sophocles's *Antigone*, ends in tragedy. The standoff between Faith and Enlightenment—Hegel's labels for the kinds of positions held by early modern Pietists and their secular rationalist opponents—devolves into a seemingly intractable culture war. Both of these conflicts are confronted in ways that reveal the inadequacies of those shapes of spirit; the conflicts make it clear that something is wrong with that way of organizing a community and justifying its beliefs, practices, and institutions. Again and again, Hegel describes how shapes of spirit fall apart, only to be replaced by other shapes of spirit that try to compensate for the weaknesses of what came before.[8] It is only at the end of Chapter VI that he depicts a conflict that ends in reconciliation rather than self-destruction—in part because of the conflicting parties' participation in sacramental practices of confession and forgiveness. At that point, full-fledged reciprocal recognition and what Hegel calls "absolute spirit" emerge.

Religion, Ethics, and Post-Kantian Interpretations of Hegel

But what is absolute spirit? The answer to that question is highly disputed among contemporary interpreters of Hegel. It is clear that what Hegel calls "absolute" is the shared object of religion and philosophy. It is also clear that religion and philosophy grasp the "absolute" in different forms, with religion representing it as "God" and philosophy knowing it as "spirit." But interpreters disagree about how to understand these related concepts and the significance of the differences between religious and philosophical reflections on them.

Much scholarship on Hegel contends that his philosophy is thoroughly metaphysical, an attempt to gain knowledge of the absolute through reason, and thus a rejection of Immanuel Kant's critical turn.[9] His concept of spirit, some interpreters hold, is best understood as a divine mind or supernatural entity that manifests and progressively reveals itself in history. A growing number of scholars, however, have challenged this interpretation of Hegel. Such scholars have argued that Hegel's concept of spirit is nonmetaphysical, metaphysically minimalist, and/or naturalist. On this view, *spirit* refers to the collection of norms and norm-generating practices that characterize a community. *Absolute* spirit is that range of norms and practices in which spirit has itself for an object—in and through which members of the community create, sustain, and transform its collection of norms and norm-generating practices. When members of the community are fully self-conscious of this process and their participation in it, they have achieved what Hegel calls absolute knowing. My reading of the *Phenomenology of Spirit* is indebted to this second group of scholars. As I show in the following chapters, this line of interpretation not only is equipped

SOCIAL ETHICS IN HEGEL   [7]

to make sense of some of the most challenging passages in the *Phenomenology of Spirit* but also has the advantage of connecting Hegel's epistemological and ethical thought in ways that continue to resonate for us today.

This body of scholarship is sometimes referred to as the nonmetaphysical interpretation of Hegel. That label can be confusing. Just what is being ruled out when Hegel, or an interpretation of Hegel, is called "nonmetaphysical"? Moreover, the label has had the effect of repelling readers with religious commitments, who worry that a nonmetaphysical Hegel is a Hegel stripped of religious or theological relevance. This is unfortunate. Many of the so-called nonmetaphysical interpretations of Hegel do neglect his relevance for these areas of thought, but that neglect has more to do with the particular interests of the analytic philosophers who have spearheaded this interpretation than with the interpretive moves themselves. In fact, these interpretive moves reveal aspects of Hegel's thought that ought to intrigue and engage theologians and scholars of religion. Religion is everywhere in Hegel's philosophy. To take this fact seriously, and to treat his philosophy of religion with due care, however, is not incompatible with the view that Hegel has rejected precritical metaphysics. The chapters ahead highlight the role that religious communities and practices play in Hegel's account of spirit, and chapter 5 addresses the various senses in which that account may and may not be said to involve metaphysics. In the meantime, to sidestep (some of) the confusion, I will avoid the label "nonmetaphysical" and refer, instead, to "post-Kantian" interpretations of Hegel.

Post-Kantian interpretations of Hegel emphasize Hegel's continuity with Kant and object to interpretations that cast Hegel's philosophy as engaged in the dogmatic metaphysics that Kant tried to rule out.[10] According to Robert Pippin, for instance, Hegel should not be interpreted as rejecting Kantian philosophy and reverting to Spinozistic metaphysics. Instead, he should be interpreted as endorsing and extending central aspects of Kant's project, even as he leaves others behind.[11] For the purposes of this book, the most important of these is Kant's account of the transcendental unity of apperception.

In the Transcendental Deduction in the *Critique of Pure Reason*, Kant argues that the human mind does not passively record data from the sensible world but rather engages in an active process of "unifying the manifold," that is, making judgments about how sensory material ought to be organized.[12] The experience of seeing a table, for instance, is not a matter of the object "table" impressing itself on the mind but rather an activity of organizing relevant sensory material and judging that what one is looking at is a table rather than a jungle gym or a bed. In this sense, representations of objects are normative judgments, true or false claims about the world, undertaken by "apperceiving" (that is, reflective or self-conscious) subjects or, in Kantian terminology, unities of apperception.

With Kant as his starting point, Hegel likewise argues that human beings' experiences of the world—even experiences as commonplace as seeing a

table—involve making normative judgments and, furthermore, that this practical activity is what being a subject entails. Where Hegel extends this claim,
according to Pippin, is in his insistence that these judgments are open to contestation from other self-conscious subjects. Hegel believes that people cannot
make normative judgments of the kind that characterize human beings as self-
conscious subjects unless *other* self-conscious subjects recognize or contest
these judgments. As Hegel writes, "Self-consciousness attains its satisfaction
only in another self-consciousness" (§175/144). In *Hegel on Self-Consciousness*,
Pippin reads the lordship and bondage section of the *Phenomenology* in light
of this interpretation, concluding that Hegel views self-consciousness "as always in a way provisional, as opening up a kind of gap between a subject's initial resolving and any satisfaction of its desire to confirm that what it takes to
be true or right or good is."[13] There is, in other words, a kind of provisionality
to our judgments about the world. We make judgments, and we seek confirmation or recognition that they are correct. For Hegel, self-consciousness is
not a static faculty of the individual mind but an ongoing movement or process that involves making judgments and having those judgments affirmed,
denied, or otherwise contested by someone other than oneself.

The neo-pragmatist philosopher Robert Brandom connects this post-
Kantian aspect of Hegel's thought to Brandom's own philosophy of language,
in order to develop what he calls a semantic interpretation of Hegel.[14] Like
Pippin, Brandom argues that Hegel both draws on Kant's account of the unity
of apperception and insists that such a unity of apperception must be socially
and historically situated. As noted above, Kant thinks that human beings' experiences of the world require judgments. Brandom characterizes these judgments as normative *commitments* for which human beings (as subjects) take
responsibility. As a human being interacts with the world, she acquires new
commitments, some of which may contradict other commitments that she
holds. To become a self-conscious subject—a *unity* of apperception—she must
synthesize a unified set of commitments out of such conflicts.[15]

According to Brandom, Hegel sees (as Kant did not) that this synthetic
unity has an intersubjective dimension. While Hegel agrees with Kant that the
subject is the entity who is responsible *for* his or her commitments, he goes
beyond Kant to suggest that the subject must also be responsible *to* someone or
something. Without this responsibility *to*, there is no normativity. In response
to this problem, Hegel develops what Brandom calls a "recognitive model" of
normative bindingness, in which subjects are responsible *to other subjects* for
their normative judgments, concept use, and so forth.[16] The practices of reciprocal recognition, which include taking responsibility, granting authority, and
holding oneself and others accountable, are all *social* practices. The conflicts
and reconciliations that happen as subjects try to sort out their various conflicting commitments involve members of a community contesting one another's beliefs, norms, and actions and reweaving the fabric of the community in

the face of such conflicts. In Brandom's reading of Hegel, the "inexhaustibility of concrete, sensuous immediacy guarantees that we will never achieve a set of conceptual contents articulated by relations of material inferential consequence and incompatibility that will not . . . at some point lead to commitments that are incompatible, according to those same standards. *No integration or recollection is final at the ground level*."[17] In other words, according to Brandom, people should expect that conflicts will continue to arise. The reciprocal recognition and reconciliation from which absolute spirit emerges are never more than temporary, contestable achievements. Social life must therefore involve *ongoing* practices of contestation and reconciliation.

From Epistemology to Ethics

This emphasis on the social-practical dimension of human knowing places Hegel at the forefront of an intellectual tradition that prioritizes social practice in epistemology and ethics alike. In the United States, Hegel's influence on John Dewey connects him to the tradition of inquiry that animates American pragmatism. Hegel's insistence on the social construction of norms and his recognition of what Pinkard has called "the sociality of reason" are all echoed in Dewey's democratic pragmatism. Like Dewey and other classical pragmatists, Hegel contends that knowledge emerges from the practices of people who share a community.

Meanwhile, contemporary scholars including Brandom, Pinkard, Richard J. Bernstein, Robert Stern, and Jeffrey Stout have asked whether and to what extent Hegel himself might be said to be a (proto-) pragmatist and whether pragmatism has anything to learn from Hegel.[18] Neo-pragmatist reconstructions of Hegel's thought highlight the role that practices of reasoning, deliberation, and justification play in Hegel's theory of knowledge. Despite their attention to these social practices, however, the neo-pragmatists and other Anglophone scholars sympathetic to post-Kantian interpretations of Hegel remain primarily concerned with these social practices' role in Hegel's epistemology rather than his ethics.

The intellectual tradition inaugurated by Hegel's insights into the social construction of norms and the practical basis of normative authority has a second strand, which includes many of the most influential twentieth-century continental philosophers, including Martin Heidegger, Michel Foucault, Pierre Bourdieu, and Judith Butler. Philosophers working in this strand of the Hegelian tradition have been more interested than those in the former strand in Hegel's reflections on power and his relevance for social and political thought.

At times, there has appeared to be an impasse between these two strands of this intellectual tradition. Many Anglo-American philosophers (neo-pragmatists and others) who have championed post-Kantian interpretations of Hegel have emphasized the first half of the *Phenomenology of Spirit* over the second and the epistemologically abstract over the socially, ethically, and polit-ically concrete. Consider Pippin's influential *Hegel's Idealism: The Satisfactions of Self-Consciousness*, which is often seen as a founding text of the post-Kantian line of interpretation. Pippin argues that Hegel has made his philosophical case by the end of Chapter V of the *Phenomenology of Spirit*, after Hegel's discussion of consciousness, self-consciousness, and reason but before his treatment of spirit and religion.[19] The Marxist philosopher Fredric Jameson notes that "Pippin has taught us to reread Hegel's arguments with the respect due a rigor-ous philosophizing, even though he achieves this by a modest lowering of the volume of Hegel's dialectical claims, which are surely what have always excited the latter's followers, not many of whom will be altogether content with the unpretentious Rortyan pragmatism of this new avatar."[20] Jameson worries that post-Kantian interpretations highlight the "philosophical chapters" in the first half of the *Phenomenology of Spirit* at the expense of the "non-philosophical (or 'sociological') chapters" in the second half.[21] Continental philosophers, by contrast, tend to focus on Hegel's master-slave dialectic, as well as his discus-sions of slavery, domination, tragedy, revolution and terror, and sacrifice—that is, Hegel's more obvious claims about power.

These two aspects of Hegel's thought—his epistemology and his account of power, and thus social ethics—need not be held apart. In fact, they are inex-tricably linked. This book contends that an epistemology that attends to social practices opens up to a social ethics that attends to norms, power, and conflict. In the *Phenomenology of Spirit*, Hegel shows the connection between com-munities' accounts of why the things that they believe and do ought to be be-lieved and done—that is, why they have authority—and the practices through which the members of those communities instantiate norms and adjudicate conflicts over them. That connection is at the heart of this book. As I have suggested, the transition from "shapes of consciousness" to "shapes of spirit" in the middle of the *Phenomenology of Spirit* is significant, and the second half of the text requires the careful analysis that the first half has already received from the post-Kantian interpreters. This is particularly pressing because, as Jameson notes, the social, political, and religious themes that have made the *Phenomenology of Spirit* so compelling in continental philosophical circles for the past two centuries have been neglected in this new reading of Hegel.[22] By highlighting the relationships and practices through which ethics and norms are instituted—and the dynamics of power, exclusion, and domination in them—this book bridges the gap between Hegel's post-Kantian interpreters and those animated by continental philosophy.

On my reading, Hegel anticipates many nineteenth- and twentieth-century objections to (and misreadings of) his philosophy. Those who read Hegel as a philosopher of totality, of mediation that ends in absolute spirit, have objected to his supposed claim that mediation could come to an end under present his-torical circumstances (Marx, Kierkegaard, Kojève), while others have objected to his apparent presumption that mediation could come to an end under *any* circumstances (Adorno, Foucault, Derrida). If Hegel's metaphysics are of the sort that traditional interpretations suggest—that is, if Hegel thinks that absolute spirit involves the subject's a priori knowledge of the absolute—then absolute spirit *would* entail closure.[23] But I read Hegel as a philosopher of "mediation without closure."[24] Hegel is committed to the notion that social practices stand at the center of human life. Through social practices, human beings become subjects—and through social practices, these subjects create, maintain, and transform the norms of their shape of spirit. When people reflect on these processes, Hegel claims, the search for a self-sufficient standard of knowledge comes to an end, because they become self-conscious of their participation in the practices by which they institute norms and generate authority. Nothing about this, however, necessitates the end of difference, conflict, or contestation.

In the following chapters, I develop these arguments with two broad goals in mind. The first is to explicate Hegel's *Phenomenology of Spirit* as a work not only of epistemology but also of social ethics, concerned with the evaluation of relationships, practices, and institutions. The book tracks Hegel's account of how ethical conflicts emerge and how they might be confronted and overcome. The second goal is to show the continuing relevance of Hegel's social ethics for a religiously diverse democratic society. Accordingly, this book proceeds in two parts.

Chapters 2–5 present an interpretation of the *Phenomenology of Spirit* that connects consciousness's search for the standard of knowledge to an account of the relationships and practices that communities ought to cultivate. These chapters involve close readings of a series of linked parts of Hegel's *Phenomenology* alongside analysis of the major concepts at play in them. Chapter 2 begins to make the case that, for Hegel, the authority of a community's norms is rooted in its social practices. It considers the lessons of Hegel's discussion of Sophocles's *Antigone*, in which he shows that a community that treats its norms as natural, fixed, and immediately given will be afflicted by tragedy. Chapter 3 turns from immediacy and tragedy to self-legislation and alienation through a discussion of the conflict between Faith and Enlightenment. Faith and Enlightenment believe that individuals must be able to affirm their commitments for themselves, based on objective standards that are available to all. Because they disagree about what those standards are, however, they are locked in a culture war–style impasse. The apparent intractability of their conflict stems from the two sides' inability to recognize the social practices through which members of each group authorize and contest their norms. Chapter 4 describes Hegel's alternative to domination. It compares the relationship between the lord and bondsman in the famous struggle for recognition to the relationship between the wicked and judging consciousnesses near the end of the *Phenomenology of Spirit*. In the latter section, the two individuals' conflict is transformed into a relationship of reciprocal recognition through their practices of confession and forgiveness. I describe the structure of the relationship of reciprocal recognition as one of reciprocal authority and accountability, and I show how this relationship emerges from the sacramental practices of confession and forgiveness. Chapter 5 draws out the implications of these three conflicts for Hegel's account of absolute spirit. Absolute spirit, I argue, is characterized by ongoing diversity, conflict, and disagreement, mediated by rituals of reconciliation that create and repair relationships of reciprocal recognition.

The final chapters of the book move from interpretation to application. There is no straightforward way to apply Hegel's thought to contemporary public life. Hegel's system of philosophy is marked by its own social and historical context. Hegel himself knew this. "Philosophy," as he famously wrote in the preface to the *Philosophy of Right*, "is its own time comprehended in thought" (26).[25] Nevertheless, many of the social, political, and philosophical challenges that confronted Hegel still demand attention. It seems to me that his work continues to provide philosophical resources for thinking about these challenges. Hegel's view of conflict and reconciliation—his social ethics—can help us think about the relationships and practices that sustain diverse communities.

Chapter 6 addresses the relationship between religion and philosophy. It responds to the worry that Hegel's claims about authority collapse into a naturalist view of norms and normativity that is incompatible with respect for religious difference. I engage with the work of contemporary Christian theologians concerned with the nature of authority and argue for the relevance of the Hegelian account to these concerns. While the Hegelian standpoint is at odds with some religious views, it embraces a set of practices for engaging with one another across such differences and disagreements. Finally, chapter 7 offers an account of democratic authority based in the relationships and practices of citizens. In a democratically organized community, citizens' relationships are relationships of reciprocal recognition. Insofar as we call ourselves democrats, we ought to be committed to cultivating practices in which we recognize one another's authority and hold one another accountable. These practices include some, but not all, forms of contestation and conflict, as well as practices of reconciliation. I offer examples of what such relationships and practices have looked like in democratic organizing and restorative justice.

Hegel's *Phenomenology of Spirit* offers an account of the relationships, rituals, and other social practices through which norms are created and transformed, and through which they gain or lose their authority over people and communities. The task of this book is to understand Hegel's claims about what those relationships and practices are and how they work, and to suggest how his social ethics can contribute to how we think about, and do, democracy in our own diverse communities.

CHAPTER TWO

Tragedy and the Social Construction of Norms

IN CHAPTER VI of the *Phenomenology of Spirit*, Hegel develops his idea that the standard of knowledge that consciousness seeks must emerge from the practices of people who share a community and a way of life. In terms of Hegel's epistemological project, this chapter of the *Phenomenology of Spirit* presents and interrogates accounts of the standard of knowledge as they appear, implicitly, in the beliefs, practices, and norms of communities. It is also the point at which the connection between Hegel's epistemological project and his ethical project takes shape. Because the chapter deals with accounts of the standard of knowledge as they appear in communities, it is concerned with the evaluation of relationships, practices, and institutions. It is concerned, in other words, with social ethics.

The chapter begins with Hegel's famous discussion of Greek *Sittlichkeit* and Sophocles's *Antigone*. After providing a romanticized account of Greek *Sittlichkeit*, Hegel turns to the *Antigone* to reveal the internal conflicts that plague that form of life. The play is, of course, a tragedy, and Hegel believes that it offers a paradigmatic example of the tragic conflicts that belie Greek *Sittlichkeit*'s apparent harmony. The central conflict of the *Antigone* is simultaneously a conflict between Creon and Antigone, between the roles and obligations of men and of women, and, more broadly, between human law and divine law. It is, in Hegel's interpretation, a conflict between two sets of one-sided stances, each of which stubbornly asserts itself as fixed and given. Hegel criticizes this view of norms as fixed or given, and he shows that communities that treat norms in this way are internally inconsistent and self-destructive. Their self-destruction takes the form of tragic conflict. An adequate form of life would be one that could overcome this kind of conflict—but not, I argue, conflicts of all kinds. Tragic conflict can only be overcome in a community that acknowledges that naturalized identities and obligations in fact embody normative commitments that may be open to contestation and revision—a community in which people acknowledge their responsibility for creating, sustaining, and transforming their norms.

The chapter proceeds in the following way. First, I briefly discuss the context of Hegel's discussion of the *Antigone* within the *Phenomenology of Spirit*. Second, I offer a close reading of Hegel's description of the collapse of Greek *Sittlichkeit*, drawing attention to two key concepts in the text: character and the acknowledgment of guilt. Based on this reading, I argue in contrast to some of Hegel's feminist critics that Hegel is himself a critic of naturalized gender norms and, indeed, of naturalized norms in general. Finally, I consider the implications of Hegel's view of tragedy for his social-ethical thinking about conflict and reconciliation.

The Context for Hegel's Critique of Greek Sittlichkeit

Hegel's discussion of the *Antigone* responds to a view that was widely held by his contemporaries, according to which Greek *Sittlichkeit* was a harmonious form of life that provided an appealing alternative to the fragmentation and alienation of modern life.[1] Hegel's task in this section of the *Phenomenology of Spirit* is to expose the deep contradictions at the heart of Greek *Sittlichkeit* that make it an unsupportable option for Hegel and his contemporaries.

Here, as throughout the *Phenomenology of Spirit*, Hegel alternates between two modes of analysis. In the first, he describes how the members of a shape of spirit see themselves (what he calls the shape of spirit *for itself*). In the second, he steps back to show his readers a contradiction or conflict within the shape of spirit that its members have not yet seen (i.e., the shape of spirit *for us*). One interpretive challenge facing readers of the *Phenomenology of Spirit* is to keep track of these two modes of analysis, distinguishing between those views that Hegel attributes to others and those that he endorses for himself.

In his discussion of the *Antigone*, Hegel begins with an account of Greek *Sittlichkeit for itself* before offering an account of that shape of spirit *for us*, in which he reveals its self-destructive features. While this chapter focuses on that conflict and self-destruction, it is worth briefly sketching out the apparently harmonious view of Greek *Sittlichkeit* with which Hegel begins.

Participants in the shape of spirit that Hegel calls Greek *Sittlichkeit* believe that their laws, practices, institutions, and other norms have authority simply because they have *always* had that authority. Of the Greeks' conception of their own norms, Hegel writes:

> They *are* and nothing more than that. This constitutes the consciousness of their relations. It is in that way that they count for Sophocles's Antigone as the *unwritten* and *unerring* law of the gods:

Not now and yesterday, but forever,
It lives, and nobody knows from whence it appeared.

They *are*. However much I inquire about their emergence and confine
them to their point of origin, still I have gone far beyond them, since it
is I who am henceforth the universal, and they are the conditioned and
restricted. However much they are supposed to be legitimated through
my insight, still I have already set their unwavering being-in-itself into
motion, and I regard them as something which is perhaps true for me
but perhaps not. An ethical disposition consists precisely in immovably
sticking to what is right and in abstaining from any movement, any
undermining, and any reduction. (§436/321–22)

According to the participants in this shape of spirit, the authority of the
laws that govern human activities is given. These laws simply *are*. To be ethical, on this view, consists of adherence to these fixed and given laws.

The laws that govern Greek *Sittlichkeit* have two sources: the human law
and the divine law. These are taken to be complementary. The human law has
its roots in what Hegel calls the "ethical substance" of Greek *Sittlichkeit*. Ethical substance is the normative spirit of that form of life, including the sense of
peoplehood that animates it and binds its participants. Hegel writes:

Ethical substance is thus the *actual* substance, absolute spirit *realized*
in the plurality of determinately existing *consciousnesses*. The spirit is
the *polity*, which, when we entered into the practical embodiment of
reason itself, was *for us* the absolute essence and which here emerges
in its truth *for itself* as a conscious ethical essence and as the *essence for
the consciousness* which we now have as our object. . . . As the actual
substance, it is *a people*, and as *actual consciousness*, it is the *citizens* of
the nation. (§446/329)

The ethical substance of Greek *Sittlichkeit* is given a concrete form in a body
of laws. This is the human law. Because the human law embodies the ethical
substance that animates Greek *Sittlichkeit*, it is taken as *given*. Hegel writes
that "its truth is the *validity* which is publicly open to the light of day. It is an
existence which, for immediate certainty, takes on the form of existence that
has been made freestanding" (§447/329–30). The human law, as the "freestanding" embodiment of the ethical substance, has, for the participants in
this shape of spirit, a kind of second nature or immediacy. And it is this body
of law that governs the polis and its citizens.

Standing alongside the human law is the divine law. Like the human law,
the divine law is taken as given. It consists of the "*simple* and *immediate essence* of ethical life," those laws and norms that are not considered but simply
accepted (§448/330). Such laws govern the institution of the family. Hegel

writes that "this moment expressing ethical life in this element of *immediacy*, that is, in the element of *being*, or an *immediate* consciousness of itself both as essence and as being this self in an other, which is to say, as a *natural ethical* polity—this moment is the *family*" (§449/330). The family, based in the household, is the site of the natural ethical community that takes the divine law as immediately given and authoritative for it.

The division between the human law and the divine law is accompanied by a series of other divisions—between polis and household, state and the family, and men and women. Men, as citizens, have primary identities and obligations originating in human law and the polis. Women, as noncitizens in Greek *Sittlichkeit*, have primary identities and obligations originating in the divine law and the family. The harmony that this shape of spirit claims for itself depends on the complementarity of each of these divisions. The human law and the divine law, polis and household, state and family, men and women must be reconcilable. For this to be the case, what is taken as the universal ethical substance of the state must be compatible with the natural ethical life of the family.

The harmony of Greek *Sittlichkeit* appears to be threatened by the fact that the family has a tendency to pull away from the polis, to establish itself as an independent and self-sufficient unit. But the polis has a solution for this problem: war. By waging war against an external threat, the polis binds together the disparate units that constitute it. Hegel writes that "in order not to let [the family] become rooted and rigidly fixed within this activity of isolating themselves, an activity which would otherwise let the whole come undone and the spirit within it fade away, the government must from time to time shake them to their core by means of war" (§454/335). Through war, the polis reasserts its transcendence of the family units that constitute it.

The family is bound to the polis in war through the sacrifice of its young men. Husbands, sons, and brothers become soldiers, the family's sacrifice to the state. These soldiers confront death for the sake of the polis. Hegel writes that "death is the consummation and the highest work that the individual as such undertakes for the polity" (§451/332). Faced with death, these young men transcend their familial roles, becoming bound to and identified with the polis that gives meaning to their sacrifice. Hegel writes that "by the labor the government imposes on them, those individuals, who have become more and more absorbed in their own lives and who thereby tend to tear themselves loose from the whole in striving after inviolable *being-for-itself* and personal security, are made to feel their lord, death" (§454/335).[2] By demanding the sacrifice of its citizens, moreover, the polis connects the power of the human law to the power of the divine law that governs death: "The polity therefore has the truth and substantiation of its power in the essence of the divine law and in the realm of the underworld" (§454/335).

The family and the polis are also connected in the burial rites that the women of the family are obligated to perform for men who have died in battle.

Through burial, the family takes what was assumed to be merely natural and contingent, namely *death*, and affirms its social meaning, thereby "interrupting nature's work" (§451/333). Burial reinstates the dead individual as a member of the universal ethical community. In this way, the family serves not only as a natural entity but also as a locus of ethical activity that reconciles the natural and the normative, the family and the community, and the individual and the universal. Hegel writes, therefore, that "this last duty [burial] thus constitutes the consummate *divine* law, that is, it constitutes the positive *ethical* action vis-à-vis the individual" (§452/334). In Greek *Sittlichkeit*, it is a role-specific obligation for women to conduct these rites on behalf of their male family members. This obligation links women to the sacrifices required by the polis. This becomes a crucial issue in the *Antigone*.

The family plays one other recognitive role. For a person to be an ethical subject—a locus of authority and accountability—she must be *recognized* as such by another self-conscious subject. While men are recognized as subjects through their work on behalf of the polis, women who are identified with the family and household are not. Since the relationship between husband and wife is characterized by sexual desire, and the relationship between parents and children is unequal, neither can serve as the basis for recognition in Greek *Sittlichkeit*. The relationship between brothers and sisters, however, can serve this function. The brother-sister relationship is natural but free from sexual desire, and the brother, as a member of the polis, is an ethical subject capable of bestowing recognition. One might object that the disparity between the social roles of brothers and sisters already points to a fundamental inequality in their relationship and, hence, a barrier to reciprocal recognition. At this point in the section, however, Hegel is offering an account of Greek *Sittlichkeit* for itself and is not yet evaluating whether that account is sound. On the account that Greek *Sittlichkeit* would give of itself, women can become ethical subjects through their brothers' recognition, thus securing the harmony of that shape of spirit. Like war and sacrifice, both burial and recognition connect the ethical functions of the family and the polis. The union of man and woman in the family, Hegel writes, is supposed to serve as the mediator between the two, even as man and woman take on distinct roles in Greek *Sittlichkeit* (§462/341–42).

Some commentators have noted that Hegel's dismissal of the possibility of sexual desire between brothers and sisters is puzzling here, given his later discussion of Sophocles's *Antigone*. As Judith Butler argues, for instance, Antigone is an odd representative of the principle of kinship in Greek *Sittlichkeit*, given that she is the offspring of the incestuous relationship between Oedipus and Jocasta and given the intimations of sexual desire and possible incest between Antigone and her brother, Polyneices.[3] We should remember, however, that Hegel is not yet presenting his own view of the matter. At this point, he is giving an approximation of Greek *Sittlichkeit*'s account of itself as a form of life. In using Antigone as a stand-in for "woman" and "kinship," Hegel will demonstrate that these categories are overdetermined in Greek *Sittlichkeit*. Antigone, identified as a woman, is thus understood *within Greek Sittlichkeit* as simply a bearer of divine law and a representative of the principle of kinship, despite the complex details of her genealogy, her desires and loves, and the very obvious ways in which she enters the play as a social and political agent. In this reading, it is not Hegel but Greek *Sittlichkeit* itself that ignores Antigone's particularity and the challenges it poses for the social and political arrangements of that shape of spirit.

With that, Hegel concludes his description of Greek *Sittlichkeit* as it appears for itself. The question remains whether this account of Greek *Sittlichkeit*—as a harmonious and nonalienated shape of spirit—is an adequate one. Does the shape of spirit described in the first part of Hegel's analysis hold up to scrutiny? Turning to Hegel's discussion of the *Antigone* and to his second mode of analysis, we see that his answer is a resounding no.

The Collapse of Greek Sittlichkeit

Hegel turns to Greek tragedy and, in particular, to Sophocles's *Antigone* to identify the internal inconsistencies and inadequacies of Greek *Sittlichkeit*. The *Antigone* is unparalleled in classical literature and modern Western philosophy as an ongoing source of reflection on the tensions between religion and the state, divine and human law, and agency and responsibility. Hegel was taken with these aspects of the play, turning and returning to them at several points in his work.[4]

Sophocles's *Antigone* opens on a terrible scene. Eteocles and Polyneices, the sons of the disgraced and now deceased Oedipus, have been engaged in a struggle for control of the city of Thebes. When Eteocles ascended to the throne, Polyneices gathered an army to wrest control of Thebes from his brother. Both Eteocles and Polyneices were killed in the resulting battle. Their uncle, Creon, assumed the throne and declared that Eteocles would receive a hero's burial while Polyneices would be denied burial as a traitor. Eteocles's and Polyneices's sister, Antigone, has resolved to follow the dictates of the divine law regarding her obligation to bury her kin and, thus, to bury her traitorous and disgraced brother. The play begins with a dialogue between Antigone and her sister, Ismene, in which Antigone announces her intention to bury Polyneices. Ismene refuses to help Antigone and urges her to reconsider her intention, but Antigone's mind is made up. She buries Polyneices. She is caught in the act, however, and, once apprehended, Antigone acknowledges that she has done the deed. Creon condemns her to death. Despite the protestations of his family members and advisors, Creon refuses to reconsider the condemnation until it is too late; by the time he reconsiders and takes action to free Antigone, she has committed suicide and so has her betrothed,

Haemon (Creon's son), and his mother (Creon's wife). The play ends with Antigone dead and Creon ruined. [5]

CHARACTER AND CONFLICT

Hegel begins his discussion of the *Antigone* in the section titled "Ethical action, human and divine knowledge, guilt and fate." He describes how each individual in Greek *Sittlichkeit* comes to be defined by either the human or the divine law, according to his or her gender. He writes:

> Ethical consciousness knows what it has to do, and it has decided whether it is to belong to divine or to human law. This immediacy is a *being-in-itself* and hence, as we have seen, its meaning is at the same time that of a natural being. It is nature, not the accident of circumstances or of choice, which assigns one sex to one law and the other to the other law—or conversely, it is both ethical powers which give themselves their individual existence and their actualization in the two sexes. (§464/343)

At the beginning of this passage, Hegel affirms that each individual, or "ethical consciousness," has *decided* whether to take its identity and obligations from the divine law or the human law. Although this is a decision, it takes on the *significance* of a natural distinction for the Greeks. Thus, Hegel states the Greeks' own view of the matter: that nature assigns the human law to men and the divine law to women. The Greeks believe this gender-based distinction to be natural, rather than contingent or chosen. Immediately, however, Hegel contradicts the Greeks' account, stating, "conversely," that it is the ethical powers themselves that divide and actualize themselves in men and women. Hegel is showing his hand; he will go on to argue that this gender-based division of identities and obligations is socially constructed rather than given or natural. It is not nature but the ethical norms of that shape of spirit that determine which laws apply to which people, even though the members of Greek *Sittlichkeit* do not recognize this. On their view, nature dictates which law applies to each person, depending on his or her sex. Therefore, each ethical consciousness, male or female, takes one of the ethical powers, the human law or the divine law, as determining his or her obligations. The result is that men and women experience themselves as having distinct identities and obligations, each exclusive of and opposed to the other (§465/343).

An individual's decision to follow the human law or the divine law gives rise to what Hegel calls "character." Hegel writes, "Because it has *decided* for *one* of them, ethical consciousness is essentially *character*. It is not the same essentiality of both which exists for ethical consciousness" (§465/343). What are we to make of this term "character"? We have several hints from elsewhere in the *Phenomenology of Spirit*. When Hegel uses the term in other contexts, it refers to something one-sided, and it typically carries the negative connotation of something fixed, stubborn, or incorrigible. For instance, Hegel writes dismissively of the "settled character" of the human brain in misguided scientific efforts to observe reason (§331/250) and later of the "stiff-necked selfsame character" of the judging consciousness who refuses to forgive another in his discussion of confession and forgiveness (§667/490). In his discussion of morality, Hegel provides a more explicit description of character. He writes that self-knowing consciousness is "*immediate*—just like ethical consciousness, it both knows its duty and does its duty, and it belongs to that duty as to its own nature. However, it is not *character*, as was the ethical consciousness, which on account of its immediacy is a determinate spirit and *which belongs merely to one of the ethical essentialities and has the aspect of not knowing*" (§597/442, emphasis added). Like a character in a drama, a character in the sense in which Hegel uses the term here is a person who plays out a role that has been scripted and given to her. A character is one-sided and unreflective or unknowing.

With this conception of character in mind, let us return to the passage at hand. Antigone and Creon, as woman and man, are obligated to obey the divine law and the human law, respectively; that is, each plays a given role, taking her or his character to dictate in an immediate, one-sided, and unreflective way what must be authoritative for her- or himself. Meanwhile, neither Antigone nor Creon recognizes that what is authoritative for her- or himself stems from the same ethical source as that which is authoritative for the other, namely, Greek *Sittlichkeit*. Hegel continues:

> For that reason, the opposition appears merely as an *unfortunate* collision of duty with an *actuality* utterly devoid of right. In this opposition, ethical consciousness exists as self-consciousness, and as such it sets itself to subordinate by force the actuality opposed to the law with which it is associated, that is, to dupe this opposed actuality. Since it sees right only on its own side and sees only wrong on the other, the consciousness that belongs to divine law beholds on the other side human, contingent *acts of violence*; and that consciousness which belongs to human law beholds on the other side the obstinacy and *disobedience* of inward being-for-itself. (§465/343–44)

Antigone and Creon each assume a privileged position relative to the other, condemning the other's position as merely subjective. Antigone views Creon as committing "contingent acts of violence," while Creon views Antigone as willfully disobedient in the name of self-legislation.[6] Because each character takes itself as authoritative over against the other, it proceeds in casting the other character in reductive terms. Believing that the other is merely subjective, each character believes that she or he alone follows an objective law. Hegel writes that each ethical consciousness experiences "the opposition between the *known* and the *not known*" and, therefore, the "absolute *right* of ethical *self-consciousness* comes into conflict with the *divine* right of *essence*" (§466/344). Each experiences an implicit conflict between itself and the other, between what it takes to be authoritative and what the other takes to be authoritative.

This implicit conflict becomes explicit when Antigone and Creon take action. Hegel has presented two characters, each of whom understands her or his identity and attending obligations as immediate and objective, while taking the other to be its antithesis. When Antigone and Creon take action, they each do what they are obligated to do; that is to say, they play the roles assigned to their characters. Antigone obeys the divine law by burying her brother. Creon obeys the human law and attempts to maintain social order by forbidding Polyneices's burial and condemning Antigone for breaking the law. In so doing, however, Creon and Antigone reveal a deep contradiction between the differentiated gender roles on which Greek *Sittlichkeit* stands. When Antigone buries Polyneices, she not only fulfills her obligation to the divine law but also disobeys the human ordinance against his burial. And Creon, in condemning Antigone under the human law, ignores the dictates of the divine law. Hegel writes that "the deed has merely carried out the terms of one law in opposition to the other. However, since it is interrelated in the essence with this other, fulfilling the demands of one law both arouses and provokes demands to fulfill those of the other, and, with the deed having made it so, it provokes the other as a violated and hostile essence now demanding revenge" (§468/347). Simply put, obedience to one law entails the violation—and provocation—of the other.

ACTION AND THE ACKNOWLEDGMENT OF GUILT

This is the pivotal point in the story for Hegel. Antigone is caught in the act of burying her brother and, when confronted by Creon, she acknowledges that she has committed this deed. This acknowledgment, as we will see, entails Antigone's recognition that she is *guilty* of violating the human law. In order to set up this point, Hegel abruptly turns to the Oedipus myth, in which the tragic hero unintentionally kills his father and marries his mother. Hegel writes:

> As concerns the action, only one aspect of the decision itself lies open to the light of day. . . . Hence, actuality keeps concealed within itself this other aspect which is alien to knowledge and which does not show itself to consciousness as it is in and for itself—which neither shows the son that the man insulting him and whom he strikes dead is his father, nor shows him that the queen whom he takes as his wife is his mother. In this way, a power that shuns the daylight preys on ethical

self-consciousness, a power which bursts forth only after the deed is done and when it has taken the deed in its grip. (§468/347)

Hegel suggests that "only one aspect of the decision" is initially clear to the agent. Oedipus intends to kill the man who insults him and to marry the woman whom he desires. But "actuality keeps concealed within itself" aspects of the deed that cannot become clear until the deed is done. At that point, Oedipus's actions prove to have consequences far beyond his intentions. His intended action is bound up with consequences that he neither intended nor anticipated, which is to say that the earlier antithesis between the known and the not-known falls apart. As Hegel writes, "This is so because the completed deed is the sublated opposition between the knowing self and the actuality confronting it" (ibid.). The deed binds the intention to actuality, the actual action and its consequences. Once Oedipus takes action, he can no longer deny his entanglement in something beyond the myopic story that he told himself about who he was and what he was doing. Thus, Hegel concludes, "the agent can deny neither the crime nor his guilt" (ibid.). Oedipus acknowledges and takes responsibility for the full range of intended and unintended consequences of his actions.

According to Hegel, the same is true for Antigone. Antigone takes action, burying Polyneices according to the unwritten law of the gods. Her action violates the human law that forbids Polyneices's burial. Therefore, Hegel insists, Antigone commits a crime against the human law and is guilty of the consequences. This is made more complicated by the fact that Antigone, unlike Oedipus, knows ahead of time that she is following the divine law over against the human law. Taking the latter to be merely human caprice, however, she buries her brother anyway. Because she knew of this opposition beforehand, Hegel writes, her guilt may be more inexcusable than Oedipus's, a point to which we will return momentarily.

In *Antigone's Claim*, Judith Butler criticizes Hegel's interpretation on this point. She argues that Hegel casts Antigone "not as a political figure, one whose defiant speech has political implications, but rather as one who articulates a prepolitical opposition to politics, representing *kinship as the sphere that conditions the possibility of politics without ever entering into it*."[7] Moreover, Butler continues, Hegel inaccurately describes Antigone as confessing to a crime against the human law that she defied, and then he denigrates the principle of kinship (and hence Antigone herself) in favor of the polis. Thus guilt—and the acknowledgment of guilt—plays an important role in Butler's criticism of Hegel. Butler challenges Hegel's claim that "guilt becomes explicitly experienced in the doing of the deed, in the experience of 'breaking through' of one law and in and through another, 'seiz[ing] the doer in the act.'"[8] Antigone, Butler protests, does not seem to feel guilty at all, "even as she acknowledges that the 'law' that justifies her act is one that Creon can regard only as a sign of criminality."[9] She continues:

> [Hegel] distinguishes Oedipus from Antigone, establishing the excusability of his crime, the inexcusability of hers. . . . As if taking the point of view of Creon who cannot get Antigone to perform a full enough confession for him, Hegel concludes this discussion with the claim that "The ethical consciousness must, on account of this actuality and on account of its deed, acknowledge its opposite as its own actuality, [and] must acknowledge its guilt." The opposite of her action is the law that she defies, and Hegel bids Antigone to acknowledge the legitimacy of that law.[10]

According to Butler, Hegel calls Antigone's crime "inexcusable" and wrongly casts her as acknowledging the legitimacy of the human law that she defied over and against the divine law that she obeyed.

Two crucial points in this passage from Butler require further attention. First, Butler mischaracterizes Hegel when she claims that, according to him, Oedipus's crime is excusable while Antigone's crime is inexcusable. Rather, Hegel writes: "Ethical consciousness is more complete and its guilt purer if it both *knows* the law *beforehand* and the power against which it takes an opposing stance, and it takes them to be violence and wrong, to be an ethical contingency, and then, like Antigone, knowingly commits the crime" (§469/348).[11] Hegel states that Antigone's *guilt* (not her crime) is purer (not more inexcusable) than Oedipus's, and it is important to understand exactly what Hegel means by guilt and crime in this context.[12] Throughout the section, Hegel uses the word "guilt" to refer to an objective state of affairs in which a person is responsible for the consequences of her actions, whether or not these consequences were intended. The heroic agent takes responsibility for the action in this full sense, not for the deed narrowly defined by some prior-held intention. To say that the hero acknowledges her guilt in bringing about a state of affairs that she neither anticipated nor endorsed is to say not that she feels badly about that state of affairs but that she recognizes her responsibility for it. Hegel's discussion of Oedipus is clear on this point. Although Oedipus is unaware that he is killing his father and marrying his mother, once he does the deed "[he] can deny neither the crime nor his guilt" (§468/347).[13] Antigone, who knows beforehand that she will violate the human law by burying Polyneices, has as much, if not more, reason to take responsibility for the full range of consequences of her actions. In this sense, Antigone is *objectively responsible* for the violation of the human law—she did the deed—which is the same as saying, in Hegel's words, that her guilt is purer.

This sort of guilt is not unique to Antigone, however. Hegel's interpretation implies that guilt is nearly unavoidable in Greek *Sittlichkeit* because the divisions within that shape of spirit create a situation in which a one-sided character, in playing out her role, will fulfill one law while violating another. A character may recognize her responsibility or guilt only *retrospectively*. She cannot take responsibility for her commitments prospectively because she takes the authority of the law as immediately given to her. Her responsibility is only backward-looking, never forward-looking.[14]

Antigone is held accountable for the intention and consequences of her actions, while she lacks the standing to take forward-looking responsibility for her deeds. Antigone is in a double bind, as she takes responsibility for the consequences of her actions, while failing to recognize her responsibility for the character that comprises her commitments. As we have seen, she takes her character and her commitments to be natural, fixed, and given. Under such conditions, Hegel writes:

> Innocence amounts to non-action, like the being of a stone and not even like that of a child. However, in terms of content, ethical *action* has the moment of crime in itself because it does not sublate the *natural* allocation of the two laws to the two sexes. Rather, within *natural immediacy*, it persists to an even greater degree as a *non-estranged* directedness to the law, and, as activity, it makes this one-sidedness into guilt, grapples with only one of essence's aspects, and conducts itself negatively towards the other, i.e. violates it. (§467/346)

Crime and guilt inevitably follow from Greek *Sittlichkeit*'s supposedly "natural allocation of the two laws to the two sexes." By taking these gender roles to be natural, Greek *Sittlichkeit* assumes that they are not the sort of thing for which people can take forward-looking responsibility. Nevertheless, to act out one of these gender roles, as Antigone and Creon do, leads one to take actions that actualize the human law or divine law while violating the other. This violation leads both Antigone and Creon (and, presumably, everyone else in Greek *Sittlichkeit*) to take retrospective responsibility for something that could not have been otherwise.

There is a second point in Butler's criticism of Hegel that requires further attention. When Hegel writes that Antigone must "acknowledge [her] opposite as [her] own actuality" (or, in Pinkard's translation, "must recognize [her] opposite as [her] own"), Butler is correct to suggest that Antigone's opposite is the human law and, therefore, that Hegel casts Antigone as recognizing the authority of that law. As I have argued, however, this is because the human law is part of the same *Sittlichkeit* that Antigone herself already acknowledges as authoritative. To reiterate a point made earlier, the two characters are products of—and responsible to—the same shape of spirit.

The sentence that Butler quotes in the passage above and the subsequent sentence in the *Phenomenology of Spirit*, which Hegel draws from Sophocles's text, are absolutely crucial for understanding the point that Hegel is trying to make. Let me repeat them here. Hegel writes:

> In terms of this actuality and in terms of its deed, ethical consciousness must recognize its opposite as its own. It must acknowledge [*anerkennen*] its guilt:
> *Because we suffer, we acknowledge that we have erred.*[15] (§469/348)

This passage and the ensuing paragraphs prefigure a discussion of confession and forgiveness that comes much later in the *Phenomenology of Spirit*. At the end of Chapter VI, Hegel describes two modern characters who are embroiled in a conflict of a different sort: between one who acts in the world and one who judges the other's actions. Hegel calls these two characters the "wicked consciousness" and the "judging consciousness." The wicked consciousness takes action in the world, and the judging consciousness condemns the wicked consciousness for acting in a way that sullies dutiful action with subjective intentions and desires. The wicked consciousness recognizes that this is true, not only for itself but also for the judging consciousness who has made the condemnation. The wicked consciousness realizes that the judgment made by the judging consciousness is not simply the "rightful consciousness of action" but also a form of action that can likewise be marked by subjective intentions and desires (§666/489). Therefore, the wicked consciousness confesses (*gestehen*) this realization to the judging consciousness. According to Hegel, the confession is an acknowledgment that what the wicked consciousness had taken as alien to it, namely the judging consciousness, is in fact "the same as himself" (ibid.). Hegel writes:

> His confession [*Geständnis*] is not an abasement, nor a humiliation, nor is it a matter of his casting himself aside in his relationship with the other, for this declaration is not something one-sided through which he would posit his non-selfsameness with the other. On the contrary, it is solely in consideration of his intuition of his *selfsameness* with the other that he gives expression to himself, that is, he gives expression on his own part to *their selfsameness* in his confessions, and he does this because language is the *existence* of spirit as the immediate self. He thus expects that the other will contribute his own part to this existence. (§666/490)

The confession, then, is not an admission of subjective guilt; as Hegel states, it is not an abasement or a humiliation. Rather, it is an acknowledgment of what the two individuals hold in common—in Hegel's words, their selfsameness. Thus, the wicked consciousness confesses, "I am he [*Ich bin's*]" and expects the judging consciousness to say the same. While the judging consciousness initially refuses to do so, his "hard heart" eventually breaks, he recognizes the position shared by himself and the other, and the two consciousnesses enjoy forgiveness and reciprocal recognition.[16]

The conflict and reconciliation between the wicked consciousness and the judging consciousness are crucial to the development of what I am calling Hegel's social ethics, and I look at them in much greater detail in chapter 4. At this point, however, it is worth noting that the Antigone section parallels this later discussion in three illuminating ways. First, like the wicked consciousness, Antigone acknowledges her guilt. As in the later section, this ought not to be understood as subjective guilt—feeling badly—but as objective guilt, that is, responsibility for the intended and unintended consequences of one's actions. Antigone's acknowledgment of her guilt is not an abasement or a humiliation but her recognition that the repercussions of her actions extend beyond the intentions of her one-sided character.

Second, in the acknowledgment of her guilt, Antigone's one-sided character breaks down. Like the wicked consciousness, for whom "it is solely in consideration of this intuition of his *selfsameness* with the other that he gives expression to himself," Antigone "must recognize [her] opposite as [her] own." The word that Hegel uses here, translated as "recognize," is a form of the verb *anerkennen*, which can indicate both acknowledgment and *recognition* in the sense of granting a status to something. Paul Redding helpfully parses the meaning of *anerkennen*:

> Like the English verbs "recognize" and "acknowledge," *anerkennen* has a *performative* dimension: to acknowledge another in some particular way is to acknowledge the *validity* of some implicit claim and thereby bind one's actions in relevant ways. Thus, if I acknowledge some person's greater expertise or knowledge in certain matters, I will in the future, all other things being equal, defer to that person's judgments in such matters. But the word *anerkennen* is also closely connected with its cognates *kennen* and *erkennen*, which have predominantly epistemic senses. . . . A little reflection reveals that these performative and epistemic issues are actually interwoven in quite complex ways. One does not acknowledge another *simpliciter*: one acknowledges another *as* (an expert, prime minister, honest, . . .). That is, performative acknowledgement is itself bound up with hermeneutic issues concerning the recognition of another *as* a certain kind of subject. And conversely, given that *knowing* itself involves a form of "validity claim," that of *truth*, it is bound up in complex ways with acknowledgement as an act.[17]

This word is important throughout the *Phenomenology of Spirit*, including in Hegel's discussion of reciprocal recognition (*gegenseitiges Anerkennen*) in the later confession and forgiveness section. At this point, however, we can see that through her speech act Antigone *acknowledges* her guilt, both in the epistemic sense of accepting the fact of her responsibility *and* in the practical sense of recognizing the validity of the human law that she violated, bestowing a status upon it that she did not previously. This acknowledgment or recognition, Hegel writes, "expresses the sublated conflict between the ethical *purpose* and *actuality*" (§470/348). Because Antigone's character was essentially one-sided and unreflective, it cannot survive her acknowledgment of the human law.

Third, as in the later section on confession and forgiveness, Hegel states that the confession of just one ethical consciousness is insufficient for the resolution of the conflict. He writes that "the victory of one power and its character along with the conquest of the other would thus merely be one part and would be the imperfect work which inexorably advances towards equilibrium" (§471/349). It is crucial to Hegel that *both* characters break down. We have seen how Hegel thinks that Antigone's character breaks down through her acknowledgment of the human law that she violated. Hegel then turns to Creon: "The agent gives up his *character* and the *actuality* of his self and is brought to his downfall. His *being* is to belong to his ethical law as his substance, but in the recognition of the opposition, this law has ceased for him to be his substance, and instead of achieving his actuality, the agent has achieved a non-actuality, a disposition" (§470/438). Creon's downfall comes from his recognition that the human law cannot have the immediate authority that he had ascribed to it. The character—the role that he played out—cannot survive this recognition. Creon, the character, is ruined. Indeed, both Antigone and Creon acknowledge that both the human law *and* the divine law provide partial accounts of Greek *Sittlichkeit*. Hegel writes, therefore, that "the movement of the ethical powers against each other and the individualities which set these powers into life and action have therein reached their *true end* in that both sides experience the same demise. This is so because neither of the powers has any advantage over the other that would make it into a *more essential* moment of substance" (§471/349). Human law and divine law, along with the characters that actualize these laws, have been destroyed by their conflict. Neither side—human law or divine law, man or woman, Creon or Antigone—has the standing to override the claim of the other.

Despite the similarities between these two sections of the text, Antigone fails to reconcile with Creon in the way that the wicked consciousness eventually reconciles with the judging consciousness. Why should that be? Well, despite the fact that Antigone acknowledges her responsibility for the consequences of her actions, she remains stuck in a way of thinking about norms and commitments that takes them to be natural, fixed, and given. So although she is willing to take retrospective responsibility for her action, she cannot assume prospective responsibility for it.

In this way, Antigone and Creon take their gender roles as fixed and given. They shirk responsibility for creating, sustaining, or transforming these roles. They claim responsibility only for the consequences of their actions. Creon does not acknowledge his guilt until after Antigone kills herself and Creon's wife and son have committed suicide. Only then does he cry out, "I'll never pin the blame on anyone else that's human. I was the one, I killed you, poor child. I did it. It is all true."[18] By that time, of course, reciprocal recognition and reconciliation are impossible for Antigone and Creon. Thus, while the human law is initially victorious over the divine law, the condemnation of Antigone ultimately undermines the human law itself: "The achievement of public spirit is thereby transformed into its opposite, and the public spirit experiences that its supreme right is supreme wrong and that its victory is to an even greater degree its own downfall" (§473/351).

When Butler argues that Hegel casts Antigone as acknowledging the legitimacy of the human law, she is correct. But she is only *partially* correct, for Hegel also casts Creon as acknowledging the legitimacy of the divine law. Indeed, in Hegel's discussion of the *Antigone*, both Antigone and Creon do retrospectively recognize their responsibility for the whole of Greek *Sittlichkeit*. Ultimately, however, there is no opportunity for reciprocal recognition either within the play or, as we will see, within Greek *Sittlichkeit* more broadly. Because the ancient Greeks take their immediate understanding of the human law as beyond criticism and of the divine law as infallible, there is no hope for reconciliation in this form of life. The confessions of Antigone and Creon fall on deaf ears.

The Social Construction of Gender and Other Norms

Because Hegel's discussion of the *Antigone* focuses on the conflict between male and female characters in the context of an ancient Greek society organized around strictly divided gender roles, it has been the site of ongoing debate about Hegel's views on gender. Is Hegel presenting an essentialist view of gender? Does Hegel provide resources for feminist philosophy and ethics? Readers have come to dramatically different answers to these questions. For instance, while Judith Butler accuses Hegel of gender essentialism, Robert Brandom claims that Hegel is criticizing that very thing. Indeed, Brandom goes so far as to say that Hegel's critique of gender essentialism in the Antigone section should earn Hegel a place in the "feminist pantheon." Kimberly Hutchings, meanwhile, finds resources in this section for a feminist project but argues that Hegel must be "read against himself" in the passages that follow.[19]

On my reading, Hegel's criticism of Greek *Sittlichkeit* is a criticism of a shape of spirit that takes its norms—including gender norms—to be natural and shielded from scrutiny and critique. As such, Hegel's discussion of the *Antigone* is amenable to the development of a feminist ethics. It is, moreover, an important first step in Hegel's social ethics. The final two sections of this chapter aim to make good on these two claims.

So far, Hegel has shown that Antigone recognizes that her account of what was authoritative for her was incomplete. When she acknowledges her guilt, she sheds her one-sided and unreflective character. She acknowledges that the authority of the divine law cannot be fixed or given. Unlike Hegel's discussion of the wicked and judging consciousnesses, however, his discussion of Antigone and Creon does not end with reciprocal recognition. Instead, it ends with the downfall of Thebes.

In the final paragraphs of the section, Hegel shows that it is impossible to resolve ethical conflict within this shape of spirit. He turns from the play to a broader reflection on its lessons about Greek *Sittlichkeit*, beginning with the issues of war, sacrifice, and death. As we have seen, the independence of the family threatens the unity of the polis in Greek *Sittlichkeit*. The polis responds to this threat by engaging in perpetual warfare and mandating that young men fight on its behalf. While the earlier account of Greek *Sittlichkeit* suggested that this response binds the family to the polis and overcomes the tension between the two, the *Antigone* demonstrates that it does not. Instead, warfare generates resentment, particularly on the part of women. Hegel writes that "since the polity gives itself durable existence only by disrupting familial happiness and by dissolving self-consciousness in the universal, it creates an internal enemy for itself in what it suppresses, which is at the same time essential to it, that is, it creates an enemy in the feminine [*Weiblichkeit*] itself" (§474/352). According to the norms of Greek *Sittlichkeit*, women's obligations are defined by their familial roles as sisters, wives, and mothers. War disrupts the life of the family as young men are recruited for battle and expected to sacrifice themselves to the polis. By disrupting family life and dissolving the individual and family into the polis, it creates an enemy among the guardians of the Greek family—namely, women.

This passage troubles many feminist philosophers who are repelled by the suggestion that women are an "internal enemy" of the polis and who read Hegel as affirming the gender essentialism of Greek *Sittlichkeit*. Some, like Butler, argue that as Hegel abstracts from Antigone to "womankind in general," he reduces her to a mere representative of her gender and thus "effaces her from [the] text."[20] Kimberly Hutchings, who elsewhere argues persuasively against Butler that "to read Hegel as affirming the purity of the realms of divine and human law is to read him in terms of Antigone's and Creon's mistakes about the nature of ethical life," is nevertheless puzzled when Hegel writes in this passage:[21]

> By intrigue, the feminine—the polity's eternal irony—changes the government's universal purpose into a private purpose, transforms its universal activity into this determinate individual's work, and it inverts the state's universal property into the family's possession and ornament.

In this way, the feminine turns to ridicule the solemn wisdom of maturity, which, being dead to individuality—dead to pleasure as well as to actual activity—only thinks of and is concerned for the universal. (§474/352–53)

According to Hutchings's interpretation of this passage, Hegel is making a "generalized transhistorical claim about the role of woman in relation to the community" that is at odds with his earlier criticisms of the dualisms at the heart of Greek *Sittlichkeit*.[22] Hutchings argues that contemporary readers can only account for this passage by reading Hegel against himself: "Hegel's misogyny is confirmed on Hegelian grounds."[23]

But wouldn't it be strange for Hegel to endorse a "generalized transhistorical claim" just paragraphs after arguing that Antigone's and Creon's tragic fates stem from seeing their identities and obligations as fixed and given? This is one place where Hegel's readers must consider what type of analysis Hegel is engaged in—whether he is describing Greek *Sittlichkeit* as it appears *for itself* or describing it as it appears *for us*.[24] In the passage above, it is clear that Hegel is describing Greek *Sittlichkeit*; what is not yet clear is what type of description this is and whether it amounts to an implicit endorsement or criticism of what is being described.

The passage continues as Hegel describes the irresolvable conflict at the heart of Greek *Sittlichkeit*. He writes: "The polity can only sustain itself by suppressing [woman's] spirit of individuality, and, because that spirit is an essential moment, the polity likewise creates it by its repressive stance towards it as a hostile principle" (§474/353). The paradox that he is describing is this: in order to maintain its unity, the polis requires the family to sacrifice young men to fight and die on its behalf. As the guardians of the family and household, women resent this requirement. They are repressed by the state, as Antigone's experience demonstrates, thereby generating further resentment and tension between the family and the polis, which the polis must then struggle once again to overcome. These tensions and conflicts are built into the gender roles and obligations that form the basis of Greek *Sittlichkeit*. It creates, naturalizes, and then suppresses its own "internal enemy" or "hostile principle" in women.

These problems are the result of the particular laws, practices, institutions, and other norms that characterize Greek *Sittlichkeit*; they are neither generalized nor transhistorical. Norms such as gender roles and social obligations are socially constructed. So are the beliefs and practices that govern the relation of family, polis, and external enemies. But in a community like Greek *Sittlichkeit* that takes its norms to be natural, these roles, obligations, and other commitments are all taken as fixed and given. Thus the tensions and conflicts that arise within and among individuals, families, and polis cannot be resolved. Forget about the idealized account of harmonious Greek *Sittlichkeit*; Hegel's discussion of the *Antigone* and the passages that follow it reveal

Greek *Sittlichkeit* to be burdened by the unresolvable conflict between women and men who take their ethical obligations to issue from different, at-times-conflicting, and yet nonrevisable sources. It is in this sense that, within Greek *Sittlichkeit*, the feminine generates that which is suppressed by the polis and yet essential to it. This reveals the instability, self-contradiction, and tragedy that characterize this particular form of life. Because it cannot withstand the inconsistencies between its account of itself and its actual existence, Greek *Sittlichkeit* collapses. It cannot sustain the roles and obligations that define it internally, nor can it maintain the perpetual warfare that defines its borders.

We can now understand the "transhistorical claim" that Hutchings takes Hegel to be making about women at the end of his discussion of Greek *Sittlichkeit*. This claim is best understood as one that *appears* true from within the perspective of Greek *Sittlichkeit*, a shape of spirit that Hegel has shown to be internally inconsistent and self-destructive. Hegel argues that, in Greek *Sittlichkeit*, people *believe* that their norms are natural, generalized, and transhistorical. They believe that women and men have distinct sets of identities and obligations, which are immediately given and unreflectively enacted. What Hegel has argued in this section is that these gendered characters are one-sided, inadequate, and bound for destruction just like Antigone and Creon. Thus, given what I have argued about Hegel's conception of character, the conflict of characters, and the mutual destruction of characters, we should interpret Hegel's reading of the *Antigone* as an argument about the construction of norms. Hegel shows that identities and obligations must *not* be taken as fixed and given—or generalized and transhistorical—and that ethical conflict can only be overcome in a community that acknowledges gender and other identities as normative commitments, open to revision.

This conclusion anticipates contemporary feminist insights about the social construction of gender. Hegel was not, however, a feminist. Despite his criticism of the naturalization of gender roles in the *Phenomenology of Spirit*, he expresses patriarchal and misogynistic views elsewhere in his work. Seyla Benhabib notes this disparity, arguing that Hegel "show[s] a clear awareness of the cultural, historical, and social variations in family and sexual relations. Nevertheless, although Hegel rejects that differences between 'men' and 'women' are naturally defined, and instead sees them as part of the spirit of a people (*Volksgeist*), he leaves no doubt that he considers only one set of family relations and one particular division of labor between the sexes as rational and normatively right."[25] Hegel's apparently misogynistic claims require their own analysis, and it is beyond our scope to consider them here. But it is worth noting that Benhabib's reading of Hegel's discussion of the *Antigone* in the *Phenomenology of Spirit* differs substantially from the reading presented here. According to Benhabib, Hegel's dialectic "will sweep away Antigone in its onward historical march. . . . Spirit may fall into irony for a brief historical moment, but eventually the serious transparency of reason will discipline women and eliminate irony from public life."[26] Benhabib casts the irony that women introduce into Greek *Sittlichkeit* as a form of social criticism worth preserving, but she misses Hegel's own social criticism. On Hegel's view, women appear as the "everlasting irony" of Greek *Sittlichkeit* precisely because of its naturalization of gender norms. It is neither "the feminine" nor the possibility of social criticism that is sublated in Hegel's dialectic but, rather, the notion that laws and other norms should be fixed and given. Hegel highlights the very possibility of contestation of those norms that have been taken as natural.

Tragedy and Social Ethics

Hegel is critical of Greek *Sittlichkeit* as a form of life that takes the authority of its laws and other norms to be fixed and given. Such a form of life will be self-destructive, Hegel suggests, and its self-destruction will take the form of tragic conflict.[27] Let us consider in more detail, then, how Hegel characterizes tragic conflict and its relevance for social ethics.

Tragic conflict, according to Hegel, is a particular form of conflict. Not all conflicts are properly described as *tragic* conflict and not all suffering is *tragic* suffering. Although we commonly use the word "tragedy" and its derivatives to mark particularly terrible or absurd conflicts, catastrophes, or suffering, Hegel uses the word in a more specific and narrow sense. Tragedy, on Hegel's view, is a form of ethical conflict in which two goods or rights stand in opposition to one another, such that the pursuit of one entails the relinquishment or violation of the other. Tragedy, moreover, is characterized by its inevitability, a sense in which the situation could neither have been avoided nor otherwise resolved. The conflict between Antigone and Creon is paradigmatic.

In Sophocles's *Antigone*, Antigone and Creon each hold to one of two opposing and incommensurable rights, and each advances her or his right to the exclusion of the other. This framework, and the conflict that emerges from it, is what draws Hegel to the *Antigone*. As Walter Kaufmann writes, Hegel "realized that at the center of the greatest tragedies of Aeschylus and Sophocles we find not a tragic hero but a tragic collision, and that the conflict is not between good and evil but between one-sided positions, each of which embodies some good."[28] In the *Antigone*, neither Antigone nor Creon has a monopoly on right; each advances a correct claim about the good that she or he ought to pursue according to the laws and other norms of Greek *Sittlichkeit*. Nevertheless, both Antigone and Creon commit a grave wrong in their pursuit of that good.

Sophocles's *Antigone* is also characterized by the inevitability of the conflict and its outcome. Hegel's reading of the play highlights this feature. He characterizes both Antigone and Creon as *characters*. Recall that a character, for Hegel, is a one-sided and unreflective figure. The character plays a role. It is a role over which the character does not have authority; it is given to her, written by someone or something else and unreflectively enacted. As characters in a tragic drama, Antigone and Creon must take responsibility for the terrible consequences of actions that could not have been otherwise without having been granted the authority to determine their own commitments, intentions, and deeds. Their responsibility for their actions and those action's consequences, therefore, can only ever be retrospective or backward-looking.[29]

Hegel holds that there is something wrong in a community in which moral agents take themselves to be characters who cannot claim forward-looking responsibility for themselves or their actions. To act out a role in the way that characters do—to take one's identity and obligations to be fixed, and to take the authority of the norms governing these as immediately given—is to relinquish or never have been granted the responsibility to create, maintain, and transform them. It is to refuse to recognize that a subject is a locus of authority and accountability. A character is thus a deficient subject, and a form of life in which subjects are limited to acting out the role of characters is a deficient form of life. As Hegel shows, it is a form of life plagued by tragic conflict.

One criticism of Hegel's view of tragedy is that it is too closely tied to his account of reconciliation to be particularly *tragic* at all. Martha Nussbaum levels a version of this criticism against Hegel. She contends that Hegel's interpretation of the *Antigone* "locates the deficiency of the protagonists in [their] narrowness or one-sidedness alone, not in their conflict-avoiding aims."[30] According to Nussbaum, this is indicative of Hegel's broader project of eliminating conflict from human interaction. Nussbaum argues that, according to Hegel, "from tragedy we learn not to eliminate [conflict] in the wrong way, by an exclusive attachment to one value and the disregard of others. But we also learn, by implication, how to avoid it correctly: by effecting a synthesis that will do justice to both of the contending claims."[31] On this view, Hegel's point is not only that *tragic* conflict ought to be overcome or eliminated but that all conflict ought to be overcome or eliminated through the sublation of rival positions.

This is the wrong lesson to take from Hegel's discussion of the *Antigone* and his broader view of tragedy. Hegel shows that the tragedies that afflict Greek *Sittlichkeit* are the inevitable result of that shape of spirit; they are the result of deficiencies in its laws, practices, institutions, and other norms and, above all, of deficiencies in its account of the authority of those. If the members of Greek *Sittlichkeit* saw their laws and other norms as contestable— rather than taking them as fixed and their authority as given—they would be faced with conflicts, surely, but not with *tragic* conflicts. Hegel's point here is not that every form of conflict is to be eliminated or avoided, only that the particular form of conflict that arises in Greek *Sittlichkeit* is.

Hegel does think that practices of reconciliation have a role to play in coping with conflict. The shape of spirit in which conflict and reconciliation are co-equal moments in an ongoing dialectic—the shape of spirit that Hegel calls *absolute spirit*—could not have tragic conflict as its paradigmatic form of ethical confrontation. Subjects would understand themselves to be loci of authority and accountability. The authority of their beliefs, norms, and practices would not appear to them as immediately given but would be understood as maintained and shaped by their actions and those of others in their community. Ethical conflicts would persist, but, strictly speaking, they would not be tragic conflicts in the sense that Hegel describes here.

But we are getting ahead of ourselves. There are a few more stops to make before arriving at absolute spirit. I turn now to a different type of conflict—the struggle between Faith and Enlightenment—and a different way of understanding the relationship between action and authority.

CHAPTER THREE

Culture War and the Appeal to Authority

WHEN HEGEL WRITES about the *Antigone*, he highlights the structural features of theatrical Thebes that make the play's tragic outcome inevitable. Its inhabitants have not only a bad account of what the authoritative grounds of their laws and norms might be but also the wrong sorts of relationships and practices for coping with disagreements about those laws and norms.

As a result, Hegel refuses to join his contemporaries in romanticizing Greek *Sittlichkeit*. It would be both impossible and undesirable to re-create that form of life. But neither does he romanticize the present. Hegel acknowledges that modernity *does* appear to be fragmented, with religious and philosophical movements making incompatible demands on modern subjects and claiming different grounds for those demands. Modern life appears beset by conflict, and it is unclear what standards or authorities, if any, could adjudicate between seemingly incommensurable positions. From his earliest essays, Hegel is interested in the role that *religion*—and, particularly, *religious practices*—might play in coping with such conflicts.

This chapter starts to address Hegel's interest in religious practices in processes of conflict and reconciliation. It begins with a brief discussion of Hegel's "Tübingen Essay," in which he argues that a *Volksreligion* or "religion of the people" must include practices that shape people's habits and dispositions. This discussion serves as the background for an analysis of Hegel's treatment of the conflict between Faith and Enlightenment in the *Phenomenology of Spirit*. This conflict reveals the inadequacies of both Faith and Enlightenment as shapes of spirit; in particular, Hegel argues that it reveals the inadequacy of shapes of spirit that ignore the relationship between the rituals and social practices in which its members engage and the standard that they claim to use when they assess knowledge claims. A community's rituals and social practices

are much more closely related to the standard of knowledge than either Faith
or Enlightenment is prepared to admit. The final section of the chapter, then,
steps outside of this dialectical impasse to sketch out Hegel's account of the
relation between social practices and the standard of knowledge.

A Prelude: Religious Practice in
Hegel's "Tübingen Essay"

Motivated by his concerns about the chaos and fragmentation of the rapidly
changing societies of late eighteenth- and early nineteenth-century Europe,
Hegel's early essays attempt to reconcile a conception of *Sittlichkeit* with the
loss of immediacy that accompanies modern reflexivity.[1] These essays explore
the role of religion—in some cases Christianity and in others *Volksreligion*—in
unifying a diverse and fragmented society.[2] In the "Tübingen Essay," Hegel
tries to reconcile Kantian morality, with its emphasis on rationality and the
moral law, with Hegel's own interest in *Volksreligion*. Even when people use
reason to determine the moral course of action, reason alone cannot compel
them to follow this course. Their habits, desires, and passions must be trained
to accord with reason. *Volksreligion*, Hegel argues, can do this work.

Unlike reason, *Volksreligion* comprises practices and communities that
train moral subjects. These practices and communities shape people's habits,
desires, and passions, making them compatible with rationality and morality.
In fact, Hegel argues, a religion's ability to serve this function is the measure of
Volksreligion; Hegel writes that "any religion purporting to be a *Volksreligion*
must be so constituted that it engages the heart and the imagination. Even the
purest/religion of reason must become incarnate in the souls of individuals,
and all the more so in the people as a whole" (52/37).

Unlike those who call for the interiorization or privatization of religion,
Hegel insists on the importance of its public aspects, particularly rituals and
other religious practices. As Thomas A. Lewis characterizes the "Tübingen
Essay," the young Hegel is trying to find a "middle path between radical interiorization of faith that would disregard practice altogether and what he views
as an irrational superstition that views these practices as 'mechanical opera-
tions.' He seeks to give the Enlightenment its due without allowing it to undermine a vital role for religious rituals."[3] Thus, early in the "Tübingen Essay,"
Hegel echoes a Kantian concern about religion when he states that "religion is
sheer superstition whenever I seek to derive from it specific grounds of action
in situations where mere prudence is sufficient, or when fear of divinity makes
me perform certain actions by means of which I imagine that it might be pla-
cated" (37/18).[4] But Hegel does not view all religion, or all religious rituals, as
superstitious. Quite to the contrary, he argues that *Volksreligion* is not only
compatible with but also inconceivable without such rituals.

Volksreligion, Hegel argues, involves both ceremonies and what he calls essential customs. "With regard to ceremonies," Hegel writes, "on the one hand,

no *Volksreligion* is conceivable without them; on the other, nothing is harder to prevent than their being taken by the populace at large for the essence of religion itself" (53/38). Ceremonies are *inessential* customs; they are part of the form that a religion may take, but they are not connected in any necessary way to the content of that religion. Essential customs, by contrast, embody the content of a religion. Hegel names baptism, the Eucharist, and sacrifice as examples of essential customs. The sacraments of baptism and the Eucharist, Hegel argues, are "rites involving certain extraordinary benefits which we as Christians are duty-bound to perform so as to become more perfect, more moral" (ibid.). Sacrifice, likewise, is "part of the [religion's] structure," not in terms of religion's "formal aspect" but in terms of its true content (ibid.).[5] While Hegel is not entirely clear about *what* content is embodied in these rituals, he emphasizes the rituals' essentiality or necessity as an expression and embodiment of the *Volksreligion*. Thus, in this early essay, Hegel argues that certain forms of religious practice are necessary to *Volksreligion* and that *Volksreligion* has a role to play in creating the sorts of subjects who can recognize the standard of knowledge and can act in accordance with it.

Hegel develops these ideas about rituals and social practices in the *Phenomenology of Spirit*. Although he drops the terms *Volksreligion* and "essential customs," he remains committed to the notion that certain religious practices are more than "mere embellishments," that they *do* something, at once expressing a set of commitments and actualizing those commitments in the life of a community. This notion is more complicated than simply the idea that religious practices shape habits and dispositions, although Hegel does appear to endorse that idea as well.[6] Rather, it seems that, on Hegel's account, certain forms of religious practice are wrapped up in the process by which a standard of knowledge is made authoritative, and made *known* as authoritative, for a community. Hegel's account of this process is far too complex to address in a prefatory way, however, so the remainder of this chapter and the following chapter are devoted to clarifying it.

From Greek Immediacy to Modern Alienation

Given how much has been written about the *Phenomenology of Spirit*, it is surprising that so little of the secondary literature has focused on the conflict between Faith and Enlightenment. It is often overshadowed by Hegel's discussion of Greek *Sittlichkeit* and by the final conflict and reconciliation of Chapter VI, in which absolute spirit makes its debut.[7] But the conflict between Faith and Enlightenment is a critical link between these. Hegel's discussion of that conflict offers an immanent critique of two shapes of spirit that refuse to recognize the relationship between their social practices, including religious practices, and the standard of knowledge that each takes as authoritative. In order to understand those shapes of spirit and their inadequacies, we have to backtrack for a moment to see how they emerge from the aftermath of the collapse of Greek *Sittlichkeit*.

That collapse is followed by the rise and fall of several other shapes of spirit, including Roman legal society and European aristocratic culture. As I have argued, Greek *Sittlichkeit* comes to an end when the identities and social roles that individuals experienced as immediate, fixed, and given come into conflict with one another. When this happens, the illusion of harmony is destroyed. At the end of the *Antigone*, the eponymous character is dead by her own hand and her rival, Creon, is ruined. Nevertheless, what Hegel and many of his contemporaries admired about Greek *Sittlichkeit* was their sense that individuals *should* be reconciled with the larger community of which they are a part.

The shape of spirit that follows Greek *Sittlichkeit* in the *Phenomenology of Spirit* lacks both its immediacy and this sense of reconciliation between the individual and the larger community. Whereas Greek *Sittlichkeit* was governed by what were taken to be natural identities and obligations, all of which were supposed to be reconciled in a differentiated but harmonious spirit, this new shape of spirit is governed by a conception of legal personhood that is utterly divorced from individuals' identities and commitments. Hegel writes:

> Since this determinateness [i.e., the determinateness of Greek *Sittlich-keit*] disappears, the life of spirit and this substance, which is conscious of itself in the self-consciousness of all, are both lost. In both of them, the substance emerges as a *formal universality* and no longer dwells in them as a living spirit. Instead, their simple unadulterated individuality has been shattered into a plurality of multiple points. (§475/354)

This new shape of spirit is Roman legal society, in which "persons," as bearers of legal rights, are formal members of the society but have no deeper identification with it in terms of their identities or commitments.

In Roman legal society, as Hegel describes it, legal persons have no particular affinity for the vast empire or its laws. They are not reconciled with it or with one another within it: "As a legal person, each exists for himself, and he excludes continuity with others through the absolute unaccommodating nature of his point-like existence. Those legal persons are thus in a merely negative relationship to each other in the same way that they are in a negative relationship to the lord of the world, who is himself their relation to each other, that is, their continuity with each other" (§481/358). This is a community in only the most formal sense. Legal persons are not bound together by shared beliefs or norms but by the will of the "lord of the world," or emperor, who enforces his will through coercion and the threat of violence. Like the relationship between the lord and bondsman, the relationship between the lord of the world and the legal person is a relationship of domination.

This relationship of domination is also one of *alienation*. The legal person is estranged from the larger community because the latter is governed by laws that are imposed from without: "Since the content alien to legal personality makes itself effective within it, and it makes itself effective because it is their reality, legal personality thus experiences—even more so its complete lack of substance" (§481/358). In other words, the legal person must obey laws and norms that are *alien* to it; they are not laws and norms that the legal person endorses for itself. As a result, the legal person experiences its relationship to the community as one of complete estrangement.

The result is that the legal person retreats into itself, seeking the ground for its commitments not in the lord of the world who dominates but in its own consciousness. Hegel writes that the legal person is *"driven back into itself"* (§482/359). This produces a new set of problems. Because the legal person views the individual and the community as wholly separate and utterly irreconcilable, it "falls apart into two worlds." It posits, on the one side, the empty and contentless interiority of the individual and, on the other side, the determinate but arbitrary content of the community. Each of these, then, takes shape as a distinct shape of spirit. Hegel refers to them as the world that spirit "constructs for itself in the ether of pure consciousness" and the "actual world" (§486/362–63). For the former, the standard of knowledge must rest on the side of the subject, or consciousness. For the latter, the standard of knowledge must rest on the side of the substance, or the world. After Hegel shows what form that latter takes as a shape of spirit—and reveals how it falls apart—he returns to the "ether of pure consciousness" in which Faith and Enlightenment are born.[8]

The Conflict between Faith and Enlightenment

Faith and Enlightenment are two shapes of spirit—or, perhaps more accurately, two distinct variations on a single shape of spirit—that emerge from their estrangement from the "actual world." Both Faith and Enlightenment reject the arbitrary and contingent standards of that world. Such standards cannot be binding on them; they cannot be authoritative. Faith and Enlightenment experience themselves as alienated from these standards, unable to endorse them for themselves. So, they both reject the world and turn inward, seeking authoritative grounds for belief and action within individual consciousness. Faith and Enlightenment disagree, however, about what those grounds might be. Let us consider each in turn.

FAITH

On one side is *Faith*. Faith (*Glaube*) and religion (*Religion*) are related concepts, but Hegel is careful to distinguish between them.[9] Initially, he warns his readers not to confuse Faith with religion proper. He writes that Faith is "not therefore self-consciousness of the absolute essence as it is *in* and *for itself*; it is not religion which is being considered. Rather, it is *Faith* insofar as it is a *flight* away from the actual world and thus does not exist *in* and *for itself*" (§486/363). Whereas religion, on Hegel's account, involves a community's reflection on the absolute in a way that reconciles the community and its practices with the absolute, Faith tries to flee the world and find the absolute in pure consciousness.

But Faith *cannot* really flee the world, for it is a shape of spirit. It is a form of life with its own norms, practices, and communal life.[10] In this sense, it turns out to be a *form* of religion that refuses to recognize the relationship between the absolute and Faith's concrete social life. Hegel explains:

> Just as *religion*—for it is clear that it is religion that is being spoken of—comes on the scene here as the Faith belonging to the world of cultural development, religion does not yet come on the scene as it is *in and for itself.*–It has already appeared before us in other types of determinateness, namely, as the *unhappy consciousness,* as a shape of the substance-less movement of consciousness itself.–In ethical substance it also appeared as a faith in the netherworld. However, consciousness of the isolated spirit is not really *Faith,* not really the essence posited in the element of a pure consciousness which lies beyond the actual. Rather, Faith itself has an immediate presence; its elemental unit is the family.– However, religion has here partly emerged from the *substance* and is the pure consciousness of that substance; this pure consciousness, the *essence,* is in part alienated from its actual *existence.* Thus, it is, to be sure, no longer the movement of substance-less consciousness, but it still bears the determinateness of opposition to actuality as *this actuality* itself, and it is the opposition to the actuality of self-consciousness in particular. It is thus essentially merely a *Faith.* (§527/392)

Hegel tries to clarify his claim that Faith is not "religion *in and for itself*" by comparing Faith to two other forms of religion that appeared earlier in the *Phenomenology of Spirit.* The first of these is the unhappy consciousness. The unhappy consciousness is a shape of consciousness, rather than a shape of spirit; consciousness has not yet taken the social-practical turn that it takes at the beginning of Chapter VI. Therefore, its account of the standard of knowledge is necessarily independent of any norms, social practices, or institutions.

The second form of religion that Hegel mentions in this passage is "faith in the netherworld," the religion of Greek *Sittlichkeit.* He notes that, despite the name, this is not *really* Faith insofar as it affirms the authoritativeness of its social arrangements and practices. Although Hegel has already shown how Greek *Sittlichkeit's* account of this authoritativeness fails, it is distinct from Faith insofar as it recognizes that its concrete social life has some relation to its standard of knowledge and account of authority.

As a shape of spirit, Faith is not *without* substance as the unhappy consciousness is. But its account of the standard of knowledge does not acknowledge that substance. Hegel writes that Faith's *essence*—what it takes to be authoritative for itself—is alienated from its *existence*—its concrete social life. Faith forms communities and those communities' members participate in religious practices, but these communities and practices do not appear in Faith's account of the authority of its commitments. This is what Hegel means when he states that, in Faith, religion does not yet appear *in and for itself*; what Faith is *actually* committed to, as revealed through its life in the world, is different from what it takes itself to be committed to.

Faith, as we have seen, rejects the authority of the "actual world" and seeks authoritative grounds for its beliefs and practices within individual consciousness. For Faith, such grounds are to be found in the experience of, and relationship with, God. Through rituals and other forms of worship, Faith prepares itself for a religious experience that would unify Faith with the triune God whom it takes as authoritative. Hegel writes that "this obedience of service and praise brings forth the consciousness of unity with the essence existing in and for itself" (§533/396). Rituals and worship, in other words, make it possible for Faith to perceive the unity of itself with the standard of knowledge and ground of authority—to perceive that standard as reconciled with itself, rather than alienated from or external to it. Such practices, however, are ongoing, for such reconciliation is never achieved once and for all. Hegel continues, "This service is merely that incessant act of engendering [the unity], an activity which never completely reaches its goal in the present" (ibid.).

In his discussion of Faith, Hegel is once again drawing on historical referents to sketch out a shape of spirit—one form that a community *could* take and the account that such a community *could* give of itself. As usual, Hegel's sketch is driven by conceptual, rather than historical, necessity. Nevertheless, in sketching this shape of spirit, Hegel seems to have in mind both Friedrich Heinrich Jacobi's claim about the primacy of faith over reason and the roots of that claim in Pietism.[11] The Pietists were skeptical of the authority of both rationalism and religious orthodoxy and, instead, focused on the authority of religious experience as a ground of belief. They emphasized the role of religious communities and practices in providing the conditions for the experience of the divine; however, the Pietists did not believe that these practices had any independent authority. To use Hegel's language, they were not taken to be *essential* for the Pietists. This view seems to inspire Hegel's claim that central to Faith's self-understanding is the notion that religious practices may be vehicles for reconciliation with the absolute without being essential or authoritative in themselves.

PURE INSIGHT (OR, ENLIGHTENMENT)

Enlightenment is also fleeing the "actual world." Like Faith, Enlightenment tries to overcome the groundlessness that plagued the previous shape of spirit by identifying objective standards for belief. It shares Faith's rejection of tradition and external authorities as providing such grounds. As Terry Pinkard has pointed out, Faith and Enlightenment share two important assumptions about the grounds of belief and knowledge: first, they share the assumption that "for an agent to know something is to submit it to certain authoritative grounds that are not themselves dependent on any transcendent source for their own authentication (although these authoritative grounds may themselves serve to authenticate belief in something transcendent)," and second, that "for an agent to know something is to be in possession of 'grounds of belief' that hold universally for all individuals."[12] While Faith claims to find nontranscendent, universal grounds for belief in its experience of unity with the absolute, Enlightenment claims to find authoritative grounds in pure insight or critical scrutiny.

For Enlightenment, only rational norms that are self-legislated can be authoritative. This is what Hegel means when he writes that "[pure insight] knows the essence not as *essence* but as the absolute *self*" (§535/397). Thus it "proceeds to sublate all self-sufficiency that is *other* to self-consciousness," that is, it critically scrutinizes and rejects every law, norm, or tradition that appears to self-consciousness as something given to it from outside of itself (ibid.).

Initially, Enlightenment does not affirm a set of commitments of its own. Instead, it claims to offer a standpoint—the standpoint of pure insight—from which to evaluate others' commitments, which appear to Enlightenment as given rather than self-legislated. Regarding itself as a neutral arbiter of this exogenous content, pure insight "is in the first place empty insight whose content appears to it as an other. Hence, in Faith it *comes across* this content in this shape which is not yet its own, as an existence totally independent of it" (§548/405). Because pure insight is supposed to offer a *universal* standard of knowledge and ground of authority, it exhorts others to adopt its rational standpoint by casting aside their own contingencies and particularities. As Hegel concludes the introduction to his discussion of pure insight: "This pure insight is thus the spirit that calls out to every consciousness: *Be for yourselves* what you all are *in yourselves—rational*" (§536/398). This is how Enlightenment confronts Faith. The resulting conflict is what Hegel calls "the struggle of Enlightenment with superstition."

THE STRUGGLE

Enlightenment recognizes what Hegel has already told his readers: that what Faith takes itself to be committed to differs from what Faith's beliefs and actions reveal it to be committed to. In an attempt to expose Faith's errors, Enlightenment launches a three-pronged attack. First, Enlightenment argues that Faith's belief in God is false. According to Enlightenment, there is no being-for-itself other than self-conscious human beings. Because Faith's God is a being-for-itself that exists in an otherworldly beyond, Enlightenment treats this being as it does all exogenous content, as mere prejudice or error.

Second, Enlightenment claims that Faith gives a bad account of how its beliefs are justified. Although Faith claims that its commitments are justified through the experiences and emotions that serve as evidence of its unity with the absolute, Enlightenment argues that the content of Faith's commitments actually depend on "individual pieces of historical evidence," contingent and particular events that cannot support these commitments. Testimony regarding miracles, the transmission of this testimony, and the interpretation of scripture are all contingent and arbitrary historical events that cannot support Faith's beliefs about God. With regard to these first two aspects of Faith, Hegel writes that Enlightenment "knows Faith to be opposed to itself and thus opposed to reason and truth. Just as in its eyes Faith is on the whole a tissue of superstitions, prejudices, and errors, the consciousness of this content is in its own eyes further organized into a realm of errors in which false insight, as the *universal social sphere* [*allgemeine Masse*] of consciousness, is immediate, naïve, and completely without any reflective turn into itself" (§542/401). According to Enlightenment, therefore, Faith's ontological and epistemological claims about God must be false.

Third and finally, Enlightenment attacks Faith's account of its actions. Faith claims to stand in an immediate relation to God, as evidenced by the emotions brought about by religious experience. These experiences, in turn, are prompted by religious practices that take place in the actual world. Enlightenment is puzzled by this account. How can the faithful come to stand in an immediate relation with God, who exists independently of human beings in an otherworldly beyond, by engaging in this-worldly practices? For Enlightenment, there is an insurmountable gap between the transcendent absolute and Faith's immanent social practices. Thus Enlightenment "finds it both foolish and wrong" that Faith's elevation above particularity "should be demonstrated *by way of the deed*, that is, this pure intention is in truth a deception which both pretends and demands to be an *inner* elevation but which takes on the affectation that it is gratuitous, foolish, and even wrong to be serious about *actually putting this into practice* and *demonstrating its truth*" (§556/412).

Enlightenment criticizes, for example, Faith's practices of sacrifice (*Aufopferung*). To demonstrate and reinforce their detachment from this world, the faithful give up certain possessions and pleasures. Enlightenment scoffs at these sacrifices, dismissing them as "wrong and useless" (§569/421). According to Enlightenment:

> The believing, faithful consciousness recognizes the actuality of possessing property and of keeping hold of it and consuming it. In claiming its property, it behaves in an even more isolated and stubborn manner, just as it has even more crudely thrown itself into its consumptive activities, since its religious activity—that of *giving up* possessions and the consumption of them—falls into the other-worldly side of this actuality, and it purchases freedom for itself on that side. In fact, through this

opposition, this service of sacrifice of both natural activities and the activities of consumption has no truth; both the retention and the sacrifice occur together *side by side*. The sacrifice is merely a *sign* that the actual sacrifice has been performed in only a small degree; hence, the sign is in fact merely a *representational thought* of the sacrifice. (§569/421)

Enlightenment argues that Faith's sacrifices are wrong because the faithful sacrifice some possessions and pleasures while holding on to others; their sacrifices can be no more than a symbol of something that they cannot achieve in actuality. Furthermore, Enlightenment claims that these sacrifices are useless because it "finds it simply inept either to discard *a* possession in order both to know and to prove that one is liberated from possession *per se* or to renounce *an* indulgence in order both to know and to prove that one is liberated from indulgence *per se*" (§570/421). Enlightenment ridicules Faith for sacrificing particular possessions or pleasures when its aim is to rid itself of the desire for *all* worldly goods: "Since in the action the *purpose*, which is a universal purpose, and the *execution* of the purpose, which is an individual activity, essentially would have to be present to consciousness in their inadequacy to each other, that action proves itself to be the sort of action in which consciousness has no share, and this action thereby in effect proves to be too *naïve* even to be an action at all. It is simply too naïve to fast in order to prove oneself freed from the pleasures of the table, and it is too naïve to rid *the body* of some other pleasure, as Origen did, in order to show that one has dismissed pleasure" (§570/422). The gap between the universal purpose of the action and what the action actually accomplishes is too great for the action to even be taken seriously. Of Enlightenment's three criticisms of Faith, this is the most important. It is through the conflict over Faith's *practices* that the conflicts over its ontology and epistemology are considered and addressed.

Faith's account of itself—particularly its denial of the authority of its practices—is indeed wrong. Faith cannot, on its own terms, say how its worship of the absolute leads to reconciliation with the absolute. Built into its account of itself is the denial of the authority of the "actual world," so it is unable to specify how its social practices could close the gap between itself and the transcendent absolute. But Enlightenment's criticism of Faith reveals something about itself, too. Enlightenment is also engaged in practices, even as it also denies the authority of the "actual world." How are the Enlightenment's practices of critical scrutiny, for instance, justified, and how can they lead to reconciliation with its conception of the absolute?

Because Enlightenment, like Faith, contends that authority must be grounded in individual consciousness, it holds that the authority of any practice must lie in the agent's *intentions* for that practice, rather than in its meaning or effects in the world. We see this emphasis on intention in Enlightenment's criticism of Faith's practices. The problem with Faith's practices, according to

Enlightenment, is that they intend to do one thing while doing something else instead. Enlightenment wrongly "puts all essentiality into the *intention*, into *thoughts*, and it thereby spares itself from actually accomplishing the liberation from natural purposes" (§571/422). This emphasis on intention blinds Enlightenment to the significance of Faith's practices—a significance that lies in their meaning and effects in the world.

Hegel insists, again and again, that the meaning of an action is irreducible to an agent's intention for that action. Meaning involves not only the agent's intention but also its consequences and others' evaluation of those consequences. By emphasizing interiorized intention, Enlightenment fails to see how social practices work in the world. It fails to see the role that social practices play in transforming the given and in creating and sustaining authority itself. Provisionally, we might say that it is through the concrete social life of the members of a community that the "ether of pure consciousness" and the "actual world" are reconciled. Neither Faith nor Enlightenment can see this from the vantage point of their shape of spirit, even as each points out the shortcomings of the other. That blindness is what leads to their self-destruction.

How Social Practices Create, Sustain, and Transform Norms

In Greek *Sittlichkeit*, individuals immediately identify with the social roles and norms that are assigned to them. This identification, however, comes at the expense of critical scrutiny of that inheritance. The authority of their social roles and norms is taken as fixed or given. What marks Faith and Enlightenment as modern shapes of spirit, in contrast to Greek *Sittlichkeit*, is their effort to find *grounds* for the authority of their social roles and norms. Both Faith and Enlightenment believe that the authority of their social roles and norms comes not from their givenness or immediacy but from their correspondence to a standard that is, in principle, available to any person at any time. When they reject the actual world in favor of the ether of pure consciousness, they reject tradition, social and political authorities, and other contingent grounds for their social roles and norms. They turn inward, seeking universal and timeless foundations for norms in religious faith or reason.

This move overcomes the problems of immediacy that plagued Greek *Sittlichkeit*, but it creates a new set of problems for Faith and Enlightenment. They become alienated from their actual existence in the world. Faith, which claims that the standard of knowledge is accessed through the religious experience of the absolute, cannot give a satisfactory account of the role that worship plays in creating or sustaining norms within the community. Enlightenment, which claims that the standard of knowledge is to be found in universal and timeless reason, refuses to acknowledge its own practices of critical scrutiny as creating or sustaining norms. Moreover, it misunderstands the significance of action in this process. Both of their accounts of the standard of knowledge fail to address the socially and historically situated practices in which they are engaged; they are, in a sense, alienated from their own actions.

Faith's strength lies in the very practices that Enlightenment criticizes. Practices of worship and sacrifice, for instance, connect Faith to the absolute. Nevertheless, Faith does not know this to be the case. Therefore, its account of the relationship between these practices and the authority of its commitments is flawed. Faith claims that the rituals that it performs, and the community with which it performs them, prepare the way for religious experience but are not in themselves essential or authoritative. It is the religious experience itself that provides authoritative grounds for belief and action. Religious practices are, as Pinkard writes, mere "auxiliaries" to what is truly authoritative for Faith.[13] Faith asserts that the standard of knowledge is wholly independent of concrete social life.

What Hegel calls Faith, however, is not disembodied belief. It is, as Hegel puts it, "the spirit of a religious community" (§549/406). For it to be *spirit*, furthermore, "an essential moment [of Faith] is the activity of the religious community itself" (ibid.). From the activity—the religious practices—of this community emerge its norms and standards. Faith does not recognize this. Although Hegel's account of the conflict between Faith and Enlightenment reveals their problems through their criticisms of, and responses to, one another, it is worth stepping back from the details of their dialectical impasse to consider what's at stake here for Hegel's broader account of action and authority.

Recall, from chapter 1, Pippin's argument that Hegel both draws on Kant's account of the unity of apperception and insists that such a unity of apperception must be socially and historically situated. Pippin argues that, with Kant as his starting point, Hegel describes our experience of the world as an ongoing practice of making judgments about the way the world is. The practice of making judgments, furthermore, is what being a subject entails. Where Hegel extends this claim, according to Pippin, is in his insistence that these judgments must be open to contestation from other self-conscious subjects. Hegel argues that we cannot make normative judgments of the kind that characterize human beings as self-conscious subjects unless *other* self-conscious subjects are in a position to affirm or contest *our* judgments. These others not only judge our self-determined judgments; they are also the condition for the possibility of our judgments in the first place. In order to have meaningful commitments, an individual must be a part of a community in which the concepts entailed by those commitments have determinate content.

Robert Brandom's semantic interpretation of Hegel elucidates this complex relationship among commitments, concepts, determinate contents, and communities. Broadly speaking, Brandom agrees with the aspects of Pippin's interpretation of Hegel discussed above, although Brandom characterizes normative judgments as *commitments* for which subjects take responsibility.

Commitments—including judgments about the way things are—involve concepts. For example, my commitment to the statement "The United States is a democracy" involves the concepts "United States" and "democracy." Each of these concepts, in turn, has content—that is, it *means* something. In order for my commitment to be contentful or meaningful, the concepts contained within it and the relationship among those concepts must themselves be meaningful. And the way that concepts become meaningful is through their use. The concept "democracy" has come to mean what it does through countless instances of the concept being used to describe particular social and political arrangements, and those uses being either accepted or rejected. Excepting cases of metaphor, a statement like "this book is a democracy" will cause most anyone in hearing distance to judge me to be confused or incompetent. The concept "democracy" typically does not apply to a book (with something like Walt Whitman's *Leaves of Grass* being the metaphorical exception). But if I state that "the United States is a democracy," the same people are likely to grant that I am a competent concept-user, even if they disagree with my proposition. In that case, I may spark a debate about the concept "democracy," its content, and its legitimate application. Democracy may be a *contested* concept, but it is a *contentful* one nevertheless.[14]

In this way of thinking about concepts, their content is neither entirely up for grabs nor ever settled once and for all. This is because the determinate content of concepts comes from the way that people have used those concepts.[15] When I say that "the United States is a democracy," my interlocutors and I rely on the way that people have previously used the concept "democracy" in order to make sense of my proposition. Those past uses include not only those of political philosophers who have defined the term but also those of journalists who have written about politics, teachers who have given civics lessons, grassroots leaders who have organized citizens, politicians who have campaigned for votes, and citizens who have debated this or that public policy. Contentful concepts are bequeathed to us by these past concept-users, and their past use governs our current use. Nevertheless, we continue the process of specifying the content of concepts as we continue to use old concepts in new situations. Past use governs current use, but it never completely forecloses the possibility of new uses that expand, contract, or revise a concept's content. This is how our concepts evolve.

In order to have contentful commitments—commitments like "the United States is a democracy" as opposed nonsensical commitments like "this book is a democracy"—a subject must be in community with other thinking, acting, and judging subjects who share a set of concepts and a set of practices by which those concepts are used, debated, and revised. This is partly because, as we have seen, the content of the concepts that make up our commitments depends on past concept use. But there is a second aspect to Hegel's claim about the social-practical or intersubjective nature of normativity, and this second point concerns the way that actions express commitments and generate authority.

While Hegel agrees with Kant that the subject is the entity who is responsible for his or her commitments, he goes on to suggest that the subject must be accountable *to* someone. Without this accountability, Hegel contends, there is no normativity. The practices of reciprocal recognition, which I discuss at length in chapters 4 and 5, include taking responsibility for one's commitments, granting authority to others to make and judge commitments, and holding oneself and others accountable for concepts used and commitments held.[16] In and through such practices, commitments, concepts, and their contents are made explicit and available for affirmation, disagreement, or revision.

Enlightenment, as we have seen, "puts all essentiality into the intention." Enlightenment thinks that what is essential or authoritative about an action is the subject's intention for it—her commitment to it under a particular description. Enlightenment fails to see that as a commitment, the subject's intention depends on past social practices for its contentfulness *and* on present social practices for its authoritativeness. In other words, the essence or authoritativeness of the action cannot be limited to the subject's intention for it after all.

When a person undertakes an action, she puts her commitments at risk by subjecting them to the judgment of others. For an action to be *my* action, an intentional action, I have to make a commitment to it. When I act, I make my commitment explicit and I petition the community to recognize my action as mine under the description that matches my commitment. As Brandom writes, "The truth of the performance, what it is in itself, is expressed in *all* of the descriptions of what is actually achieved, all of the specifications of the content in terms of its consequences. These descriptions are available in principle to anyone in the community to recognize the performance under or to characterize its content."[17]

To say that action involves risk is to acknowledge that a subject cannot unilaterally dictate the meaning or content of her action or the community's evaluation of the commitments expressed in the action. This should sound like the claim made earlier about concepts, in which for me to state a proposition like "the United States is a democracy" is to subject my use of the concepts in the proposition (as well as their relation in the proposition itself) to the judgment of other concept-users. Stating a proposition is, of course, one kind of action. What Brandom claims, however, is that all sorts of actions work in this way, making commitments explicit and further determining the content of those commitments in roughly this way. As Brandom writes:

> Th[e] notion of *determinate* conceptual contents is ultimately intelligible only in terms of the *process* of determin*ing* such contents—making them *more* determinate—by seeking the objective fulfillment of subjective practical commitments. If we are to understand the sense in

which subjective commitments and the objective states of affairs they are fallibly responsible to or authoritative over are determinately contentful, we must understand how the processes and practices that are the exercise of intentional agency are intelligible *both* as the mere expression, revelation, and translation from subjective to objective form of already fully determinate contents *and* simultaneously as the means by which initially *less* determinate contents *become more* determinate: the process of *determining* conceptual contents.[18]

People's actions express their already held commitments and submit them to potential challenges by making them explicit. Through action, commitments are expressed and embodied, evaluated in terms of the action's intention and its consequences, potentially transformed in light of this evaluation, and reintegrated in this new form into the subject's set of commitments.

Hegel holds that Faith's religious practices, which Enlightenment has denounced as wrong and useless, are among its greatest strengths. Through these practices, the faithful express their commitments and submit them to other members of the community for evaluation and transformation. Although Faith does not recognize these shared practices as authoritative or essential, Hegel argues that they are. He writes that "*obedience and activity* are a necessary moment through which the certainty of existence within the absolute essence comes about. . . . The absolute essence of Faith is essentially not the *abstract* essence which is supposed to lie in an other-worldly beyond of the faithful consciousness; rather, it is the spirit of the religious community, the unity of that abstract essence and self-consciousness" (§549/406–7). The absolute essence—what is self-sufficiently authoritative—for Faith turns out not to be the experience of unity with the transcendent absolute but the participation in the "spirit of the religious community"—the norms, practices, institutions, and other aspects of Faith's communal life. Faith's sacrifices and worship practices are *necessary moments* that unify the members of the community with that which is actually absolute for them.

Nevertheless, Faith is an *alienated* shape of spirit. Dean Moyar has argued that Hegel's account of alienation is closely related to his account of intention. Moyar describes both in terms of G. E. M. Anscombe's formulation of intentional actions as those to which the question "why did you do that?" pertains.[19] In Anscombe's account, the answer to this question identifies the subject's intentions, the reasons that make the action worth doing for the subject. An *alienated* subject does act intentionally, such that the "why" question pertains, but she is unable to provide reasons for her action that would satisfy the one who asks the question. As Moyar argues, "One is alienated when one recognizes the need to give reasons for one's action, yet those reasons are either unavailable or fail to count as reasons."[20] Alienation is the result of a fundamental failure of recognition.

Alienation in this sense only emerges at a certain point in the *Phenome-nology*'s conceptual progression because the related account of intention only emerges at a certain point. Antigone did not attempt to answer the "why" question, providing reasons for her action to Creon. Nor did Creon ask. In Greek *Sittlichkeit*, one acted the way one did simply because that was the way that things were to be done. That is what makes that shape of spirit *immediate*. Faith and Enlightenment, by contrast, give reasons for their beliefs and actions, and they sense the need to give authoritative reasons. That is what launched Faith and Enlightenment on their search for the grounds for belief in the first place.

This account of alienation as a failure to recognize another's ability to give authoritative reasons for her action highlights the social dimensions of alienation. Faith's grounds for belief, and the reasons that it gives to justify its practices, satisfy the "why" question within the religious community itself. With regard to sacrifice, Faith's answer to the "why" question is "to vanquish desire for worldly goods." With regard to the Eucharist, its answer might be "to make God present" or "to bring about an immediate relation to God." But these practical claims make no sense to Enlightenment, which asserts that only certain kinds of reasons (largely, those based on theoretical reason or empirical evidence) count as satisfactory reasons. As Moyar notes, "The Enlightenment assumes that its question, 'Why?' must be answered in a certain way, a way that faith cannot answer and remain the distinctive practice that it is."[21] Faith, therefore, is alienated in this sense of being unable to provide reasons for its actions that could satisfy the Enlightenment.

Ultimately, in its conflict with Enlightenment, Faith cannot shield itself against the barrage of criticisms leveled against it by its opponent. It cannot provide a satisfactory response to Enlightenment's criticisms of its beliefs and actions because in Faith's own account of itself its communities and religious practices are inessential to its commitments. Its norms lose their apparent authority; the beliefs and practices no longer seem to demand Faith's allegiance. Faith's practical response to Enlightenment's attack is an attempt to further disengage itself from the world, stripping itself of doctrine and religious practices in favor of an increasingly contentless emotionalism. As Hegel writes, "Faith has thus lost the content that brought its element into fruition" and it descends into "pure longing." In this contentlessness, it looks more and more like the deism of some Enlightenment thinkers, who affirm that the universe was created by a supreme being who set in motion the laws of nature but who reject doctrine, ritual, and formal worship all together. Hegel continues:

> [Faith's] truth is an empty *other-worldly beyond* for which there is no longer any adequate content to be found since everything now stands in a different relationship.–Faith has in fact thereby become the same as Enlightenment, namely, the consciousness of the relation between

the finite existing in itself and a predicate-less, unknown and unknowable absolute. The only distinction is merely *that Enlightenment* is *satisfied*, whereas Faith is the *unsatisfied* Enlightenment. (§573/509–10)

Faith is unable to provide any account of the grounds of its belief and action once it strips itself of content in this way. Because Faith claimed that the unmediated relationship to the absolute, attested to by a religious experience of this reconciliation, served as the standard of knowledge, the fact that it can no longer say anything determinate about who God is and what God requires of human beings presents a deep threat to the possibility of knowledge. In other words, absent any content, it is impossible to specify what the faithful can claim to know on the basis of religious experience.

Enlightenment, meanwhile, recognizes the role that self-conscious individuals play in generating norms. Hegel suggests that Enlightenment is correct when it says that "what Faith takes to be the absolute essence is a being of Faith's own consciousness, is its own thought, is something generated by consciousness" (§549/406). Pure insight, Hegel writes, is "conscious of itself as the *mediating* movement, that is, it is aware of itself as *activity*, as engendering" (ibid.). But it does not see that this self-legislation is only possible in the context of a community of other self-conscious subjects. It is not a solitary activity but a social one. Hegel writes that this is what Enlightenment is *in itself*; "it is the still unconscious activity of the pure concept which, to be sure, comes back round to itself as object but which takes this object for an *other* and which is also not even aware of the nature of the concept, namely, that the concept is what-is-without-distinction which absolutely divides itself" (§565/418–19). Enlightenment fails to see that what it takes as authoritative depends on a community of other subjects and their shared practices.

Neither Faith nor Enlightenment recognizes that the other affirms something that it itself lacks. For Faith, this is Enlightenment's insight about self-legislation. For Enlightenment, this is the determinate content generated (although unacknowledged) by Faith's community and practices. But because these two shapes of spirit are alienated from one another—unable to answer the "why" question with reasons that the other would even count as reasons—neither can recognize the insights of the other. Moreover, because they are both premised on the division between the "ether of pure consciousness" and the "actual world," neither is able to affirm the relationship between its standard of knowledge and the social practices in which it engages.

Standing back from Faith and Enlightenment as they appear *for themselves*, Stephen Crites concludes that "*we* see in this exchange of insults merely the pathos of two mutually uncomprehending positions. It is not even tragic, like the conflict between divine and human law in the ethical world, since it is not a conflict between two actual rights, but a polemic between blindness and emptiness, the two sides of an alienated mind."[22] Throughout the section,

Hegel often steps back to show us what these two positions hold in common, what each fails to see about itself and the other, and what modernity might learn from each. Yet, in the context of their struggle, neither learns anything about itself from the other. As Crites suggests, this is not tragedy. It is culture war, early modern style.

Conclusion

Faith and Enlightenment are both conceptually and practically inadequate shapes of spirit. They are conceptually inadequate insofar as they are unable to reconcile their account of themselves and their standard of knowledge with their embodied existence—particularly their social practices. They are practically inadequate insofar as the structure of these shapes of spirit leads to their alienation from one another—their utter failure to recognize the other as a locus of authority. The result is a conflict that leads to the destruction of both.

In this section, Hegel intimates that, properly understood, a community's religious practices ought to be linked to its account of authority and the absolute. In the "Tübingen Essay," as we have seen, Hegel argues that the essential customs of a *Volksreligion*—particularly its sacraments and sacrifices—could be a source of unity among disparate individuals. Religious practices, Hegel claims, can train subjects' habits and dispositions to accord with the dictates of reason. He remains committed to this idea throughout his work. But by the time Hegel writes the *Phenomenology of Spirit*, his view of religious practice is more complex. It is not only the case that religious practices are able to cultivate or habituate rational subjects; more important, perhaps, such practices enable participants' commitments to become contentful, to be generated, sustained, and transformed over time.

To call these practices a source of unity, however, may be misleading. The phrase may imply the "end of history" reading of Hegel, in which the emergence of absolute spirit entails the homogeneity of subjects who have overcome difference and conflict once and for all. This is certainly not what I mean. Rather, Hegel holds out the promise that if subjects understand what they are *in themselves*—socially and historically embedded subjects, engaged in ongoing norm-generating practices—their conflicts will take on a new air. According to Hegel, if subjects understand themselves in this way, they should expect that conflicts will arise as they go about the everyday human business of making commitments and taking action in light of incomplete information about the world, reevaluating those commitments and actions in the face of new information or novel situations, and holding themselves and members of their community accountable for their commitments and practices.

In order to do this work, communities need *both* an adequate account of their standard of knowledge *and* the right sorts of relationships and practices. One challenge is to figure out what these practices are and to cultivate them. As we will see, Hegel is not making a formal point about action here; not every form of action or practice will do. In the Faith and Enlightenment section, Hegel suggests that the very practices that Enlightenment regarded as superstitious—including sacraments and sacrifice—are crucial for contestation, confrontation, and reconciliation. A more detailed account of these practices comes in his discussion of the judging and wicked consciousnesses, and their mutual confession and forgiveness, to which we now turn.

CHAPTER FOUR

Rituals of Reconciliation

AT THE HEART of Hegel's social ethics is his idea of reciprocal recognition. This chapter gives an account of that idea and of the way that social practices make relationships of reciprocal recognition possible. This account takes us through Hegel's discussion of the deformed social relationship between lord and bondsman and into the conflict and reconciliation between what Hegel calls the wicked and judging consciousnesses. These consciousnesses confess to and forgive one another, and Hegel shows that in and through their confession and forgiveness they enter into a new relationship—one of reciprocal recognition that overcomes the domination and alienation of earlier shapes of spirit.

The Concept of Recognition

Hegel's concept of recognition has received considerable attention in recent years, not only from philosophers with exegetical and epistemological concerns but also from political theorists who have developed the idea of a Hegelian politics of recognition as a response to the problems of subordination, exclusion, and marginalization in diverse communities.[1] In spite of this proliferation of scholarship on recognition, however, one of the most influential accounts of Hegel's concept of recognition remains Alexandre Kojève's *Introduction to the Reading of Hegel*. That text, the published version of a series of lectures delivered in Paris in the 1930s, is credited with having revived Hegelian philosophy in twentieth-century France, where it became the interpretation of Hegel with which a generation of continental philosophers wrestled.[2]

In Kojève's interpretation of the *Phenomenology of Spirit*, the struggle for recognition stands front and center. In his *Introduction to the Reading of Hegel*, this is literally true, as the introductory essay in the volume is a commentary on the lordship and bondage section of the *Phenomenology of Spirit*, presented as an interpretive key to the rest of Kojève and Hegel's texts. Because Kojève's lectures were assembled for publication by others, this order of presentation is not his own, although it is consistent with his emphasis throughout the lectures on the struggle for recognition.

In what is perhaps the most famous section of the *Phenomenology of Spirit*, Hegel describes a self-consciousness that takes another self-consciousness as its object. Each views the other as alien to itself, and each desires the elimination of the other. They enter into a life-and-death struggle until one self-consciousness admits that it would rather give up the object of its desire than lose its life. It surrenders and becomes the slave; the other is its master (§178–89/145–50).[3] Kojève interprets this section as a description of the original occasion of an essentially human phenomenon: the desire and the struggle to be recognized by another human being. He calls this the "desire for recognition." Kojève argues that the desire and struggle for recognition distinguish humans from nonhuman animals:

> To be *human*, man must act not for the sake of subjugating a *thing*, but for the sake of subjugating another *Desire* (for the thing). The man who desires a thing humanly acts not so much to possess the *thing* as to make another *recognize* his *right* . . . to that thing, to make another recognize him as the *owner* of that thing. And he does this—in the final analysis—in order to make the other recognize his *superiority* over the other. It is only Desire of such a *Recognition* (*Anerkennung*), it is only Action that flows from such a Desire, that creates, realizes, and reveals a *human*, non-biological I.[4]

Kojève argues that, for Hegel, the desire for recognition and, thus, for domination is *essential* to human personhood, to the "human, non-biological I."

Kojève reads the rest of the *Phenomenology of Spirit* as a set of variations on this foundational theme, in which an individual desires the recognition of another, fights the other to secure that recognition, and satisfies his or her desire only when the other submits. In his reading of Hegel, not only the human being but also history itself is driven by this desire for recognition, a desire with violent and dominating consequences. Kojève writes that "history must be the history of the interaction between Mastery and Slavery: the historical 'dialectic' is the 'dialectic' of Master and Slave."[5] According to Kojève, the relationship between master and slave appears over and over again as the inevitable outcome of a primordial human desire for recognition.

Recent work on Hegel's concept of recognition challenges Kojève's interpretation. In *Hegel's Hermeneutics*, for instance, Paul Redding identifies a set of contradictions in Kojève's interpretation of Hegel's concept of recognition. Redding notes that Kojève sometimes identifies recognition as the precondition for human reality, as when he writes that "human reality can be begotten and preserved only as a 'recognized' reality."[6] Yet Kojève's idea of a primordial *desire* for recognition, which gets the first recognitive relationship off the ground in the life-and-death struggle, presupposes a human reality prior to the existence of recognitive relationships or social structures. We see this second idea at work in the passage quoted above, in which *desire* for recognition "creates, realizes, and reveals" the human being. Redding writes:

> The contradictory nature of these accounts is apparent in the circularity that dogs Kojève's account of the "first" or "original" struggle for recognition. Read as the most basic context within which recognition can occur, the struggle provides an initial *context* within which human intentionality can emerge. And yet for Kojève the struggle is itself motivated by a distinctly human motive—the desire for the "essentially nonvital" end of "pure prestige." That is, while the struggle is conceived as brought about by, *born from*, human desire—the desire for recognition—it is also seen as providing a necessary condition for the emergence or *birth of* the only sort of being capable of having that motive.[7]

This circularity, Redding argues, exposes the flaws of Kojève's reading.[8]

Redding also suggests that there is little textual evidence to support Kojève's interpretation. He notes that the phrase "desire for recognition" does not appear in the section on the life-and-death struggle or its resolution and, furthermore, that when Kojève claims that "according to Hegel, Man is nothing but Desire for Recognition," his textual support is Hegel's quite different sentence, "der Mensch *ist* Anerkennen," or "the human being *is* recognition."[9] According to Redding, Kojève's interpretation elevates one instance of the struggle for recognition and makes it paradigmatic of recognition itself, rather than attending to the different forms that recognition takes in each particular context Hegel describes.[10]

In his own interpretation of the lordship and bondage section, Redding argues that the life-and-death struggle and its resolution present one particular—and, indeed, deficient—recognitive relationship. In the life-and-death struggle, Hegel presents two consciousnesses whose desires come into conflict, giving rise to the new desire, "the desire to eliminate the other."[11] Unlike the previous desire, the object of this desire is not a thing but another being. Through the struggle, each consciousness comes to see that itself and the other are in the same situation—each is a desiring consciousness whose object is also a desiring consciousness. As Redding writes, "Each can recognize that the annihilation each means for the other is simultaneously meant for itself. Thus each now has the opportunity to grasp the 'doubled meaning' of the process in which they are involved."[12]

According to Redding, the "doubled meaning" of the struggle for recognition is the interpretive key to this complex Hegelian concept. He writes:

> Each combatant is a living "Subject-Object" able to recognize itself in an inverted form in that Subject-Object facing it. More specifically, from X's particular perspective, Y is presented as an objective Subject-

Object, that is, an objective being with intentionality. Because X can see its own intentional desire reflected back to it in Y's action, it can grasp *itself* as the subject of that intention. But it can only recognize Y's behavior as intentional because that behavior is directed toward an *object*, and X itself is that object. So X's recognition of Y's behavior as intentional, a recognition that is a precondition for grasping its own subjectivity, also implies that X must grasp its own *objectivity*. It is thereby that each Subject-Object becomes self-conscious of itself *as* Subject-Object.[13]

Hegel's concept of recognition captures the intersubjective structure of self-consciousness itself, as each being, through the struggle, comes to recognize itself as a subject (*being for itself*, in Hegel's terms) as well as the object of another's desire (*being for an other*). Self-conscious subjectivity requires the acknowledgment of this doubled subject-object relation, which is simultaneously a self-relation and self-knowledge mediated through another. To put it another way, to be a self-conscious subject is to be recognized as such by another.

As noted earlier, the German word *Anerkennung*, like its English translation "recognition," has both an epistemic and a practical sense. To recognize something is both to identify it (in an epistemic sense) and to bestow a status on it (in a practical sense). If the United States recognizes Canada as a sovereign state, for example, it both identifies and treats Canada as sovereign in the relevant ways. If the United States were to send its troops into the streets of Toronto and no one in the international community objected, however, there would be an important sense in which Canada turned out not to be sovereign after all. In order to be sovereign, a state must be recognized—both identified and treated—as such. Something similar happens in Hegel's discussion of lordship and bondage. In the resolution of the life-and-death struggle, the lord acknowledges that the bondsman is a subject, but he treats him as if he were merely an object. The lord refuses to *treat* the bondsman as a locus of authority; he refuses to recognize the bondsman's authority in practice. Meanwhile, the lord demands that the bondsman treat him as authoritative.

The relationship between the lord and bondsman is characterized by domination. The lord exercises power over the bondsman but denies accountability. The bondsman is accountable to the lord but has no independent authority. It is a relationship of *deformed* recognition. Hegel argues that the deformations of this relationship make it self-undermining. Thus, as Robert R. Williams argues, "Hegel's master and slave is but an important first phase of unequal recognition that *must* and *can* be transcended. It is not the final, but merely a transitional, inherently unstable, configuration of intersubjectivity."[14] Williams argues Kojève's overemphasis on master-slave relations has made Hegel "appear vulnerable to rather obvious criticisms, particularly

criticisms oriented on the other, otherness, and difference."[15] As a result of Kojève's influence, those working in the continental philosophical tradition have
often wondered whether Hegelian recognition is possible without domination,
particularly when parties to the recognitive relationship have unequal access
to social, economic, or political power.

While Williams is right to raise questions about the centrality of master-
slave relations to Kojève's interpretation of the *Phenomenology of Spirit* as a
whole, there is value in Kojève's attention to deformed social relationships,
including relationships of domination, in which one person is dependent on
the arbitrary will of another. Almost every shape of spirit that Hegel describes
fails to give an adequate account of the authority of its beliefs, practices, and
norms. If that authority is arbitrary or one-sided, then those beliefs, practices,
and norms can only be maintained by deception or the threat of violence. As
Pippin writes, "Hegel's claim to philosophical immortality rests on this novel
attempt to make this distinction between putative claims to normative legitimacy that are in reality exercises of coercive power for the sake of unequal
advantage (nonreciprocal recognitive statuses), and successful claims to normative legitimacy, to do so by beginning with an image of a situation regulated
exclusively by exercises of power, and to show that the ultimate unsustainabil-
ity of such a relation can be demonstrated 'experientially,' or 'internally,' that
ultimate achievement of agent status requires a recognitive social status that
cannot be achieved by exercises of power alone."[16] By focusing on the lord and
bondsman, Kojève trains our eyes to see the arbitrary will-to-power in many
social relationships and forms of life. Now, when we look, we can see domination not only in the relationship between the lord and bondsman but in other
relationships as well: in Creon's condemnation of Antigone and his failure to
listen to her claims, or in Enlightenment's attack on Faith and its refusal to
recognize the faithful as loci of authority.

But the lordship and bondage section is not Hegel's final word on social
relationships. The effort to move beyond deformed relationships and to establish relationships of reciprocal recognition does not end with the struggle
between the master and slave. Rather, it ends much later in the *Phenomenology of Spirit*, where Hegel describes a conflict between two figures whom he
calls the wicked and judging consciousnesses. These two figures confess to
and forgive one another, initiating a relationship in which each sees and treats
the other as a locus of authority and accountability. Their relationship of reciprocal recognition depends not on the triumph of one over the other but on
rituals of confession and forgiveness through which their ongoing conflicts
might be mediated.

Kojève offers an account of reciprocal recognition that is marred by his earlier interpretation of the struggle for recognition. Because Kojève treats the
desire and struggle for recognition as essential to human sociality—and because he thinks that domination is implicit in this struggle—he characterizes

the achievement of reciprocal recognition as a radical break in human history at which point the struggle for recognition is finally overcome. The struggle for recognition and the resulting relations of domination cease only at the "end of history," when human beings achieve a shape of spirit that can universally satisfy the desire for recognition and "dialectically overcome" mastery and servitude. Kojève writes that "history stops when Man no longer acts in the full sense of the term—that is, when he no longer negates, no longer transforms the natural and social given through bloody Fighting and creative Work. And Man no longer does this when the given Real gives him full satisfaction (*Befriedigung*) by fully realizing his Desire (*Begierde*, which in Man is a Desire for universal recognition of his unique personality—*Anerkennen* or *Anerkennung*)."[17] Thus, according to Kojève, the *Phenomenology of Spirit* culminates with the not-yet-realized community in which the desire that drives human history is fully satisfied and in which humans no longer engage in the work of creating and transforming norms, laws, and social structures.

But Kojève's "end of history" view does not make sense of Hegel's discussion of ongoing practices of confession and forgiveness and their role in creating and sustaining relationships of reciprocal recognition. In the rest of this chapter, I explicate the confession and forgiveness section and clarify its implications for Hegel's account of reciprocal recognition.

As he often does in the *Phenomenology of Spirit*, Hegel first presents a new shape of spirit as those within it would characterize it and then presents how he thinks it comes into conflict on its own terms.[18] I follow Hegel's presentation of the section in the same fashion. This requires, first, a discussion of the shape of spirit from which the two conflicting consciousnesses emerge, namely, "conscience." Second, I outline the conflict and its resolution and connect the concept of reciprocal recognition that emerges to insights from chapters 2 and 3 about ritual and, more broadly, social practice. Finally, I discuss the role of practices of confession and forgiveness in the emergence of reciprocal recognition and absolute spirit. When Hegel describes these practices, he draws heavily on Luther's sacramental theology. The logic and structure of the sacraments, Hegel suggests, model the way that social practices, properly understood, can symbolize and actualize relationships of reciprocal recognition.

Conscience

First we need to understand the shape of spirit from which the wicked and judging consciousnesses emerge, which Hegel calls "conscience." Immediately prior to introducing conscience, he discusses a shape of spirit called the "moral worldview." The moral worldview holds, first, that one can identify the moral course of action through introspection of one kind or another; second, that the moral course of action, although self-legislated, nevertheless constitutes an objective and universal duty, such that any individual in the same set of circumstances could and should come to the same conclusion about the moral course of action; and, third, that in taking action, one must be motivated by duty alone in order for the action to count as morally good.[19] The challenge facing the moral worldview, however, is to account for the way that a particular individual's determination of duty can be reconciled with an objective or universal morality. Hegel shows that the moral worldview is unable to provide such an account and, therefore, that it "falls to pieces" (§631/463).

To solve the problems of the moral worldview, a subsequent shape of spirit would need to preserve its idea of self-legislation while overcoming its inability to reconcile the subjective and objective points of view. The shape of spirit that tries to achieve this is "conscience."[20] Like the moral worldview, conscience looks within itself to determine what is authoritative for it. Unlike the moral worldview, however, conscience does not claim that every individual could or should arrive at the same determination about the moral course of action. Whereas the moral worldview thought that morality comprised a set of universal duties, conscience conceives of only one duty: the duty to act in accordance with one's own convictions. This is how conscience claims to overcome the problem of the moral worldview; in conscience's self-understanding, each individual has the same *formal* duty (the duty to act in accordance with one's own convictions), while each supplies his or her own *content* for that duty (the content of the convictions themselves). Thus conscience claims that moral duty is universal, objective, *and* self-legislated.

Conscience also thinks that it has an advantage over the moral worldview insofar as it can avoid the problem of conflicting duties. Whereas the moral worldview was plagued by the problem of multiple and conflicting duties, such that individuals could violate one duty by fulfilling another, conscience has but one duty and does not fear such conflict. Hegel writes:

> It does not conduct itself as the *positive universal medium* within which the many duties, each on its own, would acquire unshakable substantiality so that *either* no action could take place at all, since every concrete case contains opposition per se (and moral cases contain oppositions among duties), since there would thus always be *one* aspect, *one* duty which would be *violated* in the determination of action—*or*, if action does take place, the violation of one of the conflicting duties would actually come on the scene. Conscience is even more so the negative "one," that is, the absolute self which effaces all these diverse moral substances. It is simple action in terms of duty, an action which does not fulfill just this or that duty but which rather knows and does what is concretely right. (§635/467)

According to conscience, the positive universal duties posited by the moral worldview led to either paralysis or tragic conflict since an adherent of the moral worldview could not fulfill one of its moral duties without violating another. Conscience therefore casts itself as a godlike, self-sufficient being whose single duty is to know and to actualize its conviction.

Conscience does not weigh the circumstances or consequences of its actions, for "this actuality is an absolute plurality of circumstances which infinitely divides itself and spreads out backwards into its conditions, sideways into its juxtapositions, and forwards into its consequences" (§642/472). Conscience cannot anticipate all of the conditions, juxtapositions, and consequences of its actions, and it acts without full knowledge of them. Nor can conscience fulfill all of the duties posited by the moral worldview: "Conscience knows that it has to choose among them and to decide because in its own determinateness or in its own content, none of them is absolute, but rather only *pure duty* is absolute" (§643/472). None of this matters to conscience, for the only *absolute* that it recognizes is its own conviction. Because conscience has only one absolute duty, and because the content of this duty depends solely on its internal conviction, neither conflicting duties nor external circumstances and consequences concern it.

Action is initially important to conscience's account of normative authority. To do its duty, an individual must know its conviction and actualize it. This happens in action. Action is "merely the translation of its *individual* content into the *objective* element within which it is universal and is recognized, and it is precisely in the content being recognized that the deed is made into an actuality" (§640/470). An action, on conscience's account, is a conviction that has been translated into an objective form, in which others can recognize it and affirm that the individual has done its duty by knowing this conviction and expressing it: "Its *being-known* is what is recognized and is what *as such* is supposed to have *existence*" (§650/478). Recognition, according to conscience, consists of other individuals' affirmation that the conscientious individual knows and actualizes its convictions.

But what could it mean for others to *recognize* something like convictions, if these are understood as wholly internal states of affairs to which only the individual has access? That is, how can the community assess whether a conscientious individual has fulfilled its duty if it has not only *privileged* but also *exclusive* knowledge of its commitments? In such an account, others can know the conscientious individual's conviction only when its action amounts to a declaration of its conviction. In language, the individual declares its conviction or intention. Hegel writes that "this expression is the true actuality of the activity, that is, is what makes action valid" (§653/479). The individual's declaration validates the action itself. He continues, "Consciousness expresses its *conviction*, and this conviction is that solely within which the action is a duty. It also *counts as* duty solely by virtue of its having *expressed* the conviction, for universal self-consciousness is free from the *merely existent determinate* action. In its eyes, the *action* as *existence* counts for nothing. Rather, what counts is the *conviction* that the action is a duty, and this is actual in language"

(§653/479). The conscientious individual communicates its self-certainty, the knowledge of its duty, through the declaration of its conviction. Like Enlightenment, which claims that the significance of an act lies in the subject's own intention rather than in the act, its consequences, or others' evaluation of it, conscience claims that the significance of an act lies in the individual's own conviction, which is *expressed* in its action. According to conscience, others do not evaluate the act in itself; they simply confirm or deny that the subject's act has expressed her conviction.

Action has already lost its initial centrality in conscience's account of itself and its standard of knowledge. Whereas conscience initially claimed that the individual had to take action in order to translate its conviction into an external and objective form in which it could be recognized, it now claims that the individual must simply assure others that it knows its duty and how to fulfill it. Hegel continues, "To realize the action does not mean here that one translate its content from the form of a *purpose*, that is, from *being-for-itself*, into the form of *abstract* actuality. What it means is that one translate it from the form of immediate self-certainty which knows its own knowledge, that is, its being-for-itself, as the essence, into the form of an *assurance* that consciousness has a conviction about its duty, and that as conscience, duty knows *from its own resources* what duty is. This assurance thus guarantees that consciousness is convinced that its conviction is the essence" (§653/479–80). In addition to downgrading action in its account of its standard of knowledge, conscience implicitly affirms that the content of the conviction and the meaning of the action are determined by the individual. Other conscientious individuals are not essential for the determination of content and meaning but merely for the affirmation of them.

Nevertheless, conscience claims that it achieves a community of reciprocal recognition among conscientious individuals. Each assures the other members of the community of its own sincere convictions, and each recognizes the assurances of others as evidence that the moral duty is being fulfilled. Stephen Crites provides a helpful example of how the recognition of moral conviction works in this shape of spirit. In his example, two conscientious individuals pursue different courses of action when faced with the question of whether or not to bear arms in a war. Each acts according to his conscience, and each recognizes the conviction of the other:

> If I choose to bear arms in warfare—and for the conscientious person such a course is a matter of personal choice and conviction, not as for the citizen of the ethical world a duty simply entailed in citizenship— such an act is subject to multiple interpretations. You may suspect that I am naturally bloodthirsty, or an adventure-seeker, or that I want to impress susceptible women, and so on and so forth. You can never know, on the basis of my deed, whether I am acting conscientiously or

not. Suppose you refuse to bear arms, a refusal subject to an equal variety of possible motives. Still, if you refuse on grounds of conscience you may respect my decision if you believe that it, too, is based on honest conviction, and I may reciprocate with the same understanding. But how can we be sure one another's motives are pure? . . . Answer: I must tell you that I am defending my country as a matter of conscience, and you must likewise speak the conviction according to which you refuse. Of equal importance, furthermore, is the condition that we must believe each other. It is not a matter of arguing our respective cases. It is sufficient to convince each other of the sincerity of our convictions.[21]

A U.S. citizen drafted to military service may become a conscientious objector, refusing to serve if his religious or moral convictions lead him to oppose war. According to the Selective Service System, the conscientious objector's convictions "may be moral or ethical; however, a man's reasons for not wanting to participate in a war must not be based on politics, expediency, or self-interest."[22] In arguing the case for conscientious objector status, the individual must convince the Selective Service of his commitment to pacifism but not the merits of pacifism itself. As in Crites's example, to be recognized as a conscientious objector is to have the relevant community affirm that one's conviction is sincere.

This form of recognition proves to be deficient. Conscience envisions itself as a community of absolute and self-sufficient individuals. Each of these individuals "conducts a worship service within himself, for his action is the intuiting of his own divinity" (§655/481). When these individuals gather together, "this solitary worship service is at the same time essentially the worship service of a *religious community*" in which each declares its own convictions and worships the divinity within itself (§656/481). Their practices of declaration and affirmation amount to mere self-congratulation and sanctimony. Hegel writes that "the spirit and the substance of their bond is thus the reciprocal assurance of both their mutual conscientiousness and their good intentions; it is the rejoicing over this reciprocal purity, the refreshment received from the glory of knowing, expressing, fostering, and cherishing such excellence" (§656/481). The members of this community affirm the authenticity of one another's convictions but do not hold one another accountable for the content, context, and consequences of their actions. The glue that binds the community together is its members' mutual "rejoicing over this reciprocal purity."

The assurance that members of the community provide one another is contentless, for each individual can only provide empty affirmation of the other's claim about its conviction. There can be no question, in conscience's account of itself, of whether the conviction is good or right or true. Hegel writes that "its intention, as a result of being its own intention, is what is right, and the only requirement is that it should both know this and state its conviction that its knowing and willing are right" (§654/480). This self-certainty—the sense that only the individual can know its own intentions and, moreover, that it can know them perfectly—mars conscience's account of intention. If the individual has privileged and infallible access to its intentions, and if the deed and its consequences have no relevance for the community's assessment of it, then members of the community can do nothing but nod in assent to the conscientious individual's statement of its convictions. Moreover, if the determination of content lies entirely in the hands of the individual, then the social practice of mutual assurance adds nothing. In a stunning passage, Hegel concludes that "absolute self-certainty is immediately converted into a dying sound, into the objectivity of its being-for-itself, but this created world is its *speech*, which it has likewise immediately heard and whose echo is all that returns to it" (§658/483).

Throughout the *Phenomenology of Spirit*, as we have seen, consciousness has been searching for an account of the standard of knowledge—the yardstick against which beliefs and actions can be judged. It has come to realize that this account must address the concrete forms of social life in which knowledge claims are made, acted upon, judged, and so forth. Conscience represents a breakthrough for consciousness insofar as it is aware of the role that *action* plays in mediating between individual self-consciousness and embodied social life. Conscience's understanding of how action plays this role, however, remains insufficient. Because conscience views action as the translation of subjective content into objective form, authority remains one-sidedly subjective. Conscience takes the content or meaning of an action to be fully captured by the individual's conviction. Other members of the community can affirm the declared conviction, but they cannot judge it. Their affirmation, therefore, is contentless; it adds nothing to the conviction that the subject already holds. The "solitary worship service" that each individual conducts has no rituals or social practices that express or generate shared beliefs or values of the community. There is only the declaration of subjective conviction and the empty affirmation of it. Knowing that the affirmation of the community is contentless—a mere echo of the individual's own declaration—conscience realizes that it has not resolved the problems facing the moral worldview after all. The moral worldview was unable to provide an account of how the individual's determination of duty was reconciled with an objective or universal morality. In similar fashion, conscience cannot provide an adequate account of how the individual's action fulfills the universal duty. The mutual assurances of conscientious individuals, which were initially taken as the community's recognition of the fulfillment of that duty, turn out to be empty.

Unlike the triune God worshipped by Faith, who unites spirit and substance by entering the world as the incarnate Son, the internal divinity worshipped by the conscientious individual refuses to engage in the world of action and judgment. Hegel writes that conscience "lacks the power to empty itself [*die Kraft der Entäußerung*], that is, lacks the power to make itself into a thing and to suffer the burden of being" (§658/483).[23] Like the moral worldview before it, therefore, conscience becomes paralyzed: "it lives with the anxiety that it will stain the glory of its inwardness by means of action and existence," for it no longer has any assurance that its action is right (§658/483). Its sole activity is a kind of yearning, "which merely loses itself as it becomes an essenceless object, and as it goes beyond this loss and then falls back on itself, it merely finds itself as lost.—In this transparent purity of its moments, it becomes an unhappy, so-called *beautiful soul*, and its burning embers gradually die out, and as they do, the beautiful soul vanishes like a shapeless vapor dissolving into thin air" (§658/484). Thus, with its inadequate account of both action and recognition, conscience fades away.

The Conflict between the Wicked and Judging Consciousnesses

The speech act that conscience believed to reconcile the objective, universal consciousness and the subjective, particular self—the declaration and affirmation—merely echoed the subjective position of the conscientious individual. Instead of resolving the problems of the moral worldview, conscience "falls apart into the non-selfsameness of individual being-for-self, and each consciousness is likewise reflected out of its universality and utterly back into itself," such that each conscience can only look inward for the content that makes its actions meaningful. This disparity reveals the "opposition of individuality both to other individuals and to the universal" and, Hegel writes, "it is this relationship and its movement which must now be examined" (§659/484). The final conflict in Chapter VI begins here.

The individual "exempts himself from the universal"; for him, "duty is only a matter of words and counts as a being for an other." Thus the individual thinks that "it, as *this* self, generates its own content" (§659/484). Hegel continues:

As empty knowledge, [conscience's] pure self is without content and without determination. The content which it gives to knowledge is taken from its own self *as this* determinate self, that is, from itself as a natural individuality, and in speaking of the conscientiousness of its action, it is indeed conscious of its pure self. However, in the *purpose* of its action as the actual content of the action, it is conscious of itself as this particular individual, of what is both for itself and for others, and it is conscious of the opposition between universality, that is, duty, and its being reflected into itself from out of universality. (§659/484–85)

The individual believes that the content of its norms and its actions come from within itself, even as it recognizes the opposition that this creates between the demands of duty and its own actions. It is still caught up in conscience's duality of subjective content and objective form. Having found no way to reconcile the two, this individual embraces its subjectivity.

In declaring its independence from duty and from objective universal content, however, the conscientious individual sets itself apart from other individuals. Unsurprisingly, this leads to conflict. The conflict that Hegel describes is the "non-selfsameness of [this individual's] particular individuality with respect to another individual" (§660/485), or the conflict between two particular individuals. Hegel initially calls these two figures the particular consciousness and the universal consciousness, but he comes to refer to them as the wicked consciousness and the judging consciousness. The first is the individual just described, who believes that all content or meaning is merely subjective. The second takes up the position of the universal consciousness, holding that there are duties with objective content that do not simply arise from within a particular individual. Hegel writes:

> Confronting this inward determination is thus the element of existence, that is, the universal consciousness, to which universality, that is, duty, is to an even greater degree the essence; this is in contrast to individuality, which exists for itself as opposed to the universal, something which, to the universal consciousness, counts merely as a sublated moment. To the latter universal consciousness which clings tenaciously to duty, the first consciousness counts as *evil* because it is the non-selfsameness between its *inwardly-turned-being* and the universal, and since the first consciousness at the same time also expresses its activity as selfsameness, as duty and conscientiousness, the universal consciousness takes it to be *hypocrisy*. (§660/485)

The latter consciousness accuses the former of evil and hypocrisy. It is evil because it believes there is an opposition between its own conscience and the requirements of moral duty; and it is hypocritical because it "demonstrat[es] its respect for both duty and virtue by *seeming to be* both of them and then using that semblance as a mask to hide itself both from its own consciousness and no less from the consciousness of others; it does this as if the recognition of the opposition would in itself imply the selfsameness and correspondence of the two" (§661/485–86). In other words, the wicked consciousness claims that it is both dutiful and virtuous, but it acts according to its own subjective convictions. All the while, it lies to itself and to others about the opposition of duty and conscience. As we have seen, its attempt to reconcile its particular self with the universal consciousness by assuring the community about its intentions and thereby securing the community's recognition of its action as conscientious produces a "dying sound," a hollow echo of the subjective position of the individual.

But, Hegel continues, the judging consciousness is also unable to reconcile the positions of the particular and universal, or the subjective and objective points of view. Hegel writes that since the judging consciousness "proclaims hypocrisy to be bad, base, etc., then in making such a judgment, it is appealing to *its own* law in the same way that the *evil* consciousness appealed to *its own law*" (§663/487).[24] He continues:

> In both of them, the aspect of actuality is distinct from that of speech; in one of them, the distinction is made through the *self-interested ends* of action, and in the other, it is made through the *lack of action* per se, for the necessity of action is implied in talking about duty, since duty without deeds is something that simply has no meaning at all. (§664/487)

The judging consciousness talks about duty when it judges the wicked consciousness, but it does not itself engage in dutiful action. The judging consciousness's only action is judging, and it denies that this counts as an action. Although Hegel notes that "judging is also to be regarded as a positive action on the part of thought, and it has a positive content," the judging consciousness does not view its judgment as a positive action with positive content (§665/488).

The judging consciousness *does* view the wicked consciousness's action in these terms. In the wicked consciousness's action, the judging consciousness sees "an *intention* and a self-serving *motive* which is different from the action itself. As every action is capable of being taken in respect to its dutifulness, so too can every action be taken from the point of view of *particularity*, for as an action it is the actuality of an individual" (§665/488). The judging consciousness claims that the wicked consciousness acts with an impure or subjective intention and, with echoes of Enlightenment's view of intention, that the intention or motive of the action is the only relevant criterion of its meaning or moral value. Furthermore, Hegel states, every action can be assessed this way, since every action is the action of a particular individual: "duty for duty's sake, this pure purpose, is the non-actual. It has its actuality in what individuality does, and as a result, the action has the aspect of particularity in itself.—No man is a hero to his valet, but not because that man is not a hero, but rather because the latter is—a valet, a person with whom the hero deals not as a hero but as someone who eats, drinks, gets dressed, that is, the valet generally deals with him in the individuality of his needs and views" (§665/489).

For the judging consciousness, every action is suspect. Because actions are taken by individuals, the motive of fulfilling one's pure duty is always marred by the particularity of the individual agent. In taking this position, however, the judging consciousness exposes *itself* as base and hypocritical. Hegel writes, "The judgmental consciousness is itself thereby *base* because it divides up the action, and it both produces and clings to the action's non-selfsameness with itself. Furthermore, it is *hypocrisy* because it pretends that such judgment is not merely *another manner* of being evil but is rather itself the *rightful consciousness* of action" (§666/489). In describing the judging consciousness as base, Hegel uses the word (*niederträchtig*) that he uses throughout the *Phenomenology of Spirit* to describe one who is alienated, who cannot reconcile his subjective experience with concrete existence. The judging consciousness is base and, hence, alienated because it distinguishes between its apparently pure mental states, such as its convictions and intentions, and corrupt action and embodied existence. Moreover, it is hypocritical because it claims that its judgment of the wicked consciousness's action is pure in a way that the latter's action is not.

The judging consciousness holds to some aspects of conscience's earlier problematic account of authority, but it has already begun to overcome others. Hegel's concerns about conscience's account of authority can be divided into two parts. First, conscience assumes that individuals are not only privileged knowers but also infallible judges of their own intentions. It presumes that because individuals have privileged knowledge of their own beliefs, intentions, and judgments, they cannot be wrong in their assessment of their commitments. Second, it presumes that the significance of an action depends on intention alone, rather than the action, its consequences, or others' evaluation of it. The content or meaning of the action is taken to be determined solely by the agent, prior to acting, based on her intention for the action. The judging consciousness has begun to overcome the first of these two problems. The judging consciousness insists that the wicked consciousness's declared intention is false; it claims that the wicked consciousness is either mistaken or dishonest about its intention. Thus the judging consciousness tacitly acknowledges that an agent can be wrong about his or her intention. Someone might be a privileged knower without being an infallible judge of his or her intentions. In order for the judging consciousness to assess the action, it must be able to judge the wicked consciousness's intention as well as the action itself. The significance of the action is not fixed by the agent's stated intention; it is both knowable and contestable by others as well. At this point, however, the judging consciousness has not had this self-conscious realization. It still holds the belief that the content or meaning of an action derives solely from the agent's intention.

Thus the wicked and judging consciousnesses still see themselves as opposed to one another. That changes in the very next paragraph. The wicked consciousness realizes that the judging consciousness has taken him to be "alien and not the same as himself," and he also realizes that "the judgmental consciousness, in terms of the way that consciousness is constituted, is the same as himself" (§666/489). The wicked consciousness recognizes the validity of the judging consciousness's judgment—that he is a particular and fallible individual—but he recognizes that this is equally true for the judging consciousness himself. On this basis, the wicked consciousness *confesses* to the judging consciousness:

> As [the wicked consciousness] intuits this selfsameness and *gives expression to it*, he *confesses* this to the other, and he equally expects that the other, who has in fact put himself selfsame to him, will reciprocate his *speech* and in his own words will express their selfsameness so that recognitional existence will make its appearance. His confession is not an abasement, nor a humiliation, nor is it a matter of his casting himself aside in his relationship with the other, for this declaration is not something one-sided through which he would posit his non-selfsameness with the other. On the contrary, it is solely in consideration of his intuition of his *selfsameness* with the other that he gives expression to himself, that is, he gives expression on his own part to *their selfsameness* in his confessions, and he does this because language is the *existence* of spirit as the immediate self. He thus expects that the other will contribute his own part to this existence. (§666/489–90)

In his confession, the wicked consciousness acknowledges that he, like the judging consciousness, is a particular individual whose actions express his particular commitments. Recall Hegel's insistence that the confession is "not an abasement, nor a humiliation, nor is it a matter of his casting himself aside." Confession entails neither the domination of the confessing (wicked) consciousness by the judging consciousness nor the assimilation of the confessing consciousness into a homogenizing universal consciousness. Rather, the confession is an expression of "their selfsameness" as particular and fallible individuals subject to the judgment of others.

Confession is not only an acknowledgment of particularity; if it were, it would not be an advance over the wicked consciousness's initial standpoint. It is also an acknowledgment of a kind of universality. Like conscience, which used language to express and actualize its convictions in an objective form, the wicked consciousness uses language to express and actualize its confession. Hegel emphasizes the role of language in this passage, even in his italicization of the phrases "gives expression to it," "confesses," and "speech" at the beginning of the section. Language mediates between the particular subject and the universal spirit: "language is the existence of spirit as the immediate self."

On the face of it, the difference between confession and declaration (such as the conscience individual's earlier declaration of its convictions) may appear slight. Both are speech acts that connect the individual to another or a community in an attempt to overcome one-sided subjectivity and objectivity. The declaration, however, is an individual's statement of its conviction or intention prior to acting. The community affirms that the conscientious individual has really had this conviction, but neither the completed act nor its consequences are part of their judgment. The wicked consciousness, by contrast, confesses *after* it has taken action and another has issued an initial judgment of that action. With its confession, the wicked consciousness relinquishes its initial view that its actions could only be justified by its personal and subjective convictions. In its confession, the wicked consciousness demonstrates that it has given up its view that no one else could have anything to say about its commitments, insofar as it revises its assessment of itself and its action in response to the judgment of the other. In this sense, its confession entails its acknowledgment of the social context in which content or meaning is determined. Eventually, both the judging and the wicked consciousnesses realize that the judgment contributes to the content or meaning of the action; not all content can come from the conviction or intention of the agent. While the community of conscientious individuals understood themselves as individually determining the content of their convictions and actions, the confessing community tacitly acknowledges that the content and meaning of one's convictions, intentions, and actions depend not only on one's own determination of them but also on the judgment of others. It recognizes that content is constructed intersubjectively.

This intersubjectivity, moreover, has the doubled structure of recognition. The wicked consciousness sees itself not only as an intentional subject but also as the object of legitimate judgment by another intentional subject. Because the judging consciousness has not yet reciprocated the confession, this is not full-fledged reciprocal recognition, but Hegel is laying the foundation for that structure.

The judging consciousness hears the confession of the wicked consciousness, but it refuses to respond. This initial refusal reverses the situation of the two consciousnesses, and the wicked consciousness now judges the judging consciousness for the latter's failure to recognize his parity with the former. According to Hegel, "[The wicked consciousness] sees the judgmental consciousness as somebody who sets his own stiff-necked selfsame character in opposition to the confessing consciousness, and he sees the utter silence of someone who keeps himself locked up within himself, who refuses to be discarded vis-à-vis an other" (§667/490). The wicked consciousness sees the judging consciousness as a character, like Antigone and Creon in Greek *Sittlichkeit*. As a character, the judging consciousness is stubborn, one-sided, and unreflective. In further confirmation of their role reversal, the judging consciousness now appears as a beautiful soul, who cannot reconcile his "pure self" with his embodied existence in the world. The judging consciousness becomes mute. Hegel calls this the "highest rebellion of self-certain spirit," in which the judging consciousness refuses even to "put itself into communication with him—with him, who in his confession had already renounced his *separate being-for-itself*" (§667/490). In this way, Hegel writes:

> The hard heart shows itself to be the consciousness forsaken by spirit, the consciousness which denies spirit since it does not take cognizance that within its absolute self-certainty, spirit is master over every deed and over all actuality, and that spirit can repudiate them and make them into something that never happened. At the same time, the hard heart does not take cognizance of the contradiction it commits when it does not count the repudiation that took place *in speech* as true repudiation while it itself has the certainty of its spirit not in an actual action but in its inwardness and has its existence in the *speech* in which its judgment is phrased. It is therefore the hard heart himself who is putting obstacles in the way of the other's return from the deed into the spiritual existence of speech and into the equality of spirit, and by virtue of its hardness of heart, it engenders the non-selfsameness which is still present. (§667/491)

The judging consciousness refuses to acknowledge that it is not wholly self-determined, that "spirit is master over every deed and over all actuality."[25]

This phrase stops many readers in their tracks. Taken alone, it appears to provide incontrovertible evidence of both Hegel's supposed spirit monism and his difference-effacing absolutism. In A. V. Miller's well-known translation, the phrase is rendered even more problematic, as "Spirit, in the absolute certainty of itself, is *lord and master* over every deed and actuality."[26] Miller's translation, however, is misleading. While the word *Herr* (which Hegel uses in the lordship and bondage section) signifies master in the sense of a lord or ruler, the word Hegel uses here, *Meister*, signifies master in the sense of an expert craftsman or artisan, the person who has mastered a skill. This conflation in Miller's translation may lead readers to see a linguistic affinity between these two sections in the English translation that is not present in the original German text. It is crucial to preserve the distinction between the two. In this passage, spirit is not a lord who dominates or rules but a master who *shapes* deeds and actualities. This renders the passage rather similar to the position taken by many contemporary communitarians, pragmatists, and feminists, among others, that subjects are shaped by their social and historical context and that the identities, beliefs, and actions available to subjects are always constrained by that context. Understood in this way, this phrase can be read as a corrective to the absolute self-certainty of the hard-hearted judging consciousness. In effect, it is an admonishment of the judging consciousness and a reminder that the determinate content it affirms does not spring wholly from within but comes to it already shaped by spirit, that "universal" point of view secured not by a thing-in-itself but by a community existing over time. Spirit is master over deeds and actuality insofar as it comprises the social norms, context, and determinate concepts and commitments that make deeds and actuality meaningful to begin with.

The judging consciousness still will not admit this, and it clings to this irreconcilable opposition in which it can only be "pure being or empty nothingness." Thus it "breaks down into madness and melts into a yearning tubercular consumption. It thereby in fact gives up its grim adherence to *its being-for-itself*, but it only manages to engender merely the spiritless *unity* of being" (§668/491). The language here echoes §658, in which conscience wastes away, just prior to the emergence of the conflict between the wicked and judging consciousnesses.

In the next two paragraphs, however, the judging consciousness's hard heart breaks and the two consciousnesses achieve reciprocal recognition. This outcome is anticipated by what came before: "the true conciliation, which is to say, the *self-conscious* and *existing* conciliation, is in terms of its necessity already contained in the preceding. The breaking of the hard heart and its elevation to universality is the same movement which was expressed in the consciousness that confessed" (§669/491–92). In other words, the movement by which the wicked consciousness takes action, submits to judgment, and confesses is the same movement by which the judging consciousness recognizes its judgment as an action, submits to the judgment of the wicked consciousness, and forgives: "to the latter, this other, its one-sided, unrecognized judgment must be broken in the way that for the former, its one-sided, unrecognized existence of particular being-for-itself had to be broken" (§669/492). The judging consciousness therefore sees itself in the wicked consciousness and *forgives* it.

Confession, Forgiveness, and the Emergence of Reciprocal Recognition

Through their confession and forgiveness, the wicked consciousness and the judging consciousness are reconciled. Their reconciliation, moreover, marks the emergence of full-fledged reciprocal recognition and absolute spirit. Given the centrality of ritual and social practice in Hegel's account of spirit, it is not surprising to find confession and forgiveness at this crucial juncture. There are significant features of confession and forgiveness, however, that set them apart from the rituals and social practices described in earlier sections.

In chapter 2, I noted three significant similarities between the section on Antigone and the section on confession and forgiveness in the *Phenomenology of Spirit*. First, in both cases, Hegel describes an individual who takes action and who, after doing so, acknowledges that the content or meaning of the action was not determined by her or his own intention for the action alone.

Second, the individual who takes action recognizes that it has something in common with a second individual who judges that action. In the section on Antigone, Hegel describes Antigone's acknowledgment that the human law that Creon defends is part of the same shape of spirit as the divine law that she follows. This acknowledgment entails the breakdown of Antigone's one-sidedness. In the section on confession and forgiveness, Hegel describes the same phenomenon as the "intuition of [the wicked consciousness's] *selfsameness* with the other," an intuition that leads to its confession. Third and finally, in both the section on Antigone and the section on confession and forgiveness, the acknowledgment of guilt in the former and the confession in the latter, along with the breakdown of the one-sided character, are an insufficient basis for reconciliation between the conflicting parties. This is because nondominating, nonassimilating reconciliation requires the *doubled* structure of reciprocal recognition, in which *each* individual recognizes itself and the other as both subject and object. Eventually Antigone and Creon each have this epistemological realization, but they are unable to actualize the practical aspect of recognition. The wicked consciousness and the judging consciousness are reconciled only after the judging consciousness joins the wicked consciousness in acknowledging their selfsameness and after both *actualize* this selfsameness in their actions.

This acknowledgment and actualization takes place when the judging consciousness extends forgiveness to the wicked consciousness. Although Hegel uses the word "forgiveness" (*Verzeihung*) only once in this section, its importance is signaled by its appearance in the section's title, "Conscience. The beautiful soul, evil, and its forgiveness," and by its position in a crucial passage that moves swiftly from the breaking of the hard heart to the extension of forgiveness to the emergence of reciprocal recognition and absolute spirit. Hegel writes:

> The forgiveness it extends to the first [i.e., the wicked consciousness] is the renunciation of itself, of its *non-actual* essence, an essence which it equates with this other consciousness which was *actual* action, and it recognizes as good what had been determined in thought to be bad, namely, action; or to an even greater degree, it abandons this distinction between determinate thought and its determining judgment existing-for-itself, just as the other abandons its own act, which exists-for-itself of determining action.–The word of reconciliation is the *existing* spirit which immediately intuits in its opposite the pure knowledge of itself as the *universal* essence, intuits it in the pure knowledge of itself as *individuality* existing absolutely inwardly—a reciprocal recognition which is *absolute* spirit. (§670/492–93)

C. Allen Speight notes that Hegel's concept of forgiveness combines two key ideas: "(1) an overcoming of *resentment* that is based on a *revision of judgment* and (2) a recognition of conditions affecting both agency and judgment in general," such as the fallibility of agents, the self-interest of motives, and the potential for evil.[27] We can see each of these ideas at work in the passage above. The judging consciousness's forgiveness involves the revision of two judgments: its general judgment of action as bad and its specific judgment of the wicked consciousness as wicked for acting on the basis of its particularities. In its forgiveness, the judging consciousness acknowledges the fallibility of agents, the fact that agents can be wrong about the content or meaning of their own actions. This fact is as true for itself as for the wicked consciousness. The judgment that it had issued was motivated not only by a respect for universal duty but also by its own particularistic desires and intentions.

Like the confession, the forgiveness is a speech act. Hegel's phrase "the word of reconciliation" can refer literally to the words uttered by the two consciousnesses. Once again, Hegel claims that language is *existing* spirit or, in other words, that language does more than mediate between the particular and the universal, the individual and the community, but actually marries the two. Individual commitments get their content when actions, including speech acts, express those commitments in public, expose them to the judgment of others, and reintegrate them.[28] Focusing only on the linguistic aspects of confession and forgiveness misses the significance of the religious and theological content and context of these practices, however. Hegel does not discuss just any speech acts. Rather, he specifically focuses on the religiously inflected practices of confession and forgiveness, and he uses the theologically rich phrase the "word of reconciliation" to describe them. To ignore this would be to miss the absolutely crucial, if unorthodox, sense in which confession and forgiveness serve a *sacramental* function in Hegel's account.

Sacraments are rituals that involve both word and deed. On a Lutheran account, they are taken to both *symbolize* and *actualize* the absolute. The sacraments symbolize the divine reality through a visible sign, such as the bread and wine in the Eucharist, and they actualize the signified reality, as with Christ's real presence in the Eucharistic host.[29] In his early writings, Luther counted penance (or confession and forgiveness) among the sacraments, alongside the Eucharist and baptism. In "The Sacrament of Penance" (1519), for instance, Luther writes that penance consists of the three features of all sacraments: visible sign, signified reality, and faith. In the sacrament of penance, Luther identifies these three features as absolution, or the words of forgiveness; grace, or the gift of forgiveness; and faith, or the trust that one has been forgiven. The words of forgiveness are the sign, grace is the signified reality, and, finally, "the faith that believes the sacrament is what removes the sin."[30]

Hegel's account of confession and forgiveness includes each of these three features of the sacraments. Confession and forgiveness are speech acts that pair word and deed: the word of forgiveness, or, as Hegel puts it, "the word of reconciliation," is the sign, and the actualized forgiveness is the signified reality. The faith that one can and does forgive the other is the final aspect of their reconciliation. Without this faith, the confession and forgiveness would fail to reconcile. As Luther writes: "The hard hearted who do not as yet seek comfort for their conscience, have likewise not yet experienced this torment-ing anxiety. To them, this sacrament is of no use."[31] Using the same phrase as Luther (*das harte Herz*), Hegel writes that the hard-hearted judging con-sciousness must recognize that spirit is master over deed and actuality before it is able to respond to the wicked consciousness's confession. Hegel, like Lu-ther, may have in mind the hard-hearted Pharaoh of Exodus, who refuses to release the Israelites from bondage. In that case, hard-heartedness implies domination. The hard heart must break—and the attempt to dominate must be abandoned—before the confession can have its effect.

On Hegel's account of the sacramental function of confession and forgive-ness, however, it is not God but a fallible human being who judges and forgives the one who confesses. In this respect, Hegel's account combines aspects of the sacrament of penance with Luther's later description of public confession and forgiveness. In the "Exhortation to Confession" (1529), Luther writes that through public confession "we mutually confess our guilt and our desire for forgiveness (Matthew 5:23–24). Now, all of us are guilty of sinning against one another; therefore we may and should publicly confess this before ev-eryone without shrinking in one another's presence. . . . So we have in the Lord's Prayer a double absolution: there we are forgiven our offenses against God and against our neighbor, and there we forgive our neighbor and become reconciled to him."[32] On Luther's account, Christians can confess to and seek forgiveness from not only God or a priest but also one another. This is part of the work of reconciliation. When Luther writes that Christians should publicly confess without "shrinking in one another's presence," we may be reminded of Hegel's statement that the confession is "not an abasement, nor a humiliation, nor is it a matter of his casting himself aside." Moreover, echoing what Luther calls the "double absolution" of the Lord's Prayer, in which the individual and his neighbor are both the forgiver and the forgiven, the reconciliation between the wicked and judging consciousnesses entails the acknowledgment that each individual stands in the position of wrongdoer *and* judge, confessor *and* for-giver. Luther expressed a similar notion when he characterized the state of the Christian as *simul iustus et peccator* ("at the same time righteous and a sinner"). For Luther, the Christian is not partly righteous and partly sinful but both, fully and simultaneously—*totus iustus, totus peccator*.

The connection between the practices of confession and forgiveness and sacramental theology is key to understanding *why* Hegel thinks that these particular practices give rise to absolute spirit and *what* absolute spirit entails. According to Luther, the sacraments "represent" the divine, both in the sense of representing or symbolizing as sign and in the sense of *re*-presenting or actualizing as signified reality.[33] In Luther's understanding of the Eucharist, for example, Christ is represented by the bread and wine (visible sign) and actually made present in the community through the sacramental act (signified reality). In penance, likewise, the words of confession and forgiveness serve as signs of a reconciliation that is actualized in the ritual. Hegel thinks that Luther gets something right by insisting on the importance of practices of confession and forgiveness in the Christian community. Certain shared practices—sacramental practices—make it possible for communities to express their deepest commitments while making those commitments *actual* and *present* among them. Confession and forgiveness are sacramental practices in this sense.

Through their acts of confession and forgiveness, the two consciousnesses recognize themselves and one another as loci of authority and accountability. They acknowledge their selfsameness as acting and judging subjects who can be held accountable for their actions and judgments by others. These others, likewise, are also acting and judging subjects, fit to be held accountable. The wicked and judging consciousnesses acknowledge this fact not only in word but also in deed, in the confession and forgiveness that symbolize and actualize their agency, authority, and accountability. They perform—and they bring into being—a relationship of reciprocal recognition.

At the same time, confession and forgiveness symbolize and actualize absolute spirit. Absolute spirit is that collection of norms and practices through which a community creates and re-creates itself. It constitutes the standard of knowledge and the ground of authority. Absolute spirit emerges from the confession and forgiveness of the wicked consciousness and the judging consciousness. The confession and forgiveness symbolize this absolute standard and actualize it within the community through the deeds themselves. The confession and forgiveness—the two consciousnesses' acknowledgments of their selfsameness in their agency, authority, and accountability—are themselves the actualization of the absolute standard. Finally, the two consciousnesses' faith in the practices of confession and forgiveness, as part of what constitutes the absolute, is what makes it so. Initially, the emergence of absolute spirit sounds almost mystical. To the contrary, I argue in the next chapter that it is best understood as the result of the rituals and social practices of ordinary people. Hegel draws on the structure and logic of Luther's sacramental theology, but, as we will see, he naturalizes it in his account of absolute spirit.

Hegel's goal in the *Phenomenology of Spirit* has been to identify a community whose members are neither immediately identified with their norms nor alienated from them. He hopes to describe the way in which their beliefs and actions can be both self-legislated and authoritative. His discussion of confession and forgiveness suggests how Hegel thinks this works. The practices of confession and forgiveness are sacramental practices. In each, a speech act symbolizes and actualizes each individual's recognition of the other as a locus of authority and accountability. By confessing and extending forgiveness to one another, each one recognizes the authority of the other to act, to judge, and to forgive—to be, in a sense, an author of the norms by which they are bound. In recognizing this authority and accountability, they also generate it. Norms are authoritative, on this account, when they are created and sustained through the ongoing practices of subjects who recognize one another as loci of authority and accountability.

Hegel's account of confession and forgiveness, understood in this way, is more practical and substantial than some interpreters have suggested. Robert Pippin, for instance, argues that Hegel stops short of describing the institutional arrangements conducive to reciprocal recognition and only hints at the "spiritual possibility, a quasi-religious 'conversion experience,' in a community: 'forgiveness.'"[34] In Pippin's reading of the confession and forgiveness section, the wicked consciousness and the judging consciousness are in a situation of "inevitable guilt, and the drama that [Hegel] narrates leaves us only with the option of 'confessing' such guilt to others who we hope will reciprocate in a gesture that will undermine any such pretended independence and will reaffirm in mutual forgiveness our inevitable dependence."[35] Pippin argues that there is "no institutional manifestation" in this account of confession and forgiveness, and "very little" that could connect it to the concrete social and political arrangements described in the *Philosophy of Right*.[36] In Pippin's reading, Hegel's confession and forgiveness section resembles Shakespeare's tragic play *King Lear*, with Lear as the wicked consciousness who sullies moral duty with subjective desire and Cordelia as the hard-hearted judge or beautiful soul who cannot understand Lear's willingness to mix personal and familial love with public and political objectives. Eventually they privately confess and forgive but are unable to avoid their terrible and tragic fates. Pippin concludes that "the aspiration for a culminating reconciliation is everywhere in Hegel, but everywhere elusive."[37] On this reading, the practices of confession and forgiveness are a thin balm for a deep wound.

Pippin notes that "some see all this as evidence of the 'tragic nature of all social action' for Hegel, comprising both a universal dimension and an inevitable transgression of such a law," and he cites J. M. Bernstein's essay "Confession and Forgiveness: Hegel's Poetics of Action" as an example of this position.[38] According to Bernstein, confession is an admission of human particularity that cannot but transgress the universal law; forgiveness is an act of mourning this "inevitable transgression." Pippin, however, disagrees with Bernstein's reading; it is, he writes, "Hegel read through Adorno."[39] Instead, Pippin suggests that readers turn from the end of Chapter VI to the *Philosophy of Right* in order to find the fulfillment of the aspiration for reconciliation in Hegel's theory of the state.

While I agree with Pippin's claim that reciprocal recognition is only attainable and sustainable under particular social and historical conditions that must ultimately be specified, I also think that Hegel has provided more insight into reconciliation than either Pippin or Bernstein suggests. When Hegel invokes the practices of confession and forgiveness, he is not gesturing toward a vague "spiritual possibility, a quasi-religious 'conversion experience,'" but directing his readers' attention to the Christian sacraments with which they are likely already familiar. For Hegel's contemporaries, what Pippin refers to as "the option of 'confessing' such guilt to others who we hope will reciprocate" would not appear as thin and contingent as Pippin seems to think. As sacraments, confession and forgiveness both symbolize and actualize reciprocal recognition and absolute spirit. The sacrament of penance, recall, involves the word of forgiveness, the gracious gift of forgiveness, and faith that forgiveness has been offered. Public confession and forgiveness among Christians, at least in Luther's view, entails confession "without shrinking in one another's presence," with the faith or trust that the forgiveness extended to one's neighbor in the Lord's Prayer will be extended by one's neighbors to oneself as well.[40] While Hegel is not content to stop with Luther's understanding of the sacraments, the sacramental logic of confession and forgiveness is crucial to understanding reciprocal recognition and absolute spirit.

With Hegel's emphasis on confession and forgiveness and the section's implicit lessons about human fallibility and wrongdoing, certainly some form of guilt (as Pippin suggests) or transgression (as Bernstein suggests) is at play. It must be distinguished, however, from the guilt incurred by Antigone and Creon. As one-sided characters in Greek *Sittlichkeit*, Antigone and Creon had to play the roles assigned to them. Their identities were taken to be natural, fixed, and immediately given. Their actions fulfilled the roles and duties assigned to them but violated other duties under Greek *Sittlichkeit*. While they could ultimately see that their actions had significance that they did not intend, there was no way for them to revise their identities or obligations without giving up the naturalized roles that they *had to play*. Hegel thinks that modern individuals cannot think about their identities and obligations in this way. Identities, social roles, and duties are revisable—not willy-nilly, for there are others to whom each individual is accountable, but revisable nonetheless. The wicked consciousness and the judging consciousness are guilty of error—both in their actions and in their self-understanding—but they accept responsibility and remain open to the criticisms and corrections offered by others. Under the terms set by their shape of spirit, Antigone and Creon could do no such thing. That is why that shape of spirit was tragic, while the shape of spirit brought about by the wicked consciousness and the judging consciousness is not.

Through their confession and forgiveness, the wicked and judging consciousnesses reconcile and enter into a relationship of reciprocal recognition. This reconciliation and reciprocal recognition need not be read as a "culminating reconciliation" or "end of history." Just as Luther's sacramental theology understands human beings' need for grace to be ongoing, Hegel's discussion of confession and forgiveness does not suggest that relationships of reciprocal recognition are attained through a single speech act. Rather, it seems that practices of confession and forgiveness would have to be perpetual. These two consciousnesses could come into conflict again over a particular judgment one issues that the other thinks is false, or over an action that one takes that the other thinks is wrong. Reciprocal recognition entails the acknowledgment that the self and other are the kind of beings entitled to make judgments of this sort and that one had better take the judgment of the other in good faith. Pippin's emphasis on inevitable guilt and Bernstein's emphasis on the transgressive character of human action acknowledge ongoing conflict but overlook the possibility of ongoing reconciliation. The relationship of reciprocal recognition is premised on the epistemic and practical acknowledgment that oneself and the other are both subject and object, and that oneself and the other stand in equal positions of responsibility to one another for one's commitments. Confession and forgiveness are practices of contesting and revising norms and judgments within this structure of reciprocal recognition. In this view, practices of conflict and reconciliation are ongoing within relationships of reciprocal recognition.

Conclusion

In Kojève's interpretation, the struggle for recognition ceases only at the "end of history," when social life has been perfected and human beings no longer need to participate in the creation or transformation of norms, laws, and social structures. What I have tried to highlight, in the foregoing discussion of Hegel's treatment of confession and forgiveness, is an emergent form of recognition that neither has violence, domination, and assimilation at its core nor claims to have overcome conflict once and for all. In the confession and forgiveness section, Hegel presents a particular conflict that is resolved through rituals of reconciliation. Conflicts will continue to arise, individuals will continue to judge and revise judgments about their actions and the actions of others, and the dialectic of conflict and reconciliation will churn forward.

Needless to say, the end of Chapter VI is not the end of the *Phenomenology of Spirit*. Given the religious and theological content of the final paragraphs of the section on confession and forgiveness, it is not surprising to find Hegel turning to religion in the following chapter. There, he moves back through the shapes of spirit that have already been traced in order to pinpoint the religious beliefs and practices that inform those forms of life. As I have suggested, Hegel thinks that Christians get something right in their practices of confession and forgiveness. But Hegel also thinks that what religious communities get right is in the form of *representation (Vorstellung)*, which is to say that it is symbolically but not self-sufficiently true. What Hegel finds compelling in sacramental theology is the idea that certain shared practices enable communities to express their deepest commitments while making those commitments *actual*

and *present* among them. While the sacrament of penance in its representational form is predicated on the notion that it is the Christian God who is
represented and re-presented in the sacrament, in its absolute form—that is,
fully actualized and brought to self-consciousness—practices of confession
and forgiveness represent and re-present the absolute, that self-conscious and
self-sufficient standard.

In chapter 5, the final interpretive chapter of the book, I turn to the last
two chapters of the *Phenomenology of Spirit*—Chapter VII (titled "Religion")
and Chapter VIII ("Absolute Knowing")—to see how sacraments and sacrifice
are employed and transformed as the representational thinking that characterizes religion becomes the absolute knowing of philosophy.

CHAPTER FIVE

Religion, Philosophy, and the Absolute

IF SPIRIT IS Hegel's name for the collection of norms and norm-generating practices that characterize a community, *absolute spirit* is his name for the collection of norms and practices in which spirit has itself for an object—the norms and practices in and through which the members of the community create, sustain, and transform spirit itself.

This view of Hegel's concept of absolute spirit has both epistemological and ethical implications. It suggests that the standard of knowledge against which people's beliefs, actions, and norms are judged emerges from the social practices of the people who share a form of life. This idea is at the center of Hegel's epistemology. It also suggests that among these social practices ought to be rituals and other shared activities in which people recognize one another's authority and accountability. The sacrament of penance—confession and forgiveness—and certain forms of sacrifice are prime examples. These rituals bring about, and help support, relationships of reciprocal recognition that avoid domination and alienation. This idea is at the center of Hegel's ethics.

A community that has identified and fostered these sorts of practices will differ in important ways from the shapes of spirit that Hegel describes earlier in the *Phenomenology of Spirit*. Unlike Greek *Sittlichkeit*, which fails to recognize subjects' forward-looking responsibility as the authors and agents of their norms, such a community would cultivate ongoing practices in which norms are contested and critiqued. Unlike Faith and Enlightenment, which fail to note the role of social practices in generating and sustaining authority, such a community would self-consciously cultivate practices in which subjects express and embody their accountability to one another for the norms that they share.

The relationship of reciprocal recognition, Hegel suggests, *is* absolute spirit. It is the context for and the embodiment of those norms and practices in which spirit has itself for an object. He writes that "the word of reconciliation is the *existing* spirit which immediately intuits in its opposite the pure knowledge of itself as the *universal* essence, intuits it in the pure knowledge of itself as *individuality* existing absolutely inwardly—a reciprocal recognition which is *absolute* spirit" (§670/493). In the relationship of reciprocal recognition, each person recognizes herself and the other as both agent and judge, confessor and forgiver. Their confession and forgiveness occasion their recognition of themselves as both universal essence and individuality. Each is a locus of authority and accountability, responsible *to* one another *for* their commitments.

Some may worry that this interpretation, according to which absolute spirit emerges from the relationships and social practices of people who share a form of life, begs the question of whether Hegel's philosophy is best understood as a metaphysics. In the final lines of the confession and forgiveness section, Hegel writes that absolute spirit is God. He writes, "The reconciling *yes*, in which both I's let go of their opposed *existence*, is the existence of the *I* expanded into two-ness, which therein remains selfsame and which has the certainty of itself in its complete self-emptying and in its opposite.–It is God appearing in the midst of those who know themselves as pure knowledge" (§671/494).[1] In this cryptic passage, Hegel suggests that the reconciled consciousnesses are not two individuals who have become one but rather one who has become two. This one or *I*, Hegel states here, is God in the midst of the reconciled consciousnesses. As an elaboration of what absolute spirit is, this passage confuses more than it clarifies. It invokes, once again, the sacramental logic of the practices of confession and forgiveness, suggesting that God is manifest in the community in and through these practices. But what does Hegel mean by God? And what is the relationship between the ongoing practices of conflict and reconciliation and the picture of absolute spirit sketched here?

To reach any conclusions about the metaphysical dimensions of Hegel's philosophy, these questions must be addressed. This chapter addresses them by describing the relationship among God, spirit, and the absolute as Hegel describes them in Chapters VII ("Religion") and VIII ("Absolute Knowing") of the *Phenomenology*. Hegel holds that God and spirit are the religious and philosophical titles, respectively, for what is absolute. Religion and absolute knowing (that is, the philosophical standpoint) have the same object—the absolute—but their knowledge of this object has different forms. For religion, knowledge of the absolute takes the representational form of doctrine, ritual, and worship of God. For philosophy, knowledge of the absolute takes the conceptual form of self-conscious reflection on and participation in spirit. Because Hegel believes that the conceptual form of philosophical knowledge is more adequate to its object than the representational form of religious knowledge,

Hegel's readers have to be careful to avoid smuggling religious representations of who or what God is into the philosophical concept of spirit.

With this in mind, this chapter begins by considering Hegel's assertion in the preface of the *Phenomenology of Spirit* that truth is both substance and subject. This claim, and its relationship to Cartesian, Spinozistic, and Kantian accounts of the absolute, forms the philosophical backdrop for Hegel's views on God, spirit, and the absolute. Next, I compare religion's representational knowledge of the unity of substance and subject with philosophy's conceptual knowledge of this unity. I show that, for both religion and philosophy, *sacrifice* helps bring about this unity but that their different accounts of what sacrifice entails reveal the ways in which religion's representational knowledge of the absolute remains incomplete. Finally, I return to the final paragraph of Chapter VI to suggest that the God who "appear[s] in the midst of those who know themselves as pure knowledge" is understood from the philosophical standpoint of absolute knowing as the absolute spirit that is generated and sustained through practices of conflict and reconciliation.

The Unity of Substance and Subject

In the preface, Hegel claims that truth is both substance and subject: "in my view, which must be justified by the exposition of the system itself, everything hangs on apprehending and expressing the truth not merely as *substance* but also equally as *subject*" (§17/22–23). This sentence is something of a puzzle. As Peter Hodgson notes, Hegel's characterization of truth as both substance and subject brings together two traditionally opposed conceptions of the absolute.[2] Given Hegel's insistence on the insufficiency of one-sided accounts of authority, his effort to reconcile these two conceptions is not surprising.

The two conceptions of the absolute that Hegel tries to reconcile are, roughly speaking, a Spinozistic account of the absolute as substance and a Kantian account of the absolute as subject. The Spinozistic account that had been revived in Hegel's youth draws on Spinoza's emendation of Descartes's earlier conception of substance.[3] In Descartes's view, adopted by Spinoza, substance is that which exists such that it needs nothing else for its existence. Substance is, in other words, self-sufficient. Descartes went on to suggest that there were two kinds of substance: thinking substance (mind or soul) and extended substance (body). Descartes thought, moreover, that thinking substance could be either infinite or finite. While there is only one infinite substance—God—there is a plurality of independent minds, each of which is a distinct finite substance. While Spinoza embraced Descartes's account of substance as that which is self-sufficient, he rejected Descartes's divisions of substance. Instead, Spinoza argued that there was one substance. Thought and extension could not refer to different types of substance but to two of the infinite attributes of substance. What Descartes had considered finite substances—such as independent minds—were, in Spinoza's view, merely *modes* that exist within and are wholly dependent upon the one substance.

Hegel seeks a better account of difference and differentiation than he finds in this conception of substance. He denounces the Spinozistic account of substance, taken up in Schelling's conception of the absolute, that subsumes distinct entities into the one substance in which "everything is the same." Hegel calls this position an "utterly vacuous naiveté in cognition" that attempts to "pass off its *absolute* as the night in which, as one says, all cows are black" (§16/22).[4] According to this position, substance may be infinitely modified, but these modifications are essentially emanations of the same thing. This position fails to recognize the union of identity and non-identity in the absolute. For Hegel, to be *this* subject or object is to be unified with, but irreducible to, *that* subject or object. Hegel insists that this differentiation persists in the absolute. To suggest otherwise, Hegel thinks, is to render the absolute contentless.

While Descartes's divisions of substance may initially appear to provide an account of differentiation, Hegel also rejects the Cartesian position. Descartes's division of substance into thinking substance and extended substance sets up the mind-body and subject-object dualisms that Hegel is trying to overcome in the *Phenomenology*. Each shape of spirit that we have discussed up to this point initially grounds the authority of its norms in either the subjective or objective side of a subject-object divide. It is this one-sidedness in their accounts of the authority of their norms that has led to the collapse of each and every one of these shapes of spirit. On the one side, the shapes of spirit that attempt to ground the authority of their norms in *objects*, the way things are *in themselves*, cannot give an account of how these things are *for us*. In Chapter VI, this problem initially appears in Greek *Sittlichkeit*, which claims that its laws simply *are*. Because individuals take the authority of those laws as immediately given, they cannot say why the mere existence of the law should count as authoritative for them. When Antigone and Creon come into conflict over the burial of Polyneices, however, they acknowledge the one-sidedness of their positions. Neither one can say why the law she or he follows is authoritative for her- or himself or why it should count as authoritative for the other. This problem is raised to the level of self-consciousness in the Roman legal society, in which individuals cannot justify the norms, institutions, and practices that govern the social and political world.

Conversely, the shapes of spirit that attempt to ground the authority of their norms in the individual subject, the way things are *for the subject*, cannot give an account of what these things are *in themselves*. This leads to skepticism and alienation. They cannot say why their norms should count for anyone other than themselves, and they cannot even receive confirmation that their norms should really count for them. Faith and Enlightenment, for example, both place all authority on the side of the subject. As a result, they disavow their objective existence—rejecting their actual existence and actions in the world—and become alienated from it and from one another. Their concepts become contentless, like Faith's concept of God, and they become skeptical about the possibility of knowing anything concrete about the world.

The only account that can overcome these problems will be an account of why our norms are authoritative in themselves *and* for us, that is, an account that overcomes subject-object dualism. Hegel thinks that the reconciliation of substance and subject yields such an account. As with substance, we must not confuse Hegel's conception of the subject with the familiar Cartesian subject, the cogito. Instead, the starting point for Hegel's conception of the subject is the Kantian subject, the locus of responsibility.

As with the Spinozistic conception of substance, however, Hegel is not entirely satisfied with the Kantian conception of subject. Hegel draws on and transforms the Kantian subject, casting it as the entity responsible *to* others *for* its judgments, intentions, and actions. The Hegelian subject is an intersubjectively understood locus of authority and accountability. This gets to the heart of Pippin's interpretation of Hegel as a post-Kantian idealist.[5] Hegel identifies and hopes to solve a problem that he sees in Kant's two-part account of knowledge, a problem that is connected to this subject-object dualism. For Kant, sensibility and understanding are both necessary for knowledge. Sensibility receives or intuits objects in the world. The understanding applies categories to organize or classify those objects as knowledge. Hegel thinks that this account of knowledge has two built-in forms of givenness: first, the objects themselves are given to intuition, and, second, the categories are given to the understanding. Hegel thinks that Kant begins to suggest a way around this givenness in the B-version of the Transcendental Deduction. There, Kant states that the representations given in intuition must be accompanied by the "I think," or what he calls the "transcendental unity of apperception." Tensions seem to arise between Kant's account of the unity of apperception and his strict division of labor between sensibility and the understanding. If the representations given in intuition are already accompanied by the "I think," then are they not already organized in some way by the understanding? Pippin argues that Kant "clearly wants to establish that *objects* do conform to the categories, not that we must apply the categories to *whatever* sensory contact is delivered to us."[6] While this is Hegel's starting point, he also needs to wrestle with the givenness of the categories. To avoid the problem of skepticism—the gap between what appears to be true to the subject and what she can affirm as true about objects in the world— thinking cannot be the activity of the isolated subject applying her subjectively given categories to objects. As Lewis writes, "Any account of this thinking that conceives it fundamentally in terms of the activity of a particular subject falls into the contradictions traced in Kant: it presupposes the distinction between subject and world that is to be explained and is consequently unable to explain how this chasm is bridged."[7] To avoid that problem, Hegel's account of absolute knowing centrally concerns the *community* of thinking and judging subjects existing over time.

Hegel's idea of the absolute, as we will see in greater detail, reconciles substance and subject in a way that overcomes subject-object dualism. The absolute is both self-sufficient substance and self-conscious subject. The absolute cannot be an undifferentiated, and hence contentless, substance, nor can it be a Cartesian theater rent from other subjects and the world. What Hegel insists in the preface, and what he claims to have demonstrated at the end of the *Phenomenology*, is that the absolute unifies substance and subject. It is not the precritical consciousness of substance endorsed by Greek *Sittlichkeit* or Spinozistic metaphysics but a critical and self-conscious unity. It can only be achieved and recognized in a shape of spirit, a community and way of life. This practical achievement is *absolute spirit*.

Religion and philosophy involve two different forms of reflection on the absolute. Both understand that the absolute is that which unifies substance and subject; both, moreover, understand that this unity is achieved through a form of sacrifice or self-emptying (*Entäußerung*). To understand Hegel's idea of the absolute and the distinction that he makes between religious and philosophical reflection on it, we now have to consider how each accounts for the absolute and for the self-emptying that brings it about.

Religion: God as Absolute

Hegel's chapter on spirit ends, and his chapter on religion begins, with the emergence of absolute spirit. While earlier chapters of the *Phenomenology of Spirit* have discussed religion as it appears in consciousness's attempts to specify the standard of knowledge, the chapter on religion is the first to consider religious communities' reflections on that standard of knowledge.[8] It is the first to consider, as Hegel puts it, "the absolute essence *in and for itself*, the self-consciousness of spirit" (§672/495).

Religions, on Hegel's view, are shapes of spirit in which people engage in self-conscious reflection on the absolute. In this, religion shares something in common with absolute knowing, or philosophy. Both religion and philosophy have the absolute as the object of their reflection. What distinguishes religion from philosophy, however, is the form that its reflection takes. Religious reflection on the absolute has the form of *representation (Vorstellung)*.[9] Representation, or representational thought, is a mode of apprehending conceptual relations and truths in the form of discrete entities, images, and events. It captures conceptual and theoretical truths in a form that is more concrete and, thus, easier for consciousness to grasp. Hegel insists that religion's representations capture the *truth* of the absolute. Nevertheless, he also suggests that the representational form of religious reflection and knowledge is surpassed by the conceptual form of philosophical reflection and knowledge. What religion knows as God, philosophy knows as absolute spirit.

Hegel's chapter on religion considers a series of religions and their reflections on the absolute, and it is by looking at these religions and reflections that we come to understand what it is that Hegel thinks unites (and divides) religion and philosophy. As he does throughout the *Phenomenology of Spirit*, Hegel describes the progression of consciousness in conceptual rather than historical terms. The movement from one religion to another is not a matter of actual historical progression but a matter of the kind of account that a religion would have to give in order to overcome the problems in the previous account.[10] Hegel is describing conceptual possibilities here, not historical trajectories.[11]

Hegel groups these conceptual possibilities into three categories: natural religion, religion of art, and revealed religion. Natural religion involves people's reflection on and relation to the absolute in a natural object. In natural religion, people do not see themselves in that static natural object; their relation to the absolute, therefore, is not understood as a relation to spirit but to nature. Next, religion of art involves people's reflection on and relation to the absolute in forms of artistic expression. In the religion of art, people's reflection on the absolute is also the production of culture. In this way, the religion of art grasps the absolute as spirit rather than as nature, although it does not conceive of spirit as self-conscious or self-reflexive. Finally, revealed religion—the third and most conceptually adequate form of religion on Hegel's account—involves people's reflection on and relation to the absolute as self-conscious, self-reflexive spirit. In the final section of the chapter, Hegel elaborates on this claim about revealed religion.

Hegel's account of revealed religion hinges on the Trinitarian form of its conception of the absolute. As Cyril O'Regan has argued, what Hegel sees in the Trinity is "the perfect symbol for a dynamic, self-differentiating divine who necessarily becomes in and through history."[12] On this view, the Trinity involves the movement of universality into particularity and, then, the return of particularity into unity through the actions of the Son and the Spirit in the world.

What revealed religion takes as absolute—the Trinity—unifies substance and subject. It does so through two acts of self-emptying: "Spirit has two aspects in it, which are represented above as two converse propositions. One is this, that *substance* empties itself of its own self and becomes self-consciousness; the other is the converse, that *self-consciousness* empties itself of itself and makes itself into thinghood, that is, into the universal self. Both aspects have in this way accommodated each other, and their true union has thereby arisen" (§755/549). Substance empties itself to become self-consciousness. Self-consciousness empties itself to become the "universal self." These two acts of self-emptying, then, engender the unity of spirit as both substance and self-consciousness.

Hegel writes, "By virtue of their reciprocal self-emptying, that is, where each becomes the other, spirit thus enters into existence as their unity" (§755/550).

The reciprocal self-emptying that Hegel describes here parallels the acts of confession and forgiveness of the wicked and judging consciousnesses. Here, as in that earlier section, the universal standpoint takes on self-conscious individuality while the self-conscious individual takes on the universal standpoint. Their actions—the confession and forgiveness in the earlier section and the acts of self-emptying in revealed religion—reconcile these two standpoints and give rise to spirit. Moreover, these actions stand in contrast to the convictions and intentions of the conscientious individual who, Hegel writes, lacks the "power to empty itself" (§658/483).

Hegel's word for these acts of self-emptying is *Entäußerung*. This is often translated as externalization or alienation.[13] But it is the same word that Luther used to translate the Greek *kenosis* in Philippians 2:5–7, the verse that describes Christ's act of self-emptying in the incarnation:

(5) Ein jeglicher sei gesinnt, wie Jesus Christus auch war: (6) welcher, ob er wohl in göttlicher Gestalt war, hielt er's nicht für einen Raub, Gott gleich sein, (7) sondern entäußerte sich selbst un nahm Knechtsgestalt an, ward gleich wie ein andrer Mensch und an Gebärden als ein Mensch erfunden. (Phil. 2:5–7, Luther Bible)

Let the same mind be in you that was in Christ Jesus, who, though he was in godly form, did not regard equality with God as spoils, but rather emptied himself and assumed the form of a servant, [and] was formed equally like another human and fashioned as a human.[14]

The Son refuses to take his divinity as a reason to dominate others and, through his act of self-emptying, he enters into equality with human beings. His incarnation, therefore, is a self-emptying and a refusal to arbitrarily exercise power over others.[15]

These acts of self-emptying, which revealed religion takes to characterize the work of the divine in the world, are different from the renunciations and sacrifices that Hegel discusses earlier in the *Phenomenology of Spirit*. They are acts undertaken *by* the absolute, which generate the unity *of* the absolute. The renunciations and sacrifices that Hegel has described before this point, however, have been expressions of consciousness's alienation from the absolute. In those cases, consciousness believes that the absolute is something wholly other than itself. Its sacrifice is intended to strip it of whatever separates it from the absolute, thereby bringing about their reconciliation.[16] In such cases, however, consciousness's sacrifice fails to bring about the intended result. The unhappy consciousness, for instance, is characterized by its alienation from, and yearning for, the absolute. In an attempt to overcome its alienation, the unhappy consciousness tries to surrender (*aufgeben*) its possessions, desires, and even its own will in order to reconcile with the absolute. Hegel writes that "in that self-renunciation, there is a bestowal of recognition that shifts all the power of being-for-itself away from itself and instead treats this power as a gift from above" (§229/176). In its renunciation, the unhappy consciousness recognizes the absolute as the standard of knowledge and the ground of authority and attempts to surrender its own will in order to conform to that standard. Hegel writes that "its surrender of possessions and its abandonment of consumption likewise merely have the same negative significance, and the universal which thereby comes to be for it is in its eyes not its *own activity*" (§230/176–77). But its act of renunciation belies the insignificance that it claims for itself. It makes judgments and takes action, even as it disavows its authority in doing so. Other failed sacrifices for the sake of reconciliation with the absolute include the virtuous consciousness's attempt to reconcile with the universal, the noble consciousness's attempt to reconcile with the state, and Faith's attempt to reconcile with the divine.

In each of these cases, consciousness fails to see its sacrifice as an act that participates in the absolute. Because consciousness believes that the absolute is something external to itself, it comes to believe that its action cannot bring about the unity for which it yearns. Consciousness tries to efface itself, to give itself over to what it takes to be absolute. In doing so, it denies its own authority and accountability. Consciousness comes to see its sacrifice as one more contingent and particular judgment and action that estranges it from the absolute. In that way, its sacrifice reinforces the perceived estrangement between consciousness and the absolute, amplifying rather than diminishing consciousness's sense of alienation. How can it know that *this* judgment and action is not debased? In consciousness's self-understanding (in Hegel's words, *for itself*), its sense of alienation can only become more profound.

Properly understood (that is, for consciousness *in itself*), consciousness participates in the absolute through its act of self-emptying. The act reveals consciousness's status as a subject, a locus of authority and accountability. If consciousness believes that all authority lies outside of itself, then its sacrifice will fail. Consciousness, through its act of sacrifice, tries to strip itself of its particularities in order to merge with the absolute. But, in its action, it expresses and embodies a particular intention and deed for which it is responsible. Consciousness remains—and reveals itself as—a locus of authority and accountability. If, however, consciousness understands that it participates in the absolute, then it already knows that its sacrifice is an action of which it is the author and for which it is accountable. It recognizes its role, and that of its action, in the ongoing contest of authority and accountability.

The Son who enters into the world as a human being is not trying to *reconcile* with the absolute. His act participates in the absolute, and his self-emptying is an expression and embodiment of his commitment not to dominate another but to be a locus of both authority and accountability.

Self-emptying is not, therefore, a renunciation for the sake of reconciliation with the absolute; it is part of what it is to *be* absolute. Hegel writes, "Since this self-consciousness consciously surrenders itself, it is preserved in its self-emptying, and it remains the subject of the substance, but, as having emptied itself, it possesses at the same time the consciousness of this substance; that is, since, by way of its sacrifice, it *engenders* substance as subject, this subject remains its own self" (§749/545–46). Revealed religion captures the idea that the absolute is self-sufficient substance that *becomes* subject through its self-emptying. Through the incarnation, universality becomes particularity. Through the crucifixion, particularity returns to unity with universality. Spirit proceeds from the unity of the self-sufficient substance and the self-emptying, self-conscious subject: "Spirit is therefore posited within the third element, within *universal self-consciousness*; spirit is its religious community" (§781/568). This moment of unity, spirit, has its being *in* and *as* community.

Hegel argues that the doctrine of the Trinity captures the true content of the absolute. It captures the dynamism of the absolute—its movement from universality to particularity to unity—as well as the role that acts of self-emptying play in this movement. Hegel writes, "This incarnation of the divine essence, that is, that it essentially and immediately has the shape of self-consciousness, is the simple content of absolute religion. Within absolute religion, the essence is known as spirit, that is, religion is the essence's consciousness of itself as being spirit, for spirit is knowledge of itself in its self-emptying; spirit is the essence which is the movement of keeping selfsameness with itself in its otherness" (§759/552). The incarnation, in which the absolute empties itself and becomes a self-conscious human being, is the "simple content" of revealed religion. Spirit is the absolute's self-knowledge as both essence and self-emptying other—as, that is, authoritative and accountable.

Nevertheless, while Hegel holds that revealed religion captures the truth of the absolute in its doctrine of the Trinity, he also holds that it captures this truth in a *representational* form. The Trinity symbolizes the movement of the absolute, but revealed religion does not fully recognize what is signified. Consciousness takes this to be a truth about God, but not about itself. It does not recognize its own role in the absolute. Consciousness still thinks of the absolute as something alien to ordinary human consciousness. Hegel writes, "Something in [revealed religion's] object is kept secret from *consciousness* if the object is an *other* for consciousness, that is, *alien* to it, and if consciousness does not know the object as *itself*" (§759/552). God is "an other for consciousness," and the moments of the Trinity are conceived as one-time events, such as the birth, death, and resurrection of the Son. Hegel writes:

> The *past* and *remoteness* are merely the incomplete form of the way in which the immediate mode is mediated, that is, is posited universally. This latter is merely superficially plunged into the element of thought,

preserved within that element as a sensuous mode, and not posited as being at one with the nature of thought itself. It has been merely elevated into *representational thought* [*Vorstellen*], for this is the synthetic combination of sensuous immediacy and its universality, that is, thought. (§764/556)

Hegel argues that revealed religion's insights are "superficially plunged" into thought; revealed religion grasps its insights about the absolute in its representational form. It cannot see how the concrete social life of the religious community expresses and embodies this absolute.

This is not to say that revealed religion is false. Indeed, Hegel insists that revealed religion is *true*, but it is true in this representational form. He writes: "The *content* is the true content, but all of its moments, posited as lying within the element of the activity of representing, have the character of not having been comprehended. Rather, they appear as completely self-sufficient components which are *externally* related to each another" (§765/556). Revealed religion captures the truth of the absolute. But the form in which it captures and reflects on this truth obscures its *conceptual* significance.

To grasp this content as thought itself is to move from the realm of representation to the realm of concept. When the kenotic sacrifice represented in the incarnation is grasped conceptually rather than representationally, it is known to be the self-emptying of the self-conscious subject who relinquishes his absolute self-certainty in order to submit himself to the judgment of others. This insight follows from the end of Chapter VI. In the shape of spirit that Hegel calls conscience, consciousness takes itself to be a self-sufficient absolute; it believes that its own convictions and self-knowledge have independent authority. Being self-sufficient, however, it does not conceive itself as a subject who is fit to be held responsible. It fails to empty itself of its self-sufficiency and to submit itself to the judgment of others. The assurance that others extended to it was no more than a mere echo of its own conviction, now contentless and worthless. The wicked consciousness and the judging consciousness, however, overcome this impasse by relinquishing the self-certainty that Hegel describes in the earlier section on conscience. The wicked consciousness admits its fallibility but recognizes that it can also judge the other. The judging consciousness admits that it, too, is fallible and subject to criticism and correction but recognizes that this does not mean it cannot also be a judge. Each one is self-sufficient (in the relevant sense) and fit to be held responsible. Rightly understood, this is the heart of absolute spirit—the norms and practices of a community of subjects who reciprocally recognize authority, hold responsible, submit to judgment, and admit to fallibility.

The same move from representation to concept can be made with respect to other elements of religious doctrine.[17] Like the incarnation, for instance, reconciliation appears to revealed religion as "something *remote*, something far away in the *future*, just as the reconciliation which the other *self* achieved appears as something remote in the *past*" (§787/574). Revealed religion contends that reconciliation of the universality and particularity of the Father and Son was a historical event that took place and is now past. Ordinary human beings will reconcile with God in the future and in a transcendent realm. In revealed religion, once again, consciousness experiences itself as alienated from the absolute. This alienation characterizes revealed religion *for itself*, not *in itself*; in other words, in revealed religion, consciousness does not recognize that it is already reconciled with the absolute here and now.[18] Hegel writes, "Its reconciliation exists thereby within its heart, but it is still estranged from its consciousness, and its actuality is still fractured" (§787/574). Revealed religion reconciles with the absolute through its beliefs, practices, and institutions, but consciousness remains unreflective about the fact that these constitute a shape of spirit in and through which people generate and sustain the absolute.

In revealed religion, consciousness achieves reconciliation with other consciousness and with its form of life through its practices. Nevertheless, it is not fully aware that this is what it is up to. Hegel contends that the true content of the incarnation is that the absolute empties itself into the self-conscious subject, and the true content of the reconciliation is that the unified absolute comprises the self-emptying movements of the self-sufficient universality, or substance, and the self-conscious particularity, or subject. When the true content of the incarnation and reconciliation is known conceptually, rather than representationally, this content is known to be the movement of spirit itself. This brings us to philosophy and absolute knowing.

Philosophy: Spirit as Absolute

The final transition in the *Phenomenology of Spirit* turns from religion to absolute knowing. In Chapter VIII, the brief and, frankly, perplexing ultimate chapter of the *Phenomenology of Spirit*, Hegel describes the truth that revealed religion and absolute knowing have both grasped, now from the standpoint of absolute knowing, or philosophy.

The brevity (and perplexity) of Chapter VIII is often attributed to external factors that impinged on the writing of the *Phenomenology of Spirit*, including the fraught personal, financial, and political circumstances under which Hegel labored to finish the book.[19] Also, Hegel initially conceived of the *Phenomenology of Spirit* as the introduction to a much longer and more comprehensive *System der Wissenschaft*. On that conception, Chapter VIII would have been the bridge to another work in which Hegel would have filled in what he merely sketches in the *Phenomenology of Spirit*. But there is also an intrinsic reason for the brevity of the chapter: the content and object of absolute knowing is none other than the movement of spirit itself, as presented through the dialectical movements of the *Phenomenology of Spirit*. Hegel writes, "The *goal*, absolute knowing, that is, spirit knowing itself as spirit, has its path in the rec-ollection of spirits as they are in themselves and as they achieve the organiza-tion of their realm" (§808/591). The culmination of the book, in other words, is the recollection of the progression of the shapes of consciousness and shapes of spirit *in themselves* (as opposed to *for* themselves). As readers of the *Phenome-nology of Spirit*, we have followed consciousness on this voyage of discovery. In absolute knowing, consciousness does not know anything that Hegel's readers have not also experienced or encountered on this voyage.[20]

Readers cannot be faulted for initially supposing that absolute know-ing must add up to something more than this. The audacious phrase "absolute knowing" seems to imply omniscience and infallibility. Hegel's concept of the absolute, however, need not entail completeness or certainty of that sort. What Hegel is signaling with his use of the term is that here, finally, is a theory of knowledge that can adequately address the relationship between the knowl-edge claims that people make and the objects about which they make those claims. It avoids skepticism, on the one hand, and givenness, on the other. It avoids the one-sidedness that comes from the assumption that authority rests *only* on the subject *or* object side of a subject-object divide. It is a theory of knowledge that can satisfactorily answer the questions: What can subjects know about the world? How confident can we be in our knowledge? What grounds the authority of our beliefs, norms, and practices?

Absolute knowing knows the absolute to be *spirit*. Moreover, it knows that spirit is not one-sided. Hegel writes that "spirit has shown itself to us to be nei-ther the mere withdrawal of self-consciousness into its pure inwardness, nor the mere absorption of self-consciousness into substance and the non-being of its distinction" (§804/587). Spirit, as absolute, can be neither purely subjective nor purely objective. It must, somehow, unite the two. As we have seen, the unity of subject and object comes from spirit's self-emptying movement, from the dialectic of thought and action.

Like the triune God of revealed religion, spirit unifies subject and object through acts of self-emptying and reconciliation. But philosophy understands, in a way that revealed religion does not, that these acts are ongoing. The move-ment by which the absolute empties itself and enters the world as a subject, dies, and reconciles with the eternal substance is the perpetually recurring movement of spirit. Hegel writes:

> This substance, which is spirit, is its *coming-to-be* what it, the sub-stance, is *in itself*; and it is as this coming-to-be which is taking a re-flective turn into itself that spirit is truly in itself *spirit*. Spirit is in itself the movement which is cognition—the transformation of that former *in-itself* into *for-itself*, of *substance* into *subject*, of the object of *con-sciousness* into the object of *self-consciousness*, i.e. into an object that is just as much sublated, that is, into the *concept*. This transformation

is the circle returning back into itself, which presupposes its beginning
and reaches its beginning only at the end. (§802/585)

Hegel writes that spirit is the "movement which is cognition," the movement
of substance into subject and, then, the subject's reconciliation with a now-
sublated substance. It is the ongoing movement of thought and action that
takes what appears given or self-sufficient into self-consciousness and, in
doing so, transforms what was given. Absolute spirit is consciousness that
recognizes itself—its own movement through its norms and norm-generating
practices—as its object.

Philosophy, like revealed religion, knows that substance and subject are
unified through acts of self-emptying. Hegel writes that "[spirit] has shown
itself to be this movement of the self which empties itself of itself and immerses
itself in its substance, and which likewise, as subject, has taken both the inward
turn into itself from out of that substance and has made its substance into an
object and a content, just as it has sublated this distinction between objectivity
and content" (§804/587–88). Absolute spirit is both the object and the content of its thought; it knows itself to be this movement of the self through the
moments of self-emptying and reconciliation. Thus it experiences both self-
sufficient substantiality and self-conscious subjectivity in a perpetual dialectic.

Absolute knowing entails no more and no less than what we readers of
the *Phenomenology of Spirit* know at this point in the text. We have followed
consciousness on its voyage from sense-certainty to absolute knowing, and we
have seen how the inadequate theories of knowledge offered along the way
have given way to increasingly complex and adequate ones. The ideas, concepts, categories, forms, and norms involved in those earlier theories of knowledge structured what came next and our experience of it. Absolute knowing
reflects on the shapes of consciousness and shapes of spirit that have appeared
before it. It considers their strengths and weaknesses. For consciousness, the
progression of shapes of consciousness and shapes of spirit has been the object
and content of its knowledge. Consciousness thinks with and about the norms
that have been bequeathed to it by others.

The *Phenomenology of Spirit* is a story about the standard of knowledge and the ground of authority. In this sense, the story ends with absolute
knowing. Absolute knowing knows that the self-sufficient and self-conscious
standard of knowledge is expressed and embodied in the norms and social
practices of a community. At the end of Chapter VI, the wicked and judging
consciousnesses express and embody this standard of knowledge and ground
of authority through their practices of acting, judging, confessing, and forgiving. But they do not engage in self-conscious reflection on this. In Chapter VII, revealed religion expresses and embodies this standard of knowledge
and ground of authority through its practices, and it reflects on it in its doctrines. But, in revealed religion, consciousness still thinks of the absolute as

something from which it is at least partially alienated. In Chapter VIII, however, the beliefs and actions of individuals like the wicked and judging consciousnesses are recognized and reflected upon as the absolute itself. Beliefs and actions, including acts of granting authority and holding accountable, become both the object and the content of thought.

Unlike earlier shapes of spirit, which were unable to provide an adequate account of the authority of their norms, absolute knowing can give an account of its beliefs and practices that explains their *content* as well as their *authority*. It knows that beliefs and practices are contentful, or meaningful, on account of the content-generating practices of speaking and acting in a community over time. What gives them content is the history of concept use in that community. It also knows that its beliefs and practices are binding insofar as they are embedded in and sustained by relationships and practices of reciprocal recognition. These relationships and practices sustain norms and enable their scrutiny and critique.

On Conflict, Reconciliation, and Hegel's God

When the wicked and judging consciousnesses confess to and forgive one another, something else appears in their midst. Hegel calls this God. He writes that the "reconciling *yes*" of the confession and forgiveness is "God appearing in the midst of those who know themselves as pure knowledge" (§671/494). But again, what does Hegel mean by God? How much of the traditional Christian content of that term ought to be imported into our interpretation of Hegel here?

These are central questions in contemporary debates about how to read Hegel. Should he be read as a precritical metaphysician or a post-Kantian critical philosopher? Relatedly, is his philosophy an attempt to justify Christian doctrine or to overcome it? In addressing these interpretative questions, we must avoid one-sided answers. Hegel is a critical philosopher who is trying to say something about the world and our knowledge of it. He thinks that such knowledge is possible, and he wants to show *how* it is possible. His thought is profoundly shaped by, and engaged with, Christianity, but he is not content to rest with representations, or *Vorstellungen*, of the absolute. Thus he ultimately seeks philosophical answers to the questions that religion and philosophy share.

Whether or not such answers cast Hegel as a metaphysician depends, in part, on what sense of metaphysics one has in mind. On Kant's account, metaphysics involves the attempt to gain a priori knowledge of the absolute. Kant thought that such an attempt went hand in hand with speculation about a transcendent realm—a form of speculation that Hegel clearly rejects. As Frederick Beiser, a critic of post-Kantian interpretations of Hegel, writes: "If metaphysics consists in speculation about such a realm, then Hegel would be the first to condemn it as a pseudo-science. It is necessary to stress that Hegel's own concept of the infinite or unconditioned is entirely immanent: the infinite does not exist beyond the finite world but only within it."[21] What Hegel views as absolute is not at all transcendent; indeed, it is, and must be, wholly immanent.

What is less clear is whether Hegel's philosophy is a metaphysics in the former sense, an attempt to gain a priori knowledge of the absolute. Beiser insists that it is. He argues that "since Hegel thinks that philosophy attempts to know God through reason, and since he understands God to be infinite or unconditioned, it follows that his philosophy is a metaphysics, and indeed in roughly the Kantian sense; for it attempts to acquire knowledge of the unconditioned through pure reason."[22] A proper understanding of what it is for something to be "absolute," however, renders this a much less audacious claim than it initially appears to be. In the *Phenomenology of Spirit*, philosophy is not an attempt to know the infinite and unconditioned God; rather, it is an attempt to know the absolute—the standard of knowledge and the ground of authority. From the standpoint of absolute knowing, consciousness recognizes that this standard emerges from its own judgments and actions. It is not given to thought or to understanding. Hegel contends that nothing that is merely given could be absolute. Moreover, Hegel's claim to knowledge of the absolute is not vindicated a priori in the *Phenomenology of Spirit* but through dialectical reasoning about human thought and action. It seems to me that both the method and the result are so thoroughly different from the sort of dogmatic metaphysics that Kant criticized as to make the label "metaphysics" misleading, at the very least.[23]

What, then, to make of God's sudden appearance at the end of Chapter VI? Hegel's use of the term "God" squares with his view of confession and forgiveness as sacramental practices. Such practices, as we saw in chapter 4, represent the absolute—symbolizing and actualizing it in word and deed. God's appearance in the midst of those who confess and forgive is the actualization of the absolute—understood in religion's representational terms as God. But insofar as religion views its object, God, as an entity that exists apart from itself, its community, and its practices, it misses something crucial about its own participation in its object. Here, Hegel's use of the term *Entäußerung*, *self-emptying*, matters. Confession and forgiveness are acts of self-emptying that constitute the movement of the absolute, in ways that parallel the *kenosis* that characterizes the movement of the Trinity. Bear in mind, however, that the subjects who confess and forgive are ordinary consciousnesses, not the Father, Son, and Spirit. Their return to unity, through their relationships and practices of reciprocal recognition, is what Hegel names God here. It is what absolute knowing, or philosophy, calls absolute spirit.

There *is* something emergent about absolute spirit. The spirit that proceeds from the unity of substance and subject is more than the sum of its parts. It is irreducible to the dyad of wicked consciousness and judging consciousness, or Father and Son, or substance and subject. What is crucial, on this reading, is that spirit comprises the individual members of a community and it emerges and evolves in response to their social practices—including rituals like burial rites, devotional practices, confession and forgiveness, and self-emptying. When the members of a community reflect on these practices, and on their role as subjects who engage in them, they become self-conscious of their own normative authority, aware of their participation in the absolute.

At the end of the last chapter, I discussed Pippin's claim that "the aspiration for a culminating reconciliation is everywhere in Hegel, but everywhere elusive."[24] We can now see, in more detail, the ways in which Hegel does and does not offer a culminating reconciliation. The appearance of God and the emergence of absolute spirit at the end of Chapter VI is the culmination of consciousness's search for a shape of spirit that does not collapse under the inadequacies of its beliefs and practices. The emergence of absolute knowing in Chapter VIII is the culmination of consciousness's search for a theory of knowledge that makes sense of that shape of spirit. When consciousness achieves absolute knowing, it becomes self-conscious about the role that social practices play in creating and sustaining spirit—the self-sufficient and self-conscious standard. Spirit becomes its own object and content; the theory of knowledge no longer requires revision in light of consciousness's experience. In this sense, absolute knowing concludes consciousness's voyage of discovery.

In another sense, however, this voyage remains open-ended. The progression from one shape of spirit to the next has ceased because consciousness has arrived at relationships and practices of reciprocal recognition and an account of how those relationships and practices generate authority. But absolute knowing does not mark the end of mediation, contestation, or revision. In fact, these processes seem to be built into the shape of spirit and the theory of knowledge that Hegel offers at the end of the *Phenomenology of Spirit*. That shape of spirit, as we have seen, involves relationships of reciprocal recognition in which authority *and* accountability are matters of ongoing social practices such as confessing the arbitrariness and contingency that have entered into one's beliefs and actions, and forgiving others, with the knowledge that one is also fallible. The theory of knowledge, meanwhile, highlights the role that these social practices play in creating, sustaining, and transforming norms. Neither the shape of spirit nor the theory of knowledge forecloses the possibility of contestation over which gender norms ought to be endorsed, what acts counts as self-emptying, or anything else on this order. These are the very matters that are contested in the movement of spirit.

What absolute knowing does suggest is what it might take to be entitled to hold one or another view on these topics and how others ought to structure their response to such a view. Absolute knowing requires the perpetual relinquishment of the posture of self-sufficiency. In absolute knowing, the self-conscious subject knows "its limit." Hegel writes: "To know its limit means to know that it is to sacrifice itself" (§807/590). Spirit knows that knowledge *is* this ongoing movement out from itself, into the world, and back again. There is both conflict *and* reconciliation. Absolute knowing stands at the top of Hegel's dialectical ladder because underlying absolute knowing is the acknowledgment that human beings are going to get things wrong, time and time again. Human error, difference, disagreement, and the possibility of changing norms are built into the shape of spirit and the theory of knowledge.[25]

Hegel's conception of the absolute does not require the end of conflict. As Crites writes, "What Hegel calls spirit is not so diaphanous as it sounds, nor is its absoluteness so conversation-stopping."[26] Individuals still have diverse commitments, and they are bound to draw different conclusions from their experiences of the world. Unlike the members of Greek *Sittlichkeit*, these individuals do not merely play roles that are assigned to them. Rather, they recognize their individual and collective responsibility for their roles and norms.[27] When these individuals hold themselves and others responsible for their beliefs and actions, they do so from particular and contingent standpoints. Each acknowledges the corrigibility of her convictions, while rejecting the idea of a permanent gap between self-consciousness and its object.

Although Hegel has a reputation as a triumphalist thinker, his account of absolute spirit is poignant. It may overcome the formal tragedy of Greek *Sittlichkeit*—the conflict between two one-sided characters who refuse to acknowledge their own normative authority—but it provides no way out of human fallibility, finitude, loss, and impermanence. Hegel takes these features of human life seriously, building them into his account of how we believe, know, and act. The subject has to give up the self-certain posture of the conscientious individual in order to submit herself and her actions to the judgment of others. In so doing, she risks censure and misrecognition. Hegel ends the *Phenomenology* with an invocation of memory and Golgotha, reminders that history and sacrifice are the conditions for the possibility of reconciliation.[28]

Conclusion

Absolute knowing marks the point at which knowledge "no longer has the need to go beyond itself, that is, where knowledge comes around to itself, and where the concept corresponds to the object and the object to the concept" (§80/74). At the end of the *Phenomenology of Spirit*, consciousness arrives at this knowledge, and it recognizes the standard of knowledge.

Consciousness could not have arrived at this standard of knowledge without having traveled through the earlier shapes of spirit. It has learned from the strengths and weaknesses of previous accounts of the standard, and it is in a position to provide a diachronic and dialectical account of how it has incorporated their strengths and overcome their weaknesses. Unlike the members of Greek *Sittlichkeit*, those who have achieved absolute knowing realize that the authority of their norms is neither fixed nor immediately given. Unlike Faith and Enlightenment, they know that authority depends on public action as much as private reason or experience. And unlike conscience, they know that authority depends not only on subjective conviction but also on shared social practices of judgment, confession, and forgiveness. The shape of spirit that emerges with the confession and forgiveness of the wicked and judging consciousnesses involves a new account of authority and a new relationship to the conflicts that arise within it. Absolute spirit does not eliminate conflict; rather, it is characterized by agonism, ongoing difference, disagreement, and struggle in the context of reciprocal recognition, punctuated by moments of reconciliation.

The preceding chapters have offered an interpretation of Hegel's *Phenomenology of Spirit* that connects epistemological concerns about the standard of knowledge to ethical concerns about the relationships and practices that a community ought to cultivate if its members are to overcome domination and alienation. The connection lies in Hegel's account of absolute spirit—that is, his argument that the standard of knowledge and ground of authority emerge from the practices of people who share a community.

As I have discussed throughout these chapters, there are vigorous debates in contemporary scholarship about how Hegel ought to be interpreted on his own terms. First, does Hegel reject Kant's philosophical system and claim to have achieved a priori knowledge of the absolute, or does he accept and extend Kant's critique of precritical metaphysics? Second, does Hegel's absolute spirit overcome conflict once and for all, or is it a form of life in which difference and conflict persist within relations of reciprocal recognition? Regarding the first of these two questions, I have answered in accord with post-Kantian interpretations developed by philosophers and scholars of religion such as Robert Brandom, Thomas A. Lewis, Robert Pippin, Terry Pinkard, Paul Redding, and Sally Sedgwick, although I have also paid serious attention to Hegel's use of religious categories and concepts. Regarding the second question, I have argued that the ongoing social practices that sustain the form of life that Hegel calls absolute spirit involve both conflict and reconciliation. What initially appear as Hegel's epistemological concerns turn out to bear on ethical concerns about the kinds of relationships and practices that people ought to cultivate in the face of ongoing differences and disagreements.

In addition to these interpretive debates, however, there are a number of equally important and contentious debates about what contemporary perspective on religion, ethics, and politics one ought to develop when reading Hegel.[29] As abstract as it was, Hegel's philosophy was motivated by pressing social and political concerns. When Hegel wrote the *Phenomenology of Spirit*, the French Revolution and the Reign of Terror were not-too-distant memories, and the collapse of the Holy Roman Empire was at hand. What would this bigger and more diverse polity look like? What authority would it have over citizens—and what authority would citizens have over it? What beliefs, practices, and institutions would citizens need to cultivate in order to sustain it? Similar questions are with us still. What can we learn from Hegel's social ethics that might inform democratic thought and practice in a religiously diverse society?

The next two chapters turn from the interpretive debates to these contemporary religious, ethical, and political questions. I argue that a Hegelian social ethics—rooted in Hegel's account of the relationships and practices that a community ought to cultivate in order to overcome alienation and domination— remains relevant today. It can help us think about how to approach religious differences and ethical conflicts, and about the rituals and social practices that sustain the community in the face of these ongoing differences.

CHAPTER SIX

Commitment, Conversation, and Contestation

WE FIND OURSELVES, in the early twenty-first century, living in communities marked by their increasing diversity. We confess many faiths. Our beliefs and practices stem from different and, at times, incompatible sources. Theological disagreements about the existence and nature of the divine, the status of sacred texts, and the authority of religious traditions are closely connected to ethical and political disagreements. Too often, these disagreements harden into battle lines. Social and political life becomes polarized.

Hegel did not anticipate this twenty-first-century diversity, but he was familiar with deep and abiding conflicts. He understood the society that he inhabited to be the product of many such conflicts, some of which cut as deep as any conflict among religious or secular groups today. One such conflict pitted the Protestant Reformation against the Catholic tradition. Another pitted Pietist faith against secular rationalism. Hegel took these conflicts seriously. He tried to understand what sorts of beliefs and practices such conflicts entail and what it would take to resolve them without domination or alienation. The resulting social ethics is relevant to our more diverse communities today.

The following two chapters sketch out a Hegelian social ethics that attends to conflict and reconciliation in religiously diverse communities. This social ethics does not depend on a shared religious or philosophical standpoint. It does, however, presuppose a dialectical and diachronic account of how commitments and other norms are affirmed, contested, and transformed. And it involves ongoing practices of conflict and reconciliation and the cultivation of relationships of reciprocal recognition. This chapter outlines what it means to be committed to a belief, practice, or form of life and how, on this account, conflicts are to be confronted and, at times, resolved. It then turns to recent work in Christian theology that lends support, for its own reasons, to certain basic features of a Hegelian social ethics in the face of religious diversity and difference.[1] Recent ecumenical Christian theology, being in part an effort to overcome the most sorrowful rifts within the Christian tradition, has developed similarly illuminating ways of characterizing and dealing with conflict. In considering these features of a Hegelian social ethics and post-liberal, ecumenical Christian theology, we arrive at a model of public discourse that is pluralist and agonistic.

What It Means to Be Committed

In a religiously diverse society, people disagree about what to believe and to do—and about who or what ought to count as authoritative in settling such disagreements. The notion that one's own beliefs or practices are better or more truthful than the alternatives is not, in itself, a problem. That's simply what it means to be committed to them. In so far as one is committed to one's beliefs or actions, one believes and does *this*, rather than *that*, because one takes it that *this* is good, right, or true and that *that* is, at the least, less good, right, or true. Commitment of this sort involves one's endorsement of, and responsibility for, that to which one has committed oneself.

Nevertheless, it doesn't take more than a few minutes watching the news or scrolling through social media to see that disagreements often harden into fixed disputes. We disagree not only about our commitments but also about the standards for assessing such commitments—the authoritative grounds for believing, acting, and judging. Like the various forms of consciousness in the *Phenomenology of Spirit*, we disagree about which people, texts, and traditions have the authority to settle our disputes. These conflicts can appear intractable. Consider the abortion debate. Those at the poles of the debate disagree not only about whether abortion ought to remain legal but also about the relevant norms and standards that ought to be considered: the will of God, the teachings of religious traditions, the liberal conception of personhood and the rights that follow from it, scientific evidence about fetal development, moral claims about life's sacredness, and so on. No matter how forcefully each makes its case to the other, these two camps seem bound to disagree about what even counts as a good reason for or against reproductive rights. Under the present circumstances, it is hard to imagine how the abortion debate could ever be resolved. The same could be said of many contemporary ethical and political debates: we appear to be burdened with them for the foreseeable future.[2]

Some worry that the members of religiously diverse communities are condemned to the interminable conflicts of the culture wars. To avoid those conflicts, or to mitigate their worst effects, they seek to eliminate certain commitments, forms of reasoning, or appeals to authority from public discourse. I recognize the worry, but I think such proposals are misguided. Hegel can help us see how people make commitments and contest them in the midst of deep and abiding disagreement; he can also help us see how people can cope with and, at times, resolve such disagreements.

The dynamics of the culture wars are easy enough to follow. They involve two positions, each of which thinks it argues from incontrovertible principles. Because partisans disagree on these principles, however, each rejects the claims and commitments of the other. The conflict between Faith and Enlightenment displays these dynamics. Both Faith and Enlightenment think that their commitments rest on a fixed foundation. This foundation serves as the unshakable, unquestioned standard of knowledge and ground of authority. For Faith, this is religious experience. For Enlightenment, it is universal and timeless reason. Because Faith and Enlightenment disagree about what the foundation of its commitments ought to be, neither can see a way into conversation with the other. Their appeals to these foundational commitments act as conversation-stoppers, and Faith and Enlightenment find themselves locked in perpetual conflict.

Both Faith and Enlightenment have significant strengths as well as significant weaknesses. Their strengths come from their actual social practices. For Faith, these are its rituals and worship. These social practices are Faith's way of relating to, and reconciling with, the absolute. Through these social practices, Faith participates in and generates its actual standard of knowledge and ground of authority. Enlightenment's strengths lie in its practices of scrutiny and critique. Although it withholds its own foundational commitments from such scrutiny, it has cultivated the sorts of social practices that make the consideration and contestation of commitments and norms possible. The shape of spirit that overcomes Faith and Enlightenment's weaknesses must also preserve these strengths. Their weaknesses, Hegel suggests, are common to Faith and Enlightenment. Both fail to see their social practices as generating their standard of knowledge and ground of authority. Both claim, instead, that a fixed foundation can serve as such a standard. They take religious experience and reason, respectively, as the basis on which other commitments may be affirmed and held as true, right, or good.

Faith and Enlightenment's way of thinking about commitments has two problems. First, by treating religious experience or reason, respectively, as the fixed foundation on which other commitments rest, Faith and Enlightenment beg the question: Why should *that* be recognized as the standard of knowledge and ground of authority? Because neither Faith nor Enlightenment can give a non-question-begging account of its foundational commitment—its standard for evaluating its commitments and other norms—neither can address the challenges posed to it by the other. Each dismisses the other's claims and criticisms as based on false premises, superstition, wishful thinking, arbitrariness, or sin. We ought to be on guard against reductionist accounts like these, which attribute only weaknesses and no strengths to an alternate viewpoint. As Alasdair MacIntyre writes in a 1977 essay, "It is yet another a mark of a degenerate tradition that it has contrived a set of epistemological defences which enable it to avoid being put in question or at least to avoid recognising that it is being put in question by rival traditions."[3] MacIntyre, whose early debt to Hegel is often obscured in his more recent work, captures Hegel's concern about the weaknesses of Faith and Enlightenment as each closes its ears to the claims and criticisms made by the other.

Second, Faith and Enlightenment's shared weaknesses make it hard to imagine how commitments or norms could ever change, or how conflicts could ever be overcome. If its fidelity to a fixed standard is the sole criterion for the justification of a commitment or norm, how could something that people were once justified in believing or doing become something that people now take to be *un*justified? Changes of this sort have taken place many, many times, and what once appeared to be intractable conflicts about what to believe or do have also been overcome. The United States, to take one example, is no longer paralyzed by the conflict over women's right to vote—a conflict that, for generations, appeared intractable. Whereas it once appeared to many Americans as a given that women should be denied the right to vote, today it is widely accepted that women's disenfranchisement would be unequivocally wrong. How did that happen? Not, it would seem, by mere appeal to an unchanging foundational commitment.

Instead, commitments and norms regarding women's social, legal, and political standing changed, gradually, through processes of dialectical reasoning. In fits and starts, people assessed whether their gender norms were consistent with other commitments that they held and adequate to the form of life in which they lived.[4] People wrote articles and made declarations, shared stories in consciousness-raising groups, aired grievances and debated how to redress those grievances, and participated in the public theater of marches and demonstrations. They judged their commitments, and others'. They considered the strengths and weaknesses of those commitments relative to the strengths and weaknesses of past and present alternatives. In a related discussion of the gender-based division of labor, Pippin writes:

> One begins to become a "Hegelian" with the simple realization of how implausible it would be to insist that the injustice of such a basis for a division of labor, the reasons for rejecting such a practice, were always in principle available from the beginning of human attempts to justify their practices, and were "discovered" sometime in the early nineteen-seventies. And yet our commitment to such a rejection is far stronger than "a new development in how we go on." The past practice is irrational and so unjust, however historically indexed the "grip" of such a claim clearly is.[5]

It is tempting, from our present vantage point, to see this progress as inevitable. But it was not the case that people unearthed a set of timeless and universal reasons that supported a more equitable distribution of labor across gender lines that had been there, waiting to be discovered, all along. Instead, people gradually arrived at a dialectical and diachronic perspective on what it would take for current beliefs and actions to uphold the strengths and overcome the weaknesses of past views. They revised their social arrangements accordingly (although often incompletely).

Processes of dialectical reasoning take place all the time—whenever people air disagreements and evaluate the merits of alternate views. This is how people affirm, scrutinize, criticize, and reject commitments. It is also the way that norms evolve. It happens, to a certain extent, whether people acknowledge it or not. When people become aware of their role in this process, however, they are less likely to find themselves stuck in seemingly intractable conflicts. They may be more inclined to cultivate the relationships and practices that make conflict and its resolution less likely to perpetuate domination and alienation.

Hegel's conclusions about the standard of knowledge and the ground of authority lead to a form of social and political life in which these ground-level conflicts are expected to arise continually and in which the work of recognition and reconciliation is understood to always be incomplete. This is an *agonistic*, or contestatory, form of life, suited to a diverse modern society in which no one can presume that any particular norm that she endorses is endorsed by everyone else.

People affirm and change their commitments and norms through social practices. They make claims and take action. They disagree and argue. Sometimes they confess and forgive. They forge new norms out of the strengths and weaknesses of what came before. In a religiously diverse society, people come to different conclusions about what the best available beliefs and practices are with respect to religious and theological matters. In some of these cases, there are a number of different commitments that a person could be justified in endorsing, given all that remains unknown about them. This Hegelian account of what it means to be committed shows how the members of a religiously diverse society can hold contrasting beliefs, confront ethical conflicts, and, in some cases, overcome impasses among them.

This account challenges certain beliefs about what work appeals to authority can do. On this view, justification is always a matter of social practice. Appeals to the authority of God, scripture, and revelation are themselves social practices. They are someone's attempt to convince others that the called-upon authorities ought to hold weight when determining one's commitments. Each such appeal plays out against a background of more or less widely accepted assumptions, expectations, and patterns of interaction. In processes of dialectical reasoning, an authority can hold only as much weight as the members of the relevant community recognize it as holding for them. If I say that the word of God is authoritative, what I am saying is that I treat—and I think others ought to treat—scripture as a primary source of reasons for commitments. If others do not share this view, scripture turns out to lack the recognized, effective authority that I claim for it. Likewise, the apocalyptic view, that the divine will break into history to establish a wholly and radically new order, shares the problem of Hegel's "unhappy consciousness." The unhappy consciousness acknowledges God as both radically other and as the standard of knowledge and ground of authority. Its acknowledgment of God's authority, however, is itself a move in the normative sphere of making claims, granting authority, and judging (including judging what the standard *is*). The authority of apocalyptic in-breaking depends on its acknowledgment as authoritative by members of a community—acknowledged, perhaps, because it fulfills promises described in scripture and carried down in the tradition. That acknowledgment or recognition carries authority of its own, such that the in-breaking cannot be an independent or freestanding standard of knowledge. In some communities, one may count on others to share one's judgment about the authority of certain doctrines, texts, and figures. But even in a community in which everyone agrees to treat scripture, read in a particular way, as having authority, it cannot be said that this authority is independent or freestanding. It still depends on the recognition of the people who judge it to be authoritative for them.

A Hegelian social ethics does not depend on a shared religious or philosophical standpoint—although it does presume that commitments about these and other matters are affirmed, contested, and transformed through ongoing social practices. Concept-use and knowledge claims are judged according to the standards that people have available to them, those that have become available as they have evaluated the strengths and weaknesses of what came before. Such standards are not given to people through unmediated revelation or universal and timeless reason. God, scripture, or revelation—or, for that matter, a secular leader, legal document, or scientific method—cannot have independent or freestanding authority in the processes by which people affirm, contest, and transform their commitments and norms. Nevertheless, this view lends itself to a model of public discourse that is open to all. No commitment leads one to be barred from the conversation, and no one's commitments are immune from scrutiny and critique. Nor is it that (contested) authorities have no weight in public discourse. Rather, people ought to voice their commitments, appeal to the people, texts, and traditions that they believe ought to guide collective reasoning and decision making, and submit these commitments and appeals to the judgment of others. Hegel thought that the standard of knowledge and ground of authority resided in the assembly of norms and social practices of a people bound together in relationships of reciprocal recognition. But a Hegelian social ethics can leave that as an open question. The adherents of alternate views are in a position to argue for them.

Agonism, Authority, and Christian Apologetics

In *Theology without Metaphysics*, Kevin Hector describes the role of social practices in the institution and transformation of Christian commitments. In doing so, he responds to the worry that all of this emphasis on the authority of social practice is incompatible with faith in the reality of a transcendent God. Hector shows that theological concepts work in the same way as ordinary concepts. Their content or meaning is acquired and altered through use. When Christians use theological concepts in everyday life, they are both drawing on past uses of these concepts and making judgments about how they apply in novel circumstances. When a theological concept is used in a new way, its meaning subtly shifts. The legitimacy of this new use and shifting meaning— whether a Christian is justified in using the concept in this way—is a matter judged by other members of the Christian community. In particular, Hector argues, legitimacy is judged in terms of "conformity to Christ" and the tradition that follows from him.[6]

Although "conformity to Christ" initially seems to operate as a fixed standard or foundational commitment of the sort that Hegel criticized, it turns out that this standard is also wrapped up in the ongoing processes of dialectical reasoning. Christ is the standard against which theological concept use is judged, but it is the members of the Christian community who are the finite and fallible judges of whether a theological concept carries on in conformity to Christ (at least on this side of the eschaton). For example, in recent years, many congregations and denominations have debated whether and how to consecrate same-sex partnerships. One of the concepts at the center of these debates is *marriage*. Members of these congregations and denominations have asked, in essence, how does the concept of marriage apply in this situation? The resulting debates are mainly about the sorts of cases to which this concept applies: In particular, does the concept of marriage apply to commitments between two men or two women? There are related debates about the *consequences* of applying that concept to a particular situation. If the concept of marriage is rightly applied to same-sex partnerships, what ought to follow? What expectations, rights, or responsibilities are a consequence of the application of the concept? Hector argues that Christians give and evaluate answers to these questions in terms of fidelity to Christ's example and to the Christian tradition. At the same time, individual and collective judgments about what *constitutes* fidelity to Christ and the Christian tradition—even about what the relevant criteria are—remain contestable.[7]

Hector is not alone among Christian theologians in thinking of commitments and norms in this way. Post-liberal Christian theology likewise insists that theological concept-use and knowledge claims are judged in light of a community's narratives about who and what it is, rather than from some neutral standpoint outside of any such narrative. This view, developed in the work of Hans Frei and George Lindbeck, also gestures toward the role that social practices play in specifying the meaning of theological concepts and in authorizing religious commitments. In *The Nature of Doctrine*, Lindbeck argues that religious propositions are a kind of grammar, "communally authoritative rules of discourse, attitude, and action."[8] Like grammatical rules, Lindbeck argues, doctrines are guides or principles that govern claim-making. In other words, they are norms. These norms guide the use of other theological concepts and claims, as judged by members of the community. Just as a speaker who uses English-language concepts but strings them together in an unintelligible sequence will be viewed as an incompetent language-user by English speakers, a person who uses concepts of God, sin, and grace but ignores the Church doctrines that meaningfully structure claims about how these concepts apply to the world will likely be viewed skeptically by other Christians. Lindbeck argues that doctrines "indicate what constitutes faithful adherence to a community."[9] Although post-liberal theology has been criticized as excessively concerned with the continuity and coherence of the Christian tradition, Lindbeck's account of doctrine need not rule out doctrinal dispute and change. English speakers can disagree about the use or application of grammatical rules without abandoning English grammar. Christians, likewise, can disagree about how doctrines ought to be used, revised, or discarded in changing circumstances without abandoning Christian doctrine altogether. While it is true that this is not a view disposed toward radical theological revolution, it is well suited to ongoing contestation and even thoroughgoing reform.

Traditions change as the people who participate in them go about the everyday business of life. Perhaps they encounter new situations or changing circumstances. They try to make sense of these with the concepts, doctrines, commitments, and norms that they hold. As they do so, a number of things can happen. They may find that they are able to assimilate these new experiences into their existing set of commitments and norms. As Lindbeck argues, "The reasonableness of a religion is largely a function of its assimilative powers, of its ability to provide an intelligible interpretation on its own terms of the varied situations and realities adherents encounter."[10] It "absorbs the world" into its own commitments and norms. Alternately, adherents of a tradition may find that their experiences and encounters *cannot* be assimilated. In some cases, these experiences and encounters reveal inadequacies and inconsistencies among people's previously held commitments. People may need to revise, resignify, or even reject particular commitments in order to fix or eliminate these inadequacies and inconsistences.

Similar challenges present themselves when people with different commitments engage with one another. Lindbeck's *The Nature of Doctrine* is intended, in part, to assist in ecumenical conversations across lines of Protestant-Catholic difference. Second-generation post-liberal theologians retain this emphasis on ecumenism with, for scholars like William Placher and William Werpehowski, increased attention to contact and conversations between Christians and non-Christians. Placher and Werpehowski reject the idea that such conversations can or should proceed on the basis of universally acceptable reasons, as well as the idea that people's differences and disagreements are so profound that they cannot talk to one another at all. What Placher calls "unapologetic theology" and what Werpehowski calls "ad hoc apologetics" are approaches to public discourse that affirm real and abiding differences while encouraging the proliferation of conversations among people from different traditions.[11] Because there is no incorrigible foundational commitment from which all of one's other commitments proceed, one perfectly good way to begin a conversation is to find a single point of agreement and to proceed from there. People can begin their conversations about what to believe and to do *anywhere* within their broader network of commitments, and then they can move outward from that point, investigating and interrogating their commitments as they go. Deeper agreement, if it comes at all, comes only piece by piece.

Ad hoc apologetics, like other processes of dialectical reasoning, begins in the middle of things. Questions about what we ought to believe and to do are answered through dialectical and diachronic accounts of the strengths and weaknesses of alternate views. As Werpehowski argues, "Any argument for the scheme over religious and nonreligious competitors must be cumulative in character; it must show the way in which the scheme makes better sense of the features of reality than do the alternatives."[12] My commitment to a particular use of a concept, or to an interpretation of a doctrine, or to a way of living out a tradition ought to be based on my assessment of that commitment's superiority to alternatives; that is what it means to be committed and to take responsibility for that commitment. At the same time, such assessments are always themselves context dependent. I cannot step outside of my commitments to evaluate them wholesale.

Someone might object that Lindbeck's claim to "absorb the world" into the world of scripture is just one more way that a particular tradition can refuse to engage in conversation across difference. It effaces the difference between itself and the other, by translating the other into its own terms, rather than engaging in public discourse and critical self-examination. The criticism is fair enough. Lindbeck's way of talking about these issues, particularly his quietism on matters of truth and justification in *The Nature of Doctrine*, leaves him open to that kind of interpretation. Nevertheless, there are more generative ways of interpreting his claim. Bruce Marshall's work on theology, truth, and justification can help us see this. Marshall argues that our judgments are made and evaluated in the context of other commitments and norms that we hold. When we encounter something unfamiliar, we first try to make sense of it in light of whatever else we hold to be true. In this, Marshall draws on Donald Davidson's principle of charity in interpretation. When another person says something that I cannot make sense of, I map the unintelligible concepts onto my own and I attribute more familiar commitments to the speaker in order to help me interpret what they might mean. To the degree possible, I also presume the truth of that person's utterance or claim. While this has the potential to introduce a kind of self-referential bias into my interpretation of others, this is mitigated by the fact that much of what people say concerns the world that we share, even if we grasp and express the features of this world in radically different ways. The principle of charity makes a descriptive claim; according to Davidson, this simply *is* how we go about trying to understand one another most of the time. We cannot help interpreting others and their commitments as belonging to the same world we are in. We also cannot help interpreting them from our point of view in that world. This fact is the basis of interpretation.

Marshall uses Davidson's principle of charity to develop a compelling account of what it might be to "absorb the world." He argues that "the goal of interpretation is to find a way of understanding a discourse which allows it to be held true, that is, to find a place for it within the world or 'domain of meaning' opened up by the scriptural text."[13] Marshall goes on to say that "the theological project of 'absorbing the world' is the ongoing effort by the Christian community and individual members to construe novel, unfamiliar, or 'alien' sentences in a way which *both* (a) constitutes the best available interpretation of those sentences and (b) allows them to be held true."[14] Ultimately, some claims will be inassimilable into the world of scripture; these claims will either be regarded by Christians as false or will be the starting point for critical scrutiny of the tradition itself. The adequacy of a tradition, according to Lindbeck and Marshall, depends on its "assimilative power," its ability to give an account on its own terms of a wide variety of claims made about the world. Because people continually find themselves in novel situations, this is an ongoing process. They are continually trying to understand others in light of the commitments that they hold; they are continually adjusting their commitments as they discover inadequacies and incompatibilities. Meanwhile, a pluralist society is one in which many such traditions can "reasonably claim significant assimilative power." The debates or disagreements among such traditions will be sorted out, if at all, "only gradually over a long period of time."[15]

Davidson's principle of charity, and Marshall's use of it, offers a way of thinking about how conversations might move forward between those who disagree about metaphysical commitments. Indeed, what is Hegel doing at the end of the *Phenomenology of Spirit* if not absorbing the world in this way? Hegel ascribes true beliefs to Christians. He claims that revealed religion and philosophy have the same content—the absolute. But ultimately, he describes this content and Christian doctrines about it in terms of his own philosophical commitments. He claims that his account is the best one that anyone has been able to give so far. Like the Christian who "absorbs the world" into the world of scripture, Hegel places his own account at the end of a dialectic. He claims that his philosophical account of the absolute constitutes the best available interpretation of Christian doctrines and allows them to be held true, at least in representational form.

Hegel believes that he has given a compelling account of the strengths of revealed religion. This account includes, prominently, revealed religion's ways of relating to the absolute through practices of confession, forgiveness, and sacrifice. Hegel believes that philosophy preserves these strengths in its account of recognition and reconciliation, while overcoming what he sees as the weaknesses of revealed religion—especially the lingering alienation between the human beings who engage in these practices and the absolute. From the standpoint of Hegel's philosophy, revealed religion makes true claims about the absolute while nevertheless understanding the absolute in a limited and representational form.

Hegel and Lindbeck are not the only ones to engage in this kind of assimilative activity. Davidson's principle of charity suggests that most people do it, most of the time, as they try to make sense of the world and to justify their own judgments about it. Moreover, whether or not one agrees with Hegel's claims about religion and philosophy, his account of dialectical reasoning helps us see how we might approach the differences between them. If Hegel is right about the role of practices of contestation, recognition, and reconciliation in this process, there is no reason to be alienated by others' claims to dialectical superiority.

A naturalist may agree with Hegel's assessment of revealed religion while nevertheless recognizing the authority of someone else to dispute this assessment. She can give an account of the other's strengths in light of her own commitments and norms. At the same time, she can regard the other as a potential judge and critic of these commitments and norms. She is open to the possibility that some of them will turn out to be inadequate or inconsistent and that the other's account will expose this. She recognizes that she may need to confess to, or seek forgiveness from, the other for mistaken claims, judgments, actions, or attributions.

Christian theological accounts of dialectical reasoning employ some concepts and commitments that a naturalist account does not. These might include the sin that clouds understanding or the grace that guides finite and fallible human beings from falsity toward truth. Even if Christians and naturalists agree on something like the priority of social practices in the institution and justification of norms, they are likely to disagree about the persons who are engaged in these practices.[16] Commentators among both the Christians and the naturalists have suggested that these substantive disagreements make public discourse impossible or incoherent. Some of them, such as Richard Rorty, argue that religion is inherently a conversation-stopper.[17] Rorty suspects that religious people are tempted to mimic Faith and Enlightenment by appealing to an independent and freestanding authority outside of human beings and their social practices. Such appeals, he thinks, destroy the conversations and debates that are necessary for democracy. But Rorty fails to see the ad hoc and agonistic conversations and coalitional politics pursued by many religious people—as well as the conversation-stopping moves made by many nonreligious people.

Other commentators, such as MacIntyre, argue that the practices of dialectical reasoning simply are not possible under modern conditions of religious and ethical pluralism. Although MacIntyre remains committed to an implicitly Hegelian account of rationality, he suspects that the denizens of modern liberal democracies are unable to engage in processes of dialectical reasoning. Our differences are too deep, and our incomplete agreement about the good leaves us unable to make sense of one another's claims about rights and justice. Our conversations, MacIntyre suggests, are rendered incoherent.[18]

I think MacIntyre goes wrong in this assessment. He assumes that agreement on the good must be total in order for conversation about rights and justice to move forward, and he assumes that the differing positions in diverse liberal societies have a foundational structure. But a Hegelian social ethics rejects both of these assumptions. Instead, it posits an evolving web of agreement that is partly about the good and partly about the right. It also holds that thinking of our conflicting positions as resting on fixed foundational commitments is both unhelpful and unnecessary. Agreement on the good is not all-or-nothing; there need only be enough overlap for us to start talking and to proceed in ad hoc ways.

Suppose the abortion debate was not imagined as a standoff between two uncomprehending positions, each of which claims unassailable principles. Could the conflict be redescribed in dialectical terms? Both poles in the abortion debate have significant strengths. The pro-life position incorporates the ideal of human equality and the principle that intentionally killing the innocent is murder. The pro-choice position, meanwhile, acknowledges the authority that human beings typically exercise over their own bodies and the intuition that an early fetus is, in many respects, very unlike the paradigmatic bearer of human rights. Neither position, it seems to me, has done a very good job accounting for the strengths of the other position. Moreover, the positions have too often closed their ears to the criticisms of the other. The result is that neither position can account for the other's strengths while overcoming its weaknesses. But nothing in this debate requires construing the positions as constructed on fixed foundational commitments or unassailable principles. I suspect that a great many people, rather than standing at one pole or the other of the abortion debate, are able to identify with some of the strengths of each position. Overcoming the polarization of the debate, however, is likely to require dialectical reasoning and imagination as people elaborate a position or a range of positions that accounts for the strengths and weaknesses of the positions as currently described.

In such cases, agreement on the good need not be an all-or-nothing matter. Conversations might begin here or there or anywhere. They can take the form of ad hoc apologetics, which begin with a single point of agreement and see where that leads. They can take the form of immanent critique that identifies the weaknesses of a tradition (either one's own tradition or a rival tradition) by identifying its inadequacies and inconsistences on its own terms. They can also begin when one tradition attempts to "absorb the world" into its own, to make sense of a rival tradition in light of the web of norms that it already holds.

Processes of dialectical reasoning can show up in all kinds of relationships—within congregations, in ecumenical and interfaith dialogues, in political coalition-building, and in and across diverse communities. Congregations and denominations regularly find themselves confronting and coping with disagreements, such as whether the clergy will officiate same-sex marriages and, if they do, how they will use and revise traditional liturgy in such rituals. Many such disagreements have to do with how concepts, doctrines, laws, and practices that are imbued with authority or sacred value ought to apply to new or changing situations. Community members and congregational leaders need good arguments, but also good practices of recognition and reconciliation, in order for their relationships and communities to emerge intact.

Conclusion

Disagreements about God, authority, and the absolute remain. That is what it is to live in a religiously diverse society. The political and ethical conflicts that currently appear intractable in such societies—including conflicts over abortion and same-sex marriage—are not disconnected from these disagreements about God, authority, and the absolute. Certain ways of approaching these ethical conflicts harden the battle lines and stop the conversation. Hegel describes how such culture war–style impasses can be confronted through dialectical reasoning.

Who knows which of our present disagreements will pass away or when? If they do, it is unlikely to be because people on one side or the other of a chasm won a war of attrition—refusing to engage with partisans on the other side—but, more likely, because they considered what they were justified in believing and doing, assessed the strengths and weaknesses of alternate views, and found ways into conversation in light of their experiences and encounters with the world and one another.

A Hegelian social ethics recommends a model of public discourse that is pluralist and agonistic. It includes all comers and encourages them to approach one another as loci of authority and accountability. They ought to be willing to allow their own commitments to be scrutinized and critiqued, just as they would scrutinize and critique others. Conversation among them begins where it may and moves, in fits and starts, outward from there. Disagreements continue to arise, and so the need for conversation and contestation is perpetual.

CHAPTER SEVEN

Democratic Authority through Conflict and Reconciliation

To identify sacred mystery with every individual experience, every life, giving the word its largest sense, is to arrive at democracy as an ideal, and to accept the difficult obligation to honor others and oneself with something approaching due reverence. It is a vision that is wholly religious though by no means sectarian, wholly realist in acknowledging the great truth of the centrality of human consciousness, wholly open in that it anticipates and welcomes the disruption of present values in the course of finding truer ones.

—MARILYNNE ROBINSON, *WHEN I WAS A CHILD I READ BOOKS*

AT THE DAWN of the nineteenth century, Hegel wondered what would hold his changing society together. Would people take their identities and obligations to be fixed and given, like Antigone and Creon, leading to tragic conflicts? Would they refuse to listen to one another's claims and criticisms, like Faith and Enlightenment, turning their differences into impasses? Would they grasp at abstract and contentless freedom, like the French revolutionaries, replacing one form of domination with another? If not, what other option was there? The *Phenomenology of Spirit* is Hegel's philosophical reply to these questions—the social ethics he proposes for post-Reformation, post-Enlightenment, post-Revolutionary moderns.

A century and a half later, Hannah Arendt argued that authority had all but faded from modern social and political life. European and American political history, she suggested, was the chronicle of a series of attempts to establish, renew, or restore authority. But such attempts had always failed. "Who can deny," she asked, "that disappearance of practically all traditionally established authorities has been one of the most spectacular characteristics of the modern world?"[1] Authority, Arendt contended, is different from power.[2] Authority resides outside of power and beyond those who hold power. It commands obedience, but it does not require violence or persuasion to produce such obedience. Such authority, she suggested, is *given*; it is a shared standard for belief and action whose bindingness is self-evident to the people who take themselves to be bound by it. Arendt argued that to acknowledge the demise of authority is "to be confronted anew . . . by the elementary problems of human living-together."[3] Without a shared standard for belief and action—without *authority*—we are left with disagreement, conflict, and contestation. We are left with power and persuasion.

Hegel may have anticipated Arendt's ambivalence about the disappearance of traditionally established authorities, but he also realized that such authority was unsupportable in modern life. Nevertheless, there *is* something worth calling authority. Whatever it is, Hegel thought, it cannot be independent of human beings and their social practices. It cannot stand *outside* of disagreement, conflict, and the contest for power. Rather, it has to encompass those things, too. Hegel offered an account of the standard of knowledge and ground of authority that arose out of the social practices of people who share a form of life—practices that incorporate conflict as well as reconciliation.

Hegel's view of how these practices of conflict and reconciliation contribute to the standard of knowledge and ground of authority can help us think about *democratic* authority. It shifts our attention from legal structures and institutional apparatuses to the relationships and practices of ordinary citizens. Following democratic theorist Bonnie Honig, I use the words "citizen" and "citizenship" here to identify people engaged in a particular set of social practices. Honig argues that we ought to think of citizenship as "not just a juridical status distributed (or not) by states, but a *practice* in which denizens, migrants, residents, and their allies hold states accountable for their definitions and distributions of goods, powers, rights, freedoms, privileges, and justice."[4] A citizen is anyone who, in the words of democratic organizer Ernesto Cortés Jr., "do[es] the *work* of a citizen."[5]

Hegel holds that authority, properly constituted and rightly understood, cannot stand apart from people, their relationships, and their practices. If *democratic* authority is created and maintained through the rightly ordered relationships and practices of political actors, we need to know more about what those relationships and practices ought to look like. We need to ask: How should citizens structure their relationships? What practices should they cultivate? What form ought their conflicts to take? And how, if at all, might they repair their relationships and communities in the wake of such conflicts? These are the questions that drive this final chapter. I argue that, in a democratically organized and oriented community, citizens' relationships embody reciprocal recognition. Citizens treat one another as authoritative and accountable. I suggest that, at its best, democratic activity fosters relationships of this sort and nurtures the practices that give rise to and sustain them. Such relationships and practices are not conflict-averse. In fact, they depend on ongoing contestation and agonism. I describe the features of this form of conflict and distinguish it from other forms of conflict, including tragedy, culture war, and revolutionary terror. Finally, I turn to the practices of reconciliation that accompany ongoing contestation, including practices of forgiveness embodied in restorative justice.

The Relationships and Practices of Democratic Actors

Relationships between free and equal citizens must be relationships of reciprocal recognition. The idea of recognition at the heart of this claim, however, is significantly different from that invoked by the "politics of recognition" debated by democratic theorists in the 1990s and early aughts. At issue in those debates was an identity-based idea of recognition, according to which citizens ought to see and respect one another as bearers of particular identities. Failures of recognition, on that view, result from the refusal to see others for who they really are. As Charles Taylor writes, "The thesis is that our identity is partly shaped by recognition or its absence, often by the *mis*recognition of others, and so a person or group of people can suffer real damage, real distortion, if the people or society around them mirror back to them a confining or demeaning or contemptible picture of themselves."[6] The politics of recognition was linked to identity politics and the embrace of multiculturalism.

Criticism of the politics of recognition has taken several forms. Nancy Fraser, for example, argues that misrecognition is less a matter of a failure to see and respect people as bearers of identities than a matter of institutional patterns and social relations that perpetuate an unjust distribution of the goods of society. Kelly Oliver, meanwhile, rejects the idea of recognition in favor of what she calls *witnessing*. Criticizing Hegelian recognition as dependent on an objectifying gaze, Oliver argues that our ethical and political responsibility is to bear witness and to respond to the injustices in which we are implicated.[7] Closer to the position that I develop here is that of Patchen Markell, who criticizes the politics of recognition's emphasis on fixed and stable identities and, instead, calls for a politics of acknowledgment, in which what is acknowledged is the finitude, contingency, and flux that attend human life. Markell suggests that problems with the politics of recognition stem from ambiguities within Hegel's own idea of recognition. But, as I have argued, once Hegel's idea of recognition is understood through the relationship of reciprocal recognition that emerges with confession and forgiveness, it is indeed attentive to these features of human life. Hegel's idea of recognition is relatively consistent in its rejection of a fixed identity that precedes action, and it is much closer to Markell's politics of acknowledgment than Markell himself allows.[8]

Hegel's idea of recognition is not about the recognition of fixed *identities* but, rather, about the recognition of *subjectivities*. Read in this way—that is, through the reciprocal recognition that follows confession and forgiveness, rather than through the deformed relationship depicted in the master-slave dialectic—the gap begins to close between Hegel's idea of recognition and Oliver's witnessing or Markell's acknowledgment.[9] When we recognize one another, we bestow a status on one another that at once authorizes us as participants in the world-building activities of making claims and taking action *and* admits the likelihood that our claims and actions will be marked by contingency, arbitrariness, and fallibility. These are the markers of subjects, loci of authority and accountability. Once we follow Hegel's idea of recognition through to its culmination in the confession and forgiveness of the wicked and judging consciousnesses, we see that it does *not* involve the oppression, domination, or objectification of the other. To recognize another person as a subject involves knowing and treating her as authoritative and fit to be held accountable. Built into the idea of reciprocal recognition is the acceptance of human fallibility, the perpetuity of difference and contestation, and an implicit challenge to the notion of sovereign agency.

Each recognizes herself *and* the other as authoritative and accountable. As a locus of authority, one is authorized to make claims and take action. Each can expect that her voice will be heard and that her proposals and actions will be acknowledged. As a locus of authority, moreover, each is authorized to judge the claims and actions of others. She stands in the position of agent and judge. But a citizen's authority cannot be the authority of a lord who rules over others. It is not a status bestowed by the dominant on the dominated. That, as we have seen, is a deficient form of recognition. In relationships of *reciprocal* recognition, authority is paired with accountability. As a locus of accountability, each citizen is expected to take responsibility for her proposals and actions. She is held to account by her fellow citizens.

The reciprocal recognition that ideally obtains among democratic citizens includes, but is not exhausted by, accountability. Such accountability is not merely backward-looking and episodic. It does not involve only acknowledgment of, and punishment for, discrete harms. Reciprocal recognition also involves treating others and oneself as finite and fallible. Parties to the relationship at least implicitly acknowledge the perpetual risk of disagreement and conflict, the need for correction, and their vulnerability to one another. Our accountability, then, involves forward-looking moral responsibility under conditions of risk and vulnerability. We are responsible for our claims and actions as we undertake them. Their meaning and effects are not always within our control, and we may be mistaken or misunderstood. Thus practices of accountability are ongoing. They must be part and parcel of our relationships with one another as democratic actors. Here, it is helpful to think about practices of accountability-holding (as well as practices of authority-granting) as *rituals* or *sacramental practices*, as Hegel does—actions that are repeated and even habitual, and that symbolize and actualize our reciprocal agency, authority, and accountability.

If Hegel is right that these practices are capable of symbolizing and *actualizing*, bringing into being, the self-sufficient ground of authority, then we might shift our model of accountability-holding from a punitive to a generative and restorative one. As Craig Borowiak argues, accountability serves a positive and productive function in democratic communities; it "can improve understanding, transform agendas, and build community."[10] It can only do this, however, when accountability is seen as belonging to a broader context of reciprocal recognition.

Authority, Accountability, and Democratic Change

Accountability in democratically organized communities depends on the strength of the reciprocal relationships among citizens. One form of accountability is what legal and political philosopher Jeremy Waldron has called "agent accountability."[11] This is where an agent or representative acts on behalf of a person or group and therefore owes that person or group an account of his or her actions. Agents are, in this sense, accountable to those who are being represented. Waldron claims—rightly, I believe—that part of what makes democracy distinctive is the expectation that the government owes the people accountability of this sort. When government officials declare war, or torture prisoners, or use force against citizens, the people are due an explanation of what is being done in their name and why.[12] Another form of accountability involves the laws, standards, and institutions according to which a person will be held to account for her actions. It is important for institutions such as hospitals, universities, armies, and police forces to have transparent, justly established rules and principles to follow. It is also important for these institutions to have procedures in place for applying these rules to particular cases and for contesting their application after the fact.[13] Courts and tribunals are institutional means for holding people accountable to rules and principles that have been set forth.

These forms of accountability need to be tended to by ordinary citizens who stand in relationships of reciprocal recognition. Citizens who recognize one another as loci of authority and accountability are in a position to build coalitions and forge solidarity across difference. They are, therefore, in a position to hold elites accountable and to fight for social change. They can generate democratic authority. When citizens are alienated from one another or caught up in attempts to dominate one another, however, they are incapable of generating enough organized power or democratic authority to influence and contest official decisions effectively.

The mechanisms that are designed to hold agents and institutions accountable are, too often, feeble or absent. A president authorizes the use of torture in violation of national and international law, and he is reelected to the office. A police officer kills an unarmed black man by placing him in a chokehold, a maneuver banned by the police department that employs him; he is not indicted. Mortgage companies offer loans to people known to be unable to afford them, and those companies sell the bad loans to banks that make billions of dollars before the whole scheme collapses. Millions of people lose their homes, while banks are bailed out with taxpayer money and banking executives get million-dollar bonuses.

Such wrongs can be remedied in society only if diverse citizens' relationships are strong and healthy enough to create coalitions that can check the exercise of political and economic power and the use of force by armies and police. Those relationships themselves must be democratically organized— which is to say, they must be appropriately inclusive relationships of reciprocal recognition, sustained by practices of conflict and reconciliation. All too often, they are not. Coalitions in the struggle for justice are rarely either effective or justly structured relative to democratic ends. People who object to the current distribution of power in society are often attracted to one of three sets of social practices and organizational structures: liberal elitism; the revolutionary politics of radical intellectuals like Slavoj Žižek; or the populism of movements like Occupy. It is worth asking whether any of these attempts to achieve a just peace in society is capable of establishing authority and accountability in political, economic, and social structures or of embodying them in its own practices.

Hegel, as I have noted, was not a democrat. He supported a Prussian state with a limited monarchy and a large bureaucratic class, although he also recognized the need for the representation of citizens in the process that determines laws. In the *Philosophy of Right*, Hegel argues that such representation is not merely a matter of tallying the votes of abstract individuals or tracking the will of an indeterminate "public." Rather, it is a matter of getting the legitimate and determinate concerns of actual groups of people concretely integrated into the deliberative process. In order to do this, Hegel suggests, citizens ought to be organized into classes or "estates" (*Stände*) with common interests and concerns. Citizens then can be represented in the state as members of one of these estates—the agricultural estate, the business estate, or the bureaucratic (or "universal") estate. Through their estate and its representatives, citizens' concerns can be introduced into the deliberative process. The estates serve as a check on both the power of the sovereign and the will of the masses, such that neither is the arbitrary power of domination (§302/471).

Hegel's account of the estates and their role in deliberative processes is deeply flawed by its faith in bureaucratic rationality. Of the three estates, Hegel holds that the universal estate ought to have a privileged position in the determination of laws, for, unlike the other estates, it "has *the universal interests* of society as its business" (§205/357). Hegel suggests that the cosmopolitan and university-educated members of the universal estate would be able to distance themselves from the self-interested claims and conflicts of civil society. The civil servants who make up the universal estate "necessarily have a more profound and comprehensive insight into the nature of the state's institutions and needs, and are more familiar with its functions and more skilled in dealing with them, so that they *are able* to do what is best even without the Estates" (§301/470). Hegel assumes that the members of the universal estate are not blinkered in their view of "what is best." But Hegel's insights elsewhere—not least in Chapter VI of the *Phenomenology of Spirit*—suggest that no one is immune from the effects of arbitrariness and contingency in their beliefs and actions. Bureaucratic elites are no less in need of authority-granting and accountability-holding relationships and practices than others. Even Hegel seems to admit as much when he suggests that the expectation of public criticism has a beneficial effect on the intentions and behavior of public officials (§301/470–71). The laws, norms, and institutions that the members of the universal estate would design, apply, and uphold would be no less in need of scrutiny and critique than others.

Reading these sections of the *Philosophy of Right* nearly two centuries after Hegel wrote them, it is impossible for someone familiar with abolition, the labor movement, feminism, or the civil rights movement not to be dissatisfied with Hegel's treatment of the deliberative process. It neglects the ongoing practices of conflict and reconciliation that Hegel rightly highlights in the *Phenomenology of Spirit*. It is also excessively confident in the capacity of bureaucratic elites to transcend the conflicts that arise in civil society. Democratic movements and organizations resisting concrete forms of oppression and domination often have a better understanding of the common good than do the bureaucrats. There are interest groups to be accounted for in contemporary politics, certainly, but many such movements and organizations are directed toward the concrete realization of the common good in some important domain. Amending a constitution to outlaw chattel slavery or to guarantee women's right to vote does not come at the expense of the common good. Moreover, demands of this sort are often raised *against* an entrenched bureaucracy's view of what the common good is or ought to be.

We might think of contemporary liberal elitism as an updated version of Hegel's faith in bureaucratic rationality. Contemporary liberal elitists may reject Hegel's defense of monarchy, but they retain his faith in the rational state and the bureaucratic class that keeps it running. Such liberals sometimes claim that they, or the bureaucratic and university elites whom they support, stand above the fray. Such elites are, they suppose, in a position to design and apply the laws, norms, and institutions that are best for the common good. We have good reason to be skeptical of such claims.

Žižek, meanwhile, has generated enthusiasm on the progressive and radical Left for his trenchant critique of contemporary liberalism, capitalism, and their characteristic forms of militarism and imperialism. While Žižek is one of the most influential contemporary Hegelians, it seems unlikely that his ethical and political conclusions are compatible with the Hegelian themes of reciprocal recognition and nondomination.[14] Žižek calls for the end of the liberal capitalist system through perpetual revolution. This revolutionary movement will supposedly be led by an intellectual vanguard, the authority of which, Žižek admits, is arbitrary. He asks, channeling Nietzsche, "What kind of power (or authority) is it which needs to justify itself with reference to the interests of those over whom it rules, which accepts the need to provide reasons for its exercise? Does not such a notion of power undermine itself?"[15] According to Žižek, power is not power if it must justify itself; rather, power simply *is* authority without accountability. Therefore, Žižek argues, "Every ethical and/or moral edifice has to be grounded in an abyssal act," an act for which no reasons can be given.[16] The self-declared arbitrariness of the Leninist organizational structure that Žižek favors, in which an elite claims authority for itself and imposes its will onto others, is, in my view, a form of domination. The danger of the Leninist organizational structure is that there is nothing to prevent Stalinist outcomes except the arbitrary whims of its unaccountable leaders.

The Occupy movement, by contrast, was a leaderless collective. It was open to all; there were few, if any, barriers to entry. Participants in the movement condemned the current economic order and called for a shift in the balance of power from economic elites to the rest of society. The movement modeled "horizontalism," a set of relationships and practices that it took to be antithetical to the relationships of domination between economic elites and the 99%. It rejected hierarchy, operated through consensus decision making, and claimed no central leadership.

But with its refusal to articulate its goals and its rejection of leadership, the Occupy movement made it difficult to know on what basis participants could hold one another or other members of society accountable. Rather than eliminating relationships of domination, Occupy's horizontalism sometimes masked them. As democratic theorist Laura Grattan notes in her study of populism, Occupy's "unbending commitment to horizontalism left it ill equipped to address racial hierarchies from which the movement was not immune."[17] Grattan notes that a statement issued by one group of former Occupiers included a section titled "Leaderlessness is the new tyranny," which claimed that the official leaderlessness of the movement masked a "shadow leadership structure" that was unaccountable to individuals and communities of color inside and outside of the movement. Among this group's demands was that "the movement 'be clear about its goals, intent, and strategies to ensure that our communities . . . can make informed decisions about our participation.' The movement's refusal to name demands, that is, did not offer an unguarded sense of openness and potentiality for people who have historically experienced violent restrictions on their power."[18] Without clearly articulated goals, and without leaders authorized by the group to carry out particular tasks, it was unclear how the movement or participants within it could be held to account.

Some of the problems that faced the Occupy movement were articulated much earlier in an essay by feminist activist Jo Freeman called "The Tyranny of Structurelessness." Freeman, who founded some of the first radical feminist organizations in the country, lamented the apparently leaderless and structureless form of many early feminist consciousness-raising groups. Like Occupy, those groups rejected internal role differentiation and refused to name leaders. But that structure, Freeman argued, was neither democratic nor effective. Freeman argued that all communities have both structure and leadership. The question is whether that structure and leadership is made explicit or not. If it is not, it is effectively withheld from scrutiny and criticism. If it is, the members of the group have the means to hold those to whom authority has been delegated accountable for what they say and do on behalf of the group. This, Freeman writes, "is how the group has control over people in positions of authority. Individuals may exercise power, but it is the group that has ultimate say over how the power is exercised."[19] For Freeman, a democratically structured community has to be one in which authority and accountability are commensurate.

Compare the liberal elitist, neo-Leninist, and populist alternatives to the ethical formation, leadership development, and organizational work undertaken by members of the civil rights movement of the 1950s and 1960s. Aldon Morris's now classic study, *The Origins of the Civil Rights Movement*, describes the organized citizens who fought what he calls the tripartite system of domination: the economic, political, and personal oppression of African Americans. Black churches, he writes, "provided the movement with an organized mass base; a leadership of clergymen . . . ; an institutionalized financial base . . . ; and meeting places where the masses planned tactics and strategies and collectively committed themselves to the struggle."[20] The civil rights movement was not a bureaucratic elite, a revolutionary vanguard, or a loosely organized collection of protesters but a highly structured grassroots movement that forged solidarity among already organized churches and community organizations in the service of collective social, political, and economic goals.

Civil rights activists such as Septima Clark and Ella Baker were committed to fostering relationships and practices of reciprocal recognition among citizens. Clark was an educator and activist who, as director of workshops at the Highlander Folk School in Monteagle, Tennessee, developed the literacy and voter registration programs that later spread through the South. As Charles Payne notes, Highlander defied state laws that prohibited white and black people from eating together or sleeping in the same building. "Many visitors," he writes, "testified that the experience of egalitarian living in an interracial situation had greater impact on them than the courses and workshops."[21] Baker, who expanded the citizenship schools under the auspices of the Southern Christian Leadership Conference and later worked with the Student Nonviolent Coordinating Committee to organize Freedom Summer, was committed to what democratic theorist Romand Coles has called a "Christian prophetic discipleship." She took her role as an organizer and leader to be primarily one of "listening to and responding to the expressions of need and yearning of those to whom her Christian vocation called her to tend."[22] Both Clark and Baker saw their leadership as directed toward the development of other, local leaders. They were, in other words, committed to recognizing— and helping others recognize—the authority of fellow citizens as democratic actors. They rejected the self-sufficient authority of charismatic leaders, and they sought to democratize relationships among citizens. When Clark drafted Highlander's statement of purpose, she wrote of "broadening the scope of democracy to include everyone and deepening the scope to include every relationship."[23] The idea that the right sorts of relationships were central to the realization of the ideal of democracy guided both Baker and Clark.[24]

A similar commitment to relationships and practices of reciprocal recognition underlies the work of contemporary democratic organizers. Broad-based organizing networks, such as the Industrial Areas Foundation (IAF) and PICO National Network, focus on building democratic relationships and cultivating democratic practices among political actors in local communities.[25] Strong broad-based organizations are capable of significant political victories, but strong organizations need strong relationships and practices among democratic actors. The core of broad-based organizing is relationship-building among those actors. Through one-on-one meetings, people learn about one another's commitments and concerns and begin to treat one another as sources of reasons for their own political beliefs and actions. Without the right sorts of relationships among citizens, the coalitional politics practiced by broad-based organizations is impossible. Stout notes in his study of the ethical dimensions of grassroots organizing that "Ernie [Ernesto Cortés Jr.] calls the power that resides in a citizens' organization *relational* power, by which he means power that depends on the *quality* of the interactions among people, rather than on things like guns and money. Face-to-face interaction matters in large part because it is the main context in which representative authority in a democratic organization can be earned."[26] Stout and other religious ethicists and democratic theorists such as Luke Bretherton, Romand Coles, Laura Grattan, and C. Melissa Snarr point to local communities in which democratic authority is being generated, in which citizens are forging relationships and cultivating practices of reciprocal recognition in order to create coalitions, build power, and fight for justice.

It remains unclear whether these pockets of democratic authority can be expanded or whether enough of them can be built for democracy to thrive on a broader scale. Not enough of us are bound together in the sorts of relationships and practices that constitute democratic citizenship and generate democratic authority. Political and economic elites have too much power, and the institutions that are intended to secure people against the arbitrary exercise of power by those elites are too often degraded. In the face of these facts, people might be tempted to call for the violent overthrow of the present order in favor of a new political configuration or to throw in with a populist movement that rejects the present order and encourages various alternatives to flourish (but does not specify what those might be). But these options threaten to substitute one sort of arbitrariness for another. What is needed is not the abandonment of concrete practices of recognition, responsibility, and accountability, grounded in norms of justice and equality, but the proliferation of such practices. This is not liberal elitism, neo-Leninism, or populism; it is grassroots democracy characterized by conflict and reconciliation.

What grounds we have for democratic hope is in the examples of citizens who have engaged in these practices to make their institutions and leaders more accountable, less dominating, and more democratic. These democratic actors recognize themselves and others to be co-equal loci of normative authority. They hold one another accountable. They forge relationships, political coalitions, and organizations to help them do so. They use democratic norms to name and to resist forms of oppression and domination. They enact agonistic democratic politics, insofar as they acknowledge the finitude and corrigibility of human beings and the centrality of ongoing contestation in our pluralistic life together.

Forms of Conflict

The kind of polarization on display on political talk shows and often amplified on social media poses a significant challenge to democratic authority. Relationships of reciprocal recognition cannot be created and maintained across lines of difference unless people are willing to treat their own claims as contestable and others' as potential sources of reasons for changing their beliefs and actions. To be clear, the problem with polarization is not that it is conflictual but rather that the conflicts of polarized partisans take the form that they do. Disagreement, contestation, and conflict can and do play an ongoing role in generating and sustaining democratic authority. But conflicts come in different forms. Among these are tragic conflicts, culture war–style impasses, revolutionary terror, and agonistic contestation. Hegel helps us distinguish among these forms, and he shows why these distinctions matter. The help he provides on these points survives even when we reject his faith in the disinterested rationality of bureaucratic and university elites.

Tragedy is a form of conflict in which two goods or rights stand in opposition to one another. To pursue one is to relinquish or violate the other. Moreover, tragedy is characterized by inevitability; the conflict could not have been avoided. Tragedy ensues when people see their identities, obligations, and norms as fixed and given—when they do not or cannot take responsibility for them. When these identities, obligations, and norms are removed from the processes of justification and contestation, the incompatibilities that arise among them become irresolvable. Tragic conflicts are not to be desired but to be treated as evidence that people have not worked out adequate epistemic and practical means of coping with the differences and disagreements that arise among them.

Culture war, meanwhile, is a form of conflict in which each side claims that its own judgments are justified while denying that the other's are. Each has a reductive account of the other's beliefs and practices; it casts them as mere ideology, psychology, or political expediency, while treating its own position as immune to such reductionism. Because neither side attends to the claims of the other, both sides end up with deficient assessments of their relative strengths and weaknesses. Their conflict becomes a standoff between polarized and alienated parties. In political life, culture war–style conflicts should be seen a failure of recognition—not only of the other as a locus of authority and accountability but also of the practices that generate democratic authority.

Such conflicts can be confronted in a few different ways. They can be resolved through processes of dialectical reasoning such as those discussed in the previous chapter. Or they can be eliminated through revolutionary terror, as one side suppresses its opponent through violence or domination. Hegel considers this possibility in his discussion of lordship and bondage, and he elaborates on it in his later treatment of revolution and terror. Although I have not included a detailed discussion of revolution and terror in this book, it is worth raising here because it shows what would happen if Enlightenment gained political power and then sought to eliminate its opponents in its drive to actualize a form of absolute freedom in the absence of concrete relationships and practices of reciprocal recognition. A group of people take it upon themselves to actualize the "general will" to freedom, and they kill or otherwise suppress those whom they take to threaten their articulation of the general will. While Hegel's discussion of revolutionary terror describes what happens when Enlightenment tries to eliminate its opponents through violence in the name of freedom, the same can happen if human submission to God's arbitrary power is appealed to in order to authorize violence or coercion.

Consider Egypt's Arab Spring and its aftermath. A coalition arose in opposition to the authoritarian regime of President Hosni Mubarak. That coalition included secular activists, members of the Muslim Brotherhood, and the military. These individuals and groups were united in their opposition to Mubarak.

After Mubarak's ouster, the Muslim Brotherhood used an electoral victory to assert a sort of theocratic dominance. President Mohamed Morsi granted himself unlimited powers and cracked down on dissent. The coalition collapsed. The military took advantage of the growing unpopularity of the Muslim Brotherhood to restore its hold on power. It declared the Muslim Brotherhood a terrorist organization and it began to suppress, often violently, the dissent of secular activists and Islamists alike. It is crucial, for understanding how this played out, to notice the absence of widespread relationships and practices of reciprocal recognition among the factions of the initial coalition. Some among the liberals could articulate democratic ideals, but there was no concrete embodiment of those ideals in their relationships and practices as a whole. There was nothing like the relational organizing that Morris describes in the decades-long prehistory of civil rights victories. The military was highly organized in its ranks, and the Muslim Brotherhood was organized at the grassroots, but neither was organized around democratic ideals, and neither sought to extend reciprocal recognition to those with whom it disagreed. Hegel's analysis shows that reciprocal recognition is conceivable as an alternative to domination and revolutionary terror. This alternative, however, must be achieved through decades of relational and practical organizing at the grassroots level.

While revolutionary terror seeks the elimination of objectionable difference through violence and domination, the agonistic contestation of reciprocally recognizing subjects acknowledges the perpetuity of difference. As a form of conflict, agonistic contestation emerges from relations of reciprocity. These are the relations of those who see themselves and others as, in Hegel's words, "selfsame"—individuals who see themselves and others as moving through their shape of spirit as both subject and object, agent and judge, confessor and forgiver. This is the reciprocal recognition that *is* absolute spirit. When these relations are in place, antagonism is transformed into agonism. As William Connolly writes, "An antagonism in which each aims initially at conquest or conversion of the other can now (given other supporting conditions) become an *agonism* in which each treats the other as crucial to itself in the strife and interdependence of identity/difference."[27] Agonistic contestation is misunderstood when it is viewed as a celebration of tragedy or of antagonism. It involves perpetual contest in the context of reciprocal recognition—contest that is not only compatible with but also constitutive of authority. What Hegel calls reciprocal recognition has a close kinship with what Connolly calls relations of agonistic respect.[28]

Tragedy, culture war, and revolutionary terror undermine the accounts of authority and the social arrangements from which they emerge. Hegel argues that those accounts and social arrangements are ones we are no longer justified in upholding. Agonistic contestation, by contrast, is built into the account of authority and the social arrangements from which it emerges. It is not incidental to the account of authority; it is encompassed within it. Such contestation is an inherent part of the process by which individuals and communities make and assess claims about what is true, right, or good.[29]

In the *Phenomenology of Spirit*, the shapes of spirit, from Greek *Sittlichkeit* to conscience, try and fail to account for the authority of their norms. Reflecting on the progression of these shapes of spirit at the end of the *Phenomenology of Spirit*, Hegel's readers stand in a position to say why the normative stances that underlie tragedy, culture war, and revolutionary terror are ones that they are not justified in holding. They are in a position to see that the members of Greek *Sittlichkeit* were the authors of their gender norms, for instance; that they created and maintained their social arrangements through kinship structures and practices of warfare and sacrifice and burial; that the tragedies they suffered were not only matters of fate and contingency but also the playing out of social roles that could have been otherwise. Hegel's readers are in a position to see that the early modern culture warriors abided by norms of self-sufficient authority that hardened them to those who did not share their views; that they were blind to the religious and scholarly practices that authorized their norms. Readers are in a position to see the ways in which they are the authors (and authorizers) of their own norms, including gender norms, religious commitments, social arrangements, and political institutions, and they are in a position to call themselves and their peers to account. They can ask: Why do we have *these* norms, arrangements, and institutions?

These are not only epistemic questions but also ethical and political ones that concern how we ought to organize the communities in which we live. They are also the subject of debate. In democratic communities, ordinary citizens are the ones debating these questions, for ordinary citizens are loci of authority and accountability. Their answers, when based on forms of dialectical reasoning that account for the strengths and weaknesses of the alternatives, can authorize or unsettle their norms, arrangements, and institutions.[30] For this reason, agonistic democratic theorists emphasize debate and contestation as central to democratic thought and practice. As Honig writes, "To accept and embrace the perpetuity of conflict is to reject the dream of displacement, the fantasy that the right laws or constitution might someday free us from the responsibility for (and, indeed, the burden of) politics."[31] Hegel gives us a way of thinking about conflict that takes place within relations of reciprocal recognition and is mediated by practices of reconciliation.[32]

Practices of Reconciliation

The relationships and practices of democratic actors are not free from conflicts. Because these conflicts arise continually, the need for practices of reconciliation is perpetual. Practices in which citizens affirm or reaffirm their recognition of one another sustain democratic communities over time. For Hegel, as we have seen, the practices that bring about reciprocal recognition and absolute spirit are confession and forgiveness. Through these practices, people forge relationships with one another in which each recognizes herself and the other as agent and judge, confessor and forgiver. Each realizes, in word and deed, the corrigibility of her beliefs and actions and the fact that each stands in a position to judge the beliefs and actions of the other. These practices encompass, as well, forms of self-emptying, or *kenosis*, in which people give up the pretense to self-sufficient authority and refuse to lord over others.

Some of these are everyday practices; others have to respond to the most difficult situations in which relationships of reciprocal recognition are undermined or absent. When people distrust one another or discount one another's authority, the fabric of the community is torn. Oppression and domination, in all their forms, are incompatible with reciprocal recognition and democratic authority. To make those things possible, democratic actors have to generate trust and hope where distrust and despair reign. Practices of reconciliation are intended to do this.

Confession and forgiveness aim to right relationships that have been damaged by injustice or harm.[33] When an agent confesses, she acknowledges that injustice or harm, the damage that does to the relationship, and her responsibility for it. When an agent forgives, she acknowledges the confession and agrees to recognize the confessor as a competent agent and judge going forward.[34] Forgiveness reconciles the wrongdoer and the wronged and rights their relationship. Such practices are critical when the wronged and the wrongdoers within a community or society must find ways to move forward together, to generate authority and accountability, and to build new political institutions and practices.

This view of confession, forgiveness, and reconciliation is central to restorative justice, an alternative to traditional approaches to criminal justice. Unlike forms of justice-seeking focused on past harm and present recompense, restorative justice is forward-looking. Its aim is to reconcile the parties and to restore the relationship between them. Of course, that does not mean that it ignores the past and present dimensions of justice-seeking; it acknowledges the harm and provides restitution, but its aim is to repair the relationship that has been damaged and to reinstate the wrongdoer as a member of the community. In her work on moral repair, philosopher Margaret Urban Walker writes:

> Restorative justice embodies a view of crime or violence as a violation of people and relationships that entails an obligation to set things right, repairing victims and communities, and ideally humanizing and reintegrating offenders. The emphasis for restorative justice is on repairing relations through acknowledging the needs of victims and requiring accountability of those responsible for harm, through truth-telling, apology, and restitution or compensation.[35]

The idea of restorative justice has informed practices and institutions on scales both small and large, from local programs that teach and implement alternative conflict-resolution strategies in elementary schools to the Truth and Reconciliation Commission, which invited public testimony and discourse to grapple with the legacy of apartheid and armed resistance in South Africa.

Of course, politicians, CEOs, and celebrities make public confessions and pseudo-apologies all the time. Folks have good reason to be skeptical about the sincerity of those acts and about their potential for anything resembling democratic politics. I want to distinguish between at least some of those confessions and apologies and the sort of confession described here. For Hegel, the confession that sets the stage for reciprocal recognition is, on the one hand, not a humiliation or a throwing away of oneself; it is, on the other hand, a kind of self-emptying, a relinquishment of self-sufficient authority and an admission of one's fallibility and accountability to others. It involves, on my reading, grappling with the social dimensions of one's subjectivity and accepting the impossibility of sovereign agency. This is a demanding sort of confession, a reevaluation not only of one's actions but also of one's subjectivity and one's relation to others.

Conclusion

Democratic authority emerges where relationships and practices of reciprocal recognition are strong and widespread. The norms of a community are authoritative for its members insofar as concrete, democratically structured relationships and social practices are in place. These relationships and practices can be informal, ad hoc, and subject to contestation. They need not be institutionalized; indeed, while institutions can preserve spaces in which such relationships and practices might flourish, institutions cannot themselves generate or sustain reciprocal recognition. That is the work of citizens. The authority that emerges from these relationships and practices is not, then, freestanding. But neither is it reducible to the mere machinations of power.

In the epigraph with which this chapter began, American novelist and essayist Marilynne Robinson writes that to see the sacred in human experience and life is to "arrive at democracy as an ideal, and to accept the difficult obligation to honor others and oneself with something approaching due reverence." The ideal that Robinson writes about is "wholly religious though by no means sectarian, wholly realist in acknowledging the great truth of the centrality of human consciousness, wholly open in that it anticipates and welcomes the disruption of present values in the course of finding truer ones."[36] This is, it seems to me, a deeply Hegelian sentiment.

To arrive at democracy as an ideal involves recognizing the authority that people have as knowers and doers, as world-builders. It also involves embracing the ongoing contestation of people engaged in processes of dialectical reasoning, challenging the norms of the present in order to arrive at better, truer ones. It means treating differences and disagreements not as cause for despair or domination but as part of democracy's dialectic, in which norms are contested and authority is generated. It means acknowledging that as we face these differences and disagreements, there is no freestanding authority *out there* whose will can be immediately intuited or discerned. There are just the corrigible beliefs and practices of diverse citizens and the shape of spirit that sustains them.

Getting these beliefs and practices right is an uphill battle. We all too often fail to recognize one another as authoritative (and ourselves as accountable), and we all too often perpetuate alienation and domination in our relationships with one another. But "to honor others and oneself with something approaching due reverence" requires that we seek again and again to remake those relationships, to cultivate those practices, in which conflict and reconciliation might take place in the midst of reciprocal recognition. This, I have claimed, is the upshot of a Hegelian social ethics.

I am reminded of one of the protests that followed the Grand Jury's decision not to indict a New York City police officer responsible for the death of Eric Garner, the unarmed African American man who died of asphyxiation after the officer placed him in a chokehold in July 2014. A group of Jewish protesters sat down in the streets of the Upper West Side of Manhattan and recited the Mourner's Kaddish. Then, the protesters said the names of twenty black men who had recently been killed by New York City police officers, followed by the words, "I am responsible." For observant Jews, it is considered an obligation to recite the Mourner's Kaddish following the death of a parent. The recitation of that prayer for a group of men who were strangers to most, if not all, of the protesters was, at the least, unorthodox. But in the words that followed the prayer and the names—the words "I am responsible"—the protesters marked the expanded circle of their democratic concern and obligation. They affirmed their accountability toward these men and their responsibility for the society that did not care enough about their lives or their dignity. The protesters' accountability and responsibility were expressed and enacted in the recitation of a prayer reserved for the mourning of those in one's closest circle of loved ones. They were affirming their responsibility to fellow citizens, in a society marred by racial disparities and massive asymmetries in power. Certainly there is far more to be said and done to create the concrete social and political conditions under which racial reconciliation might be possible, not least, the proliferation of the practices of democratic organizers like Baker and Clark. But it strikes me that it is not irrelevant to that effort for these citizens to have put their bodies in the streets and to have symbolized and actualized, in word and deed, that notion at the heart of democratic authority: we are responsible.

NOTES

Chapter One: Social Ethics in Hegel's Phenomenology of Spirit

1. Hegel to Schelling, May 1, 1807, *Hegel: The Letters*, 80. Terry Pinkard discusses this episode in Pinkard, *Hegel*, 227–30.

2. Quoted in Pinkard, *Hegel*, 229.

3. For more on essence as authoritativeness, see Pinkard, *Hegel's Phenomenology*, 6.

4. The terms that Hegel uses, and which are often translated as "mastery" and "slavery," are *Herrschaft* and *Knechtschaft*. While *Herr* may be translated as "master" or "lord," *Knecht* is best translated as "servant" or "bondsman" (as opposed to *Sklav(e)*, or "slave"). Because Hegel later uses the word *Meister* to capture a different (and nondominating) form of mastery, I will avoid that translation of *Herrschaft* and will generally refer to this section as the "lordship and bondage section." It turns out to be important to preserve the distinctions among these terms, as I argue in chapter 4.

5. This definition draws from Pettit, *Republicanism*, 52, although the idea that it captures has a long history in classical republican political thought. It is worth noting that although Hegel is certainly concerned with domination in this sense, he does not consider the ideal of nondomination to be the central aim of politics as Pettit does. On Hegel's conception of freedom, see Lewis, *Freedom and Tradition in Hegel*. For a critique of Pettit's view of the supremacy of the ideal of nondomination in political life, see Markell, "The Insufficiency of Non-Domination."

6. Pinkard argues that the distinction between "shapes of consciousness" and "shapes of spirit" is the "dominant distinction in the *Phenomenology*." See Pinkard, "What Is a 'Shape of Spirit'?" 112.

7. Ibid., 114.

8. Once again, it is worth keeping in mind that the collapse of these communities or shapes of spirit is a conceptual, rather than historical, matter, although I do take Hegel to be suggesting that an actual community that organized itself in ways that echoed one or another of these inadequate shapes of spirit would suffer from the forms of conflict and self-destruction that he identifies in the *Phenomenology of Spirit*. I return to this issue throughout the book.

9. An example of this traditional view is Charles Taylor's *Hegel*, which argues that Hegel's social and political thought must be extricated from his dogmatic metaphysics. Although many contemporary interpreters disagree with Taylor's assessment of Hegel's metaphysics, Taylor's *Hegel* was an important contribution to the return to and reassessment of Hegel in contemporary Anglophone scholarship.

10. Here, I mainly discuss the work of Robert Pippin and Robert Brandom, although two other scholars who have developed post-Kantian interpretations of Hegel have deeply influenced my project. In *Hegel's Phenomenology*, Pinkard offers a philosophical reconstruction of the *Phenomenology of Spirit* in line with a post-Kantian reading of that text. It is especially useful in its explication of key Hegelian terminology. To use Pippin's words, it provides a "high-altitude picture" of Hegel's argument, although it does not tarry with the details of any particular section (Pippin, *Hegel on Self-Consciousness*, 65n7). Meanwhile, Thomas A. Lewis has connected these post-Kantian interpretations to Hegel's philosophy of religion. In *Religion, Modernity, and Politics in Hegel*, he mounts a formidable challenge to traditional interpretations of Hegel. The book considers Hegel's early theological writings,

the *Logic*, and the *Lectures on the Philosophy of Religion* at length. See also Lewis, "Religion and Demythologization." Critics of post-Kantian interpretations of Hegel include Frederick Beiser, William Desmond, Peter Hodgson, Walter Jaeschke, and Merold Westphal. As Lewis notes in his review of recent Hegel scholarship, scholars such as Jaeschke, Desmond, and Hodgson "all interpret Hegel as offering a highly rationalistic account in which God is not radically other to human beings, yet they evaluate the proposal and its relation to Christianity quite differently" (Lewis, "Beyond the Totalitarian," 564). See Beiser, *Hegel* and "Hegel, A Non-Metaphysician!"; Desmond, *Hegel's God*; Hodgson, *Hegel and Christian Theology*; Jaeschke, *Reason in Religion*; and Westphal, *History and Truth* and "Hegel and Onto-Theology," 142–65.

11. See, especially, Pippin, *Hegel's Idealism*. See also Pippin, *Hegel's Practical Philosophy* and *Hegel on Self-Consciousness*. Some critics have argued that post-Kantian interpretations make Hegel relevant to contemporary thought at the expense of accuracy. See, for instance, Beiser, *Hegel*, 53–57. Meanwhile, ongoing work in the post-Kantian line of interpretation argues that it provides a more plausible account of Hegel in his historical and intellectual context than traditional interpretations, while having the benefit of getting Hegel's philosophy of mind in the same frame as his ethical and political thought.

12. Kant, *Critique of Pure Reason*, 245–48.

13. Pippin, *Hegel on Self-Consciousness*, 60.

14. See Brandom, *Tales of the Mighty Dead*, 178–234 and *Reason in Philosophy*, 1–108. Also, Brandom has made draft chapters of his forthcoming book on Hegel's *Phenomenology of Spirit* available on his website. I am grateful to him for his permission to use and cite that material (personal correspondence, January 7, 2011). See Brandom, *A Spirit of Trust*.

15. On Brandom's account, this is both a cognitive and a practical achievement, though a rather mundane one. Part of Brandom's point, I take it, is that the sharp distinction between the cognitive and the practical does not hold for Hegel.

16. Brandom, *Reason in Philosophy*, 71.

17. Ibid., 104 (emphasis added).

18. See, for instance, Bernstein, *The Pragmatic Turn*, 89–105; Brandom, *Tales of the Mighty Dead*, 210–34; Pinkard, "Was Pragmatism the Successor to Idealism?"; Stern, *Hegelian Metaphysics*, 209–341; and Stout, "The Spirit of Pragmatism," and "What Is It That Absolute Knowing Knows?"

19. See Pippin, "Brandom's Hegel."

20. Jameson, *The Hegel Variations*, 10.

21. Ibid., 11. Jameson insists that Marxist readings of the second half of the *Phenomenology* remain the "most useful and productive commentaries" on those chapters, even while he criticizes them for their overreliance on Alexandre Kojève's interpretation of Hegel. He writes that "the fountainhead of such commentary is of course the classic lecture series of Alexandre Kojève in the 1930s, still stimulating, but about which I think some new kinds of questions can now be raised" (ibid., 11). Among the questions that Jameson asks of Kojève are whether the latter's use of the master-slave dialectic as the interpretive key to the *Phenomenology of Spirit* is justified and whether the final chapter of the book represents the "end of history." Jameson suggests—and I agree—that both of these questions should be answered in the negative. I address Kojève's interpretation of the *Phenomenology of Spirit* in chapter 4.

22. I read the second half of the *Phenomenology of Spirit* as following from, and of a piece with, the first half. On this point, I agree with Jon Stewart and Michael N. Forster, both of whom argue for the coherence and unity of the text. Both Stewart and Forster take issue with the frequent claim that the *Phenomenology of Spirit* follows no discernible plan. See Stewart, *The Unity of Hegel's Phenomenology of Spirit* and Forster, *Hegel's Idea of a Phenomenology of Spirit*. Cf. Solomon, *In the Spirit of Hegel*.

23. In "What Is Open and What Is Closed in the Philosophy of Hegel," David Kolb argues that attempts to appropriate Hegel's historicism without his supposed metaphysics have failed: "An open thinking would have difficulty comprehending and reconciling in the strong sense Hegel has in mind" (34). For Kolb, Hegel is the philosopher of closure. John W. Burbidge disagrees with Kolb. He argues that "the absolute method of knowledge involves continually taking account of the partiality in whatever has already been achieved, anticipating something else, whatever it be, that will expose how partial it is, yet being able to incorporate that novelty into a comprehensive perspective that is thereby altered and transformed" ("Hegel's Open Future," 178). More recently, in *The Future of Hegel*, Catherine Malabou has argued for the "plasticity" of human beings, God, and philosophy in Hegel's account, although she does not connect this argument to the recent Anglophone scholarship. My argument connects the "openness" or "plasticity" of Hegel's thought to post-Kantian interpretations of his epistemology and metaphysics.

24. I am borrowing Merold Westphal's felicitous phrase. Westphal does not think (as I do) that Hegel is a philosopher of "mediation without closure," but he does think that Hegel can inform such a project (*History and Truth*, xiii).

25. And, of course, from the end of the preface to the *Philosophy of Right*: "When philosophy paints its grey on grey, a shape of life has grown old, and it cannot be rejuvenated, but only understood; the owl of Minerva begins its flight only with the onset of dusk" (28).

Chapter Two: Tragedy and the Social Construction of Norms

1. See Pinkard, *Hegel's Phenomenology*, 136. Hegel himself held something like this view in his youth; many of his earliest works contrast Greek religion's ability to reconcile individuals to one another and to their society with Christianity's apparent failure to do so.

2. Translation altered slightly.

3. Butler, *Antigone's Claim*, esp. 5–6.

4. Hegel also discusses the *Antigone* in the *Philosophy of Right* and in his *Aesthetics*; this later discussion of the play is relevant to Hegel's broader theory of the tragic. See Hegel, *Philosophy of Right*, §166/318–19 and *Aesthetics*, esp. 221, 464, 1217–18.

5. Although Hegel does not offer a summary of the *Antigone* in the *Phenomenology*, he succinctly describes the play in his lectures on *Aesthetics*: "Everything in this tragedy is logical; the public law of the state is set in conflict over against inner family love and duty to a brother; the woman, Antigone, has the family interest as her 'pathos,' Creon, the man, has the welfare of the community as his. Polyneices, at war with his native city, had fallen before the gates of Thebes, and Creon, the ruler, in a publicly proclaimed law threatened with death anyone who gave this enemy of the city the honor of burial. But this command, which concerned only the public weal, Antigone could not accept; as sister, in the piety of her love for her brother, she fulfills the holy duty of burial. In doing so she appeals to the law of the gods; but the gods she worships are the underworld gods of Hades, the inner gods of feeling, love, and kinship, not the daylight gods of free self-conscious national and political life." Hegel, *Aesthetics*, 464.

6. Sophocles's *Antigone* contains the first known references to both the concept of the unwritten law and the ascription of autonomy to a person rather than to a state. (On the former, see Paul Woodruff, "Introduction to *Antigone*," in Sophocles, *Antigone*, xviii. On the latter, see Ostwald, *Autonomia*, 1. My thanks to Joseph Clair for pointing out Sophocles's novel use of the concept of *autonomos* in the *Antigone*.) In the play, Antigone asserts that she follows a law that belongs to "the gods' unfailing unwritten laws." As we have seen, Hegel quotes what Antigone says next (although the translation differs slightly): "These

laws weren't made now or yesterday. They live for all time, and no one knows when they came into the light" (Sophocles, *Antigone*, 19). The Chorus, meanwhile, accuses Antigone of being a law unto herself, that is, *autonomous*. As she proceeds toward the tomb, the chorus sings: "True to your own laws [*autonomos*], you are the only one of mortals, who'll go down to Hades while still alive" (Sophocles, *Antigone*, 36). Hegel picks up on the tension between these two types of law—the unwritten law and the self-legislated law. They are not the same thing, as Hegel points out in the passage quoted above. While Antigone takes herself to be following a law that is fixed, given, and eternal, she is accused by Creon (Hegel's account largely ignores the Chorus) of following her own whim or caprice.

7. Butler, *Antigone's Claim*, 2 (emphasis in original).

8. Ibid., 32.

9. Ibid.

10. Ibid., 33–34.

11. "Aber das sittliche Bewußtsein ist vollständiger, seine Schuld reiner, wenn es das Gesetz und die Macht *vorher kennt*, der es gegenübertritt, sie für Gewalt und Unrecht, für eine sittliche Zufälligkeit nimmt und wissentlich, wie Antigone, das Verbrechen begeht" (§469/348).

12. Butler derives this language of inexcusability from A. V. Miller's translation of the passage, although not its direct connection to crime rather than guilt. Miller's translation of the sentence is as follows: "But the ethical consciousness is more complete, *its guilt more inexcusable*, if it knows *beforehand* the law and the power which it opposes, if it takes them to be violence and wrong, to be ethical merely by accident, and, like Antigone, knowingly commits the crime." See Hegel, *Phenomenology of Spirit*, trans. Miller, 284 (emphasis added).

13. As Danielle Allen has pointed out to me, Hegel's reading of *Oedipus Tyrannus*, in which Oedipus takes full responsibility for all of the significant consequences of his or her acts, may be troubled by developments in *Oedipus at Colonus*. In that play, which takes place after *Oedipus Tyrannus* and before *Antigone*, Oedipus denies full responsibility for the consequences of the actions he believes he was fated to commit. Hegel recognizes this in his later lectures on *Aesthetics*, in which he casts *Oedipus at Colonus* as already moving beyond his conceptions of classical tragedy, action, and heroism. Hegel writes that "more beautiful than this rather external sort of denouement is an inner reconciliation which, because of its subjective character, already borders on our modern treatment. The most perfect classical example of this that we have before us is the eternally marvelous *Oedipus Coloneus*" (Hegel, *Aesthetics*, 1219).

14. I borrow the term "forward-looking moral responsibility" from Henry S. Richardson's excellent work on the subject. See "Beyond Good and Right" and "Institutionally Divided Moral Responsibility." In the latter, Richardson contrasts forward-looking moral responsibility with what J. B. Schneewind called "the divine corporation," in which a form of moral life is taken for granted and individuals act according to the rules that govern their social roles (Schneewind quoted in Richardson, "Institutionally Divided Moral Responsibility," 226). Richardson writes that "individuals are given scant responsibility for the interpretation of moral requirements. Instead, what is required of them is something more deductive or subsumptive: the mere recognition that their case falls under some previously given rule. There is no differential authorization to revise [according to one's social role] because there is simply no authorization to revise" ("Institutionally Divided Moral Responsibility," 231). I submit that this is the situation in which Hegel finds Antigone and Creon.

15. Butler notes that Antigone acknowledges her deed in this way, although her reading of this acknowledgment is quite different from my own. Like many other commentators, Butler raises questions about Hegel's translation of this last sentence from the Greek. Hegel's translation removes a crucial conditional clause from the original text. Thus what

Paul Woodruff's translation of the *Antigone* renders as "If the gods really agree with [Cre-on's judgment], / Then suffering should teach me to repent my sin" becomes Hegel's quite different phrase, "Because we suffer we acknowledge we have erred" (Sophocles, *Antigone*, 40). While Butler is correct that Hegel's translation is an unreliable rendering of Sopho-cles's text, I suggest that we follow the story that Hegel is trying to tell about character, guilt, responsibility, and acknowledgment through his idiosyncratic appropriation of the play. Butler also argues that "the verbal form of her acknowledgement only exacerbates the crime. She not only did it, but she had the nerve to *say* she did it. Thus Antigone cannot exemplify the ethical consciousness who suffers guilt; she is beyond guilt—she embraces her crime as she embraces her death, her tomb, her bridal chamber" (*Antigone's Claim*, 34). Again, I submit that Hegel invokes a conception of objective rather than subjective guilt here; thus Butler's mention of "one who suffers guilt" is misleading.

16. See §667–71/490–93.

17. Redding, *Hegel's Hermeneutics*, 103–4.

18. Sophocles, *Antigone*, 57. The "poor child" to whom Creon refers is his own son, Haemon, not Antigone. Thus Creon is acknowledging his guilt, his indirect responsibility, for the death of his son. Again, this is consistent with Hegel's emphasis on guilt as related to an individual's responsibility for the *unintended* consequences of his or her actions as well as the intended consequences.

19. See Butler, *Antigone's Claim*; Brandom, "From Irony to Trust: Modernity and Beyond," in *A Spirit of Trust*, 23; and Hutchings, *Hegel and Feminist Philosophy*. Other works relevant to these questions about Hegel's views on gender and the resources that his work provides feminist philosophy include Hoy, "Hegel, *Antigone*, and Feminist Critique"; Hutchings and Pulkkinen, *Hegel's Philosophy and Feminist Thought*; and Mills, *Feminist Interpretations of G. W. F. Hegel*. On feminist interpretations of *Antigone* more broadly, see Honig, *Antigone, Interrupted*.

20. Butler, *Antigone's Claim*, 36.

21. Hutchings, *Hegel and Feminist Philosophy*, 99.

22. Ibid.

23. Ibid. Kelly Oliver makes a more radical claim in "Antigone's Ghost." She argues that in the dialectical movement of the *Phenomenology*, "woman gets left behind as the unconscious of the family upon which all subsequent dialectical movements of the concep-tualization of Spirit rest." In this way, Hegel fails to bring to full self-consciousness all that spirit entails, thereby "undermining the entire project of that text" (70, 67).

24. This argument is similar to the strategy pursued by Hoy in "Hegel, *Antigone*, and Feminist Critique." Hoy summarizes a series of criticisms of Hegel made by feminist theo-rists, and she argues that, often, these criticisms stem from a failure to distinguish between positions that Hegel is merely describing and those he is endorsing. She writes that "ex-ploring feminist critiques of Hegel in the *Phenomenology* shows that Hegel's claims about sexual difference and gender roles need to be contextualized in terms of his dialectical strategy. Within the *Phenomenology* each shape of consciousness or spiritual world pres-ents its own ideals or conceptions of knowledge. . . . Along the way Hegel cannot rightfully be assumed to identify with any one set of claims made from within the world under ex-amination" (186).

Karin de Boer also draws on the distinction of Hegel's descriptions of Greek life as it appears "for itself" versus as it appears "for us." She argues that Hegel "does not char-acterize womanhood as 'enemy' from an external point of view, but seeks to explain how the community, presided over by the government, threatened to oppose itself to one of its inherent moments" ("Beyond Tragedy," 141). Moreover, in contrast to most readers of Hegel, de Boer argues that Hegel is no longer discussing the *Antigone* in his statement about "womankind"; rather, Hegel has turned from Sophocles's tragedies to Aristophanes's comedies, "implicitly draw(ing) on the insights of Greek comedy to argue that Greek culture, organizing its ethical life in accordance with the natural distinction between the male and female sex, contradicts the principle of individuality it harbors" (145). I take de Boer's approach to the text to be largely compatible with my own; unfortunately, a more detailed discussion of her fascinating analysis of this final section of Hegel's discussion of Greek *Sittlichkeit* and its connections to Greek comedy is beyond my scope here.

25. Benhabib, *Situating the Self*, 246.

26. Ibid., 255–56.

27. Walter Kaufmann argues that Hegel's discussion of tragedy does not add up to a "Procrustean 'theory of tragedy,'" although it "illuminated many of Aeschylus', Sophocles', and Euripedes' tragedies more than any other philosopher before or after him" (*Tragedy and Philosophy*, 200, 212). In Kaufmann's view, Hegel does not develop a one-size-fits all theory of tragic drama but rather offers instructive analyses of particular plays that illuminate aspects of agency, responsibility, and conflict. In this section, I follow Kaufmann in thinking with Hegel about ethical conflict through a discussion of tragedy.

28. Kaufmann, *Tragedy and Philosophy*, 201–2. Hegel states this more clearly in his lectures on *Aesthetics*: "The original essence of tragedy consists then in the fact that within such a conflict each of the opposed sides, if taken by itself, has *justification*; while each can establish the true and positive content of its own aim and character only by denying and infringing the equally justified power of the other. The consequence is that in its ethical life, and because of it, each is nevertheless involved in *guilt*" (*Aesthetics*, 1196); he continues, "although the characters have a purpose which is valid in itself, they can carry it out in tragedy only by pursuing it one-sidedly and so contradicting and infringing someone else's purpose" (*Aesthetics*, 1197).

29. As Brandom puts the point, "The responsibility and the authority are not commensurate" ("From Irony to Trust," in *A Spirit of Trust*, 32). Brandom's discussion of these points includes a very helpful distinction between the heroic conception of agency and the modern conception of agency (ibid., 32ff.).

30. Nussbaum, *Fragility of Goodness*, 67.

31. Ibid.

Chapter Three: Culture War and the Appeal to Authority

1. Although Hegel already recognizes in this early period that the re-creation of Greek *Sittlichkeit* is not a viable option for modern societies, he is still more enamored with Greek *Sittlichkeit* than he comes to be in the *Phenomenology of Spirit* and his later work.

2. See, especially, "The Positivity of the Christian Religion," "The Spirit of Christianity and Its Fate," and the "Tübingen Essay." All three appear in volume 1 of Hegel's collected works. The first two are published in English translation in *Early Theological Writings*. The latter is published in Hegel, *Three Essays*, 30–58. For an in-depth discussion of all three essays and, in particular, their role in the development of Hegel's thoughts on religion and politics, see Lewis, *Religion, Modernity, and Politics in Hegel*, 16–56. Fuss and Dobbins translate *Volksreligion* as "folk religion." As Lewis points out, however, "'Folk religion' too easily suggests a stress on popular, rather than elite, religion that is foreign to Hegel's usage" (*Religion, Modernity, and Politics in Hegel*, 27n33). Lewis translates *Volksreligion* as "civil religion," which he argues "better captures the public, social, and political character of Hegel's notion of a *Volksreligion*" (27). While I agree that civil religion is less misleading than folk religion, many scholars of religion will associate that phrase with the high-level discourses of elected officials and statesmen to which Robert Bellah's influen-

tial essay "Civil Religion in America" has drawn attention (*Beyond Belief*, 168–89). I do not think this quite captures Hegel's meaning either. I prefer "religion of the people," which avoids both the folksy and elitist connotations of those alternatives. As this phrase is somewhat cumbersome, however, I have left *Volksreligion* untranslated and altered the Foss and Dobbins translations accordingly.

3. Lewis, *Religion, Modernity, and Politics in Hegel*, 31.

4. Kant writes that rituals may have beneficial social functions but that the Christian conception of them is mere superstition. The Eucharist, for instance, "contains within it something great that expands the narrow, self-loving, and intolerant way of thinking of human beings . . . to the idea of a *cosmopolitan community*; and thus it is a good means for invigorating a community to the moral attitude of brotherly love as which this community is conceived." As a social practice that expands the moral sensibilities of practitioners, the Eucharist may be beneficial to the communities in which it is practiced; nevertheless, Kant continues, to believe that God's grace is made present in and through this ritual is "a delusion of religion" (*Religion within the Boundaries of Bare Reason*, 220–21).

5. While Hegel considers both sacraments and sacrifice to be "essential customs" in the "Tübingen Essay," the two types of ritual serve somewhat different functions in the *Phenomenology*. I consider Hegel's view of the sacraments in chapter 4 and consider sacrifice in detail in chapter 5.

6. Hegel pursues this point in both the *Philosophy of Right* and the *Lectures on the Philosophy of Religion*. In the latter, he argues that religion is a critical site for the "education, practice, cultivation," of a disposition toward rational self-determination (478). He thinks that individuals have the capacity for rational self-determination but that this capacity must be developed into a habit or disposition. He writes that "it is the concern of the church that this habituating and educating of spirit should become ever more inward, that this truth should become ever more identical with the self, with the human will, and that this truth should become one's volition, one's object, one's spirit" (479). As others have argued, this combination of habituation and self-determination is crucial to Hegel's concept of freedom, in which the individual identifies with the social norms (into which she has been habituated) that she can also endorse for herself as rational. See, especially, Lewis, *Freedom and Tradition in Hegel*. Hegel's attention to religious ritual should be of interest to ritual theorists. The literature on the concept of ritual is extensive, as are the contemporary debates over how ritual should be understood and theorized by scholars of religion. One significant debate is whether ritual should primarily be understood as expressive and symbolic or as effective and disciplinary. To put the question bluntly, does ritual express the already held beliefs of religious subjects or does ritual produce and transform those beliefs and the subjects themselves? While these theoretical debates are beyond my scope here, I hope that interested readers will find that Hegel's discussions of ritual provide fodder for these contemporary debates. On my reading, Hegel believes that rituals and other religious practices both *symbolize* and *actualize* a community's central commitments, at once reinscribing them and holding them up for potential scrutiny and revision. On the contemporary theoretical questions, see Asad, *Genealogies of Religion*; Bell, *Ritual Theory, Ritual Practice*; Godlove, "Saving Belief"; Hollywood, "Performativity, Citationality, Ritualization" and "Practice, Belief and Feminist Philosophy of Religion"; and Mahmood, *Politics of Piety*.

7. Notable exceptions include Brandom, "From Irony to Trust," in *A Spirit of Trust*, 75–96; Stolzenberg, "Hegel's Critique of the Enlightenment"; and Hinchman, *Hegel's Critique of the Enlightenment*. Jean Hyppolite also includes a chapter titled "The Struggle between Enlightenment and Superstition," in *Genesis and Structure of Hegel's "Phenomenology of Spirit."* Brief summaries and interpretations of the section on Faith and Enlightenment are provided in the context of extended accounts of the *Phenomenology of Spirit*, including

Pinkard, *Hegel's Phenomenology*, 165–79; Crites, *Dialectic and Gospel*, 416–31; and Jaeschke, *Reason in Religion*, 191–93.

8. The "actual world" evolves into European aristocratic culture. In this shape of spirit, the individual must become "cultured," divested of his individuality and trained to comport himself according to external standards, which are largely set by those with political power or wealth. While the German word *Bildung* generally refers positively to the product of education and cultivation, Hegel uses the term somewhat ironically here to describe a culture that is complete artifice. Through a series of complex dialectical moves, Hegel shows how the "cultured" individual comes to see that there are no authoritative grounds for the norms of this form of life. Like the legal person, the cultured individual now recognizes power and wealth as arbitrary, external authorities that he cannot endorse as authoritative for himself.

9. Although *der Glaube* carries the dual meaning of "faith" and "belief," I translate it and its derivatives as "faith," "faithful," and so forth in order to capture the religious connotation of the German word.

10. In claiming that Faith is a shape of spirit (as opposed to a "shape of consciousness"), I disagree with Forster's interpretation of Chapter VI. Forster argues that Hegel abandons his analysis of social substance around the time he introduces the world of self-alienated spirit and what Hegel calls "pure consciousness." Forster interprets Hegel as revisiting the project of the first half of the book by depicting and discussing forms of thought rather than forms of life in the second half of Chapter VI. As Forster writes, "From the section *Faith and Pure Insight* onwards—with a partial exception in the treatment of the French Revolution in the section *Absolute Freedom and Terror*—the chapter ceases to depict *social contexts*, instead focusing once again, like the earlier chapters, on very general perspectives or 'shapes of consciousness,' this contrary to the official policy stated at the beginning of the chapter that we have now left behind 'shapes of consciousness' for 'shapes of a world'" (*Hegel's Idea of a Phenomenology of Spirit*, 451). In what follows, I hope to provide evidence to the contrary; indeed, my argument is that how Faith and Enlightenment understand and shape their own social contexts is precisely the issue in this section. Thus my position is close to Brandom's when he writes that Faith and Enlightenment "comprise not only norms and the individuals subject to them, but also practices and institutions in which those norms are implicit. Faith and Enlightenment are not just theories of normativity; they are *institutionalized* theories" ("From Irony to Trust," in *A Spirit of Trust*, 76).

11. Several texts provide invaluable accounts of Hegel's religious and theological context, including Dickey, *Hegel: Religion, Economics, and the Politics of Spirit* and Olson, *Hegel and the Spirit*. In *Hegel's Phenomenology*, Pinkard also provides a brief discussion of the connection between Pietism and what Hegel calls Faith (166).

12. Pinkard, *Hegel's Phenomenology*, 166.

13. Ibid., 172.

14. According to political theorist William Connolly, political debates are essentially conceptual contests. Citizens who agree, for instance, that justice and freedom are concepts worth talking about may share an understanding of how these concepts have been used in the past but disagree about their application to novel situations. Indeed, the meaning and applications of such concepts is the kind of thing about which people are likely to disagree: "Central to politics is the ambiguous and relatively open-ended interaction of persons and groups who share a range of concepts, but share them imperfectly and incompletely. Politics involves a form of interaction in which agents adjust, extend, resolve, accommodate, and transcend initial differences within a context of partially shared assumptions, concepts and commitments. On this reading conceptual contests are central to politics; they provide the space for political interaction" (Connolly, *Terms of Political Discourse*, 6). I address the political implications of this claim about how concepts are contested in chapter 7.

15. Brandom, *Reason in Philosophy*, esp. 81–88.

16. Ibid., esp. 52–77.

17. Brandom, "Expressive Metaphysics of Agency," in *A Spirit of Trust*, 22.

18. Ibid., 14.

19. See Anscombe, *Intention*.

20. Moyar, "Self-Completing Alienation," 156.

21. Ibid., 167.

22. Crites, *Dialectic and Gospel*, 421.

Chapter Four: Rituals of Reconciliation

1. See, for instance, Honneth, *The Struggle for Recognition* and Taylor, "The Politics of Recognition." I return to the politics of recognition in chapter 7.

2. Kojève, *Introduction to the Reading of Hegel*, esp. 3–30. At one time or another, Raymond Aron, Georges Bataille, André Breton, Jacques Lacan, Maurice Merleau-Ponty, Raymond Queneau, and Leo Strauss each attended Kojève's lectures. For a consideration of Kojève's philosophy and other twentieth-century French appropriations of Hegel, see Butler, *Subjects of Desire*. Kojève's interpretation has not been particularly influential in contemporary Anglo-American Hegel scholarship. In that body of scholarship, it has largely been ignored or treated critically.

3. As mentioned earlier, Hegel's terms are *Herrschaft* and *Knechtschaft*. Because of the long tradition of translating these terms as "master" and "slave" in discussions of Kojève's work, I use the terms "master"/"mastery" and "slave"/"slavery" throughout the present discussion. Elsewhere, when Kojève's work is not at issue, I use the terms "lord"/"lordship" and "bondsman"/"bondage." See chapter 1, note 4.

4. Kojève, *Introduction to the Reading of Hegel*, 40.

5. Ibid., 9.

6. Ibid.

7. Redding, *Hegel's Hermeneutics*, 120.

8. For additional criticisms of Kojève's interpretation of the *Phenomenology of Spirit*, see Kelly, "Notes on Hegel's 'Lordship and Bondage,'" and Williams, *Hegel's Ethics of Recognition*, esp. 366–71.

9. Redding, *Hegel's Hermeneutics*, 121. Moreover, Kojève cites not the *Phenomenology of Spirit* but Hegel's Jena lectures: page 206, line 26 of volume 20 of the series of Hegel's collected works compiled and edited by Georg Lasson and, later, Johannes Hoffmeister.

10. Redding, *Hegel's Hermeneutics*, 121.

11. Ibid., 109.

12. Ibid.

13. Ibid., 111-12.

14. Williams, *Hegel's Ethics of Recognition*, 10.

15. Ibid., 12.

16. Pippin, "Brandom's Hegel," 397.

17. Kojève, *Introduction to the Reading of Hegel*, 191–92.

18. Cf. Moyar, *Hegel's Conscience*. Moyar follows Jon Stewart in designating "concept" and "experience" phases of the presentation of shapes of consciousness in the *Phenomenology of Spirit* and sees the conscience section following roughly that formulation, with the addition of a second set of concept and experience phases. Moyar argues that what Hegel presents in the concept phase of his discussion of conscience largely represents Hegel's own view of the matter. As I argue in this chapter, however, the view presented in the concept phase of Hegel's discussion of conscience must undergo one further dialectical move before reconciliation and the emergence of absolute spirit are possible. See also Stewart, *The Unity of Hegel's "Phenomenology of Spirit."*

19. Pinkard suggests that Hegel is referring to both Kantian and Pietist morality. Pinkard, *Hegel's Phenomenology*, 193.

20. This movement has often been identified with German Romanticism, as in Pinkard, *Hegel's Phenomenology*, 207–13. Beiser questions this identification, arguing that there is "too great a discrepancy between Hegel's account of the beautiful soul in the *Phenomenology* and actual Romantic attitudes and doctrines." Instead, Beiser identifies Hegel's precedents in *Sturm und Drang* and literary sources including Book VI of Goethe's *Wilhelm Meisters Lehrjahre*, titled "The Confessions of a Beautiful Soul," and Rousseau's account of the beautiful soul in *Julie, or the New Heloise*. See Beiser, " 'Morality' in Hegel's *Phenomenology of Spirit*," 222–23.

21. Crites, *Dialectic and Gospel*, 435–36.

22. Selective Service System, http://www.sss.gov/consobj.

23. Translation altered slightly.

24. Translation altered slightly. For reasons of consistency, I translate *niederträchtig* as "base" rather than "vile" (cf. Pinkard's translation). Hegel uses the word *niederträchtig*, and its opposite, *edelmütig*, throughout Chapter VI. These two terms respectively refer to individuals who are alienated, because they cannot see that their own beliefs and identities are shaped by social norms, and those who are unalienated. In his earlier discussion of the formation of Roman legal society, for instance, Hegel writes of two opposing shapes of consciousness: "one of them is a conduct towards state-power and wealth as a relation to an *equal*, the other as a relation to an *unequal*—the consciousness of the relation which is a finding-of-equality is the *noble-minded* [*edelmütige*]"; the other, by contrast, "is that of *baseness* [*niederträchtige*], which clings tenaciously to the *inequality* between both essentialities. It thus sees the power of the ruler as a shackle, as the suppression of its *being-for-itself*, and it thus hates the ruler and merely obeys him with concealed malice, standing ever ready to spring into revolt" (§499–500/372).

25. I have altered Pinkard's translation slightly, preferring the more literal "is master over" to his "has a mastery over." The German text reads: "Es zeigt sich dadurch als das geistverlassene und den Geist verleugnende Bewußtsein, denn es erkennt nicht, daß der Geist in der absoluten Gewißheit seiner selbst über alle Tat und Wirklichkeit Meister [ist] und sie abwerfen und ungeschehen machen kann" (§667/491).

26. Emphasis added. In Miller, the full sentence reads: "It does not know that Spirit, in the absolute certainty of itself, is lord and master over every deed and actuality, and can cast them off, and make them as if they never happened" (§667/406).

27. Speight, "Butler and Hegel on Forgiveness and Agency," 299.

28. Cf. Rose, *Hegel Contra Sociology*, 190–92. In Gillian Rose's reading of this passage, Hegel's point is that "words are not actions, that evil, confession and forgiveness are subjective, Christian virtues not ethical ones, and that abstract statements mask ethical actuality" (191–92). Rose's reading seems to depend on Hegel's discussion of conscience's account of itself, according to which the affirmation of the other's conviction and the issuance of judgment of another's action do not themselves count as actions that are subject to normative judgment. In my reading, however, Hegel's point in the discussion of confession and forgiveness is that conscience was *wrong* about that: these words *do* count as actions. The confession and forgiveness are simultaneously word and deed. Thus there is nothing abstract or merely subjective about the acts of confession and forgiveness; both the wicked and judging consciousnesses ultimately recognize that they are in the position of both judge and judged—that is, subject and object—and their speech acts actualize this recognition.

29. In his *Lectures on the Philosophy of Religion*, Hegel explicitly states his preference for the Lutheran account of the Eucharist over against the Catholic and Reformed accounts. According to Hegel, the Catholic doctrine of transubstantiation venerates the material host itself, while the Reformed doctrine reduces the Eucharist to its symbolic and memorial functions. The Lutheran position charts a middle course, acknowledging the

actual presence of Christ in the bread and wine, made manifest in the act of partaking: "the communion, the self-feeling presence of God, comes about only insofar as the external thing is consumed—not merely physically but in spirit and in faith." See Hegel, *Lectures on the Philosophy of Religion*, 479–81. See also Hegel's brief discussion of "*repentance* or *penitence*" immediately preceding this. As scholars like Walter Jaeschke, Cyril O'Regan, and Peter Hodgson have all noted in discussions of the *Lectures on the Philosophy of Religion*, Hegel is not endorsing a full-fledged sacramental theology in these pages, at least in any orthodox sense. As O'Regan writes, "Hegel is not so much defending a particular sacramental theology as indicating support for a sacramental *principle* that may very well apply to all reality" (*The Heterodox Hegel*, 243). Or, in Hodgson's words, "[Hegel's] account of historical details is often imprecise, and his emphasis lies on conceptual distinctions that appear in history in a variety of ways" (*Hegel and Christian Theology*, 193). For an excellent discussion of the role of the sacrament of communion in Hegel's work, see Crites, *In the Twilight of Christendom*, 49–51. Hegel's relation to Luther and orthodox Lutheranism is a matter of some debate. At this point, I claim only that the structure of the confession and forgiveness, on Hegel's account, mirrors the structure of the sacrament on Luther's. Hegel's view of God, as I will discuss in chapter 5, departs from the orthodox Lutheran view in significant ways. On that point, I follow O'Regan's interpretation. See O'Regan, *The Heterodox Hegel*; cf. Houlgate, *Freedom, Truth, and History: An Introduction to Hegel's Philosophy*; Asendorf, *Luther und Hegel*.

30. Luther, "The Sacrament of Penance," 11.

31. Ibid., 18.

32. Luther, "Exhortation to Confession." This text originally appeared in Luther's 1529 edition of the *Large Catechism*. It is included in some, but not all, editions of the *Book of Concord*. Similarly, in "The Babylonian Captivity of the Church" (1520), Luther exhorts the Church to "permit all brothers and sisters freely to hear the confession of hidden sins, so that the sinner may make his sins known to whomever he will and seek pardon and comfort, that is, the word of Christ, by the mouth of his neighbor."

33. I owe this way of putting the point to conversations with Ronald F. Thiemann.

34. Pippin, "Recognition and Reconciliation," 139.

35. Ibid.

36. Ibid.

37. Ibid., 140.

38. Ibid.; Bernstein, "Confession and Forgiveness," quoted in Pippin, "Recognition and Reconciliation," 140.

39. Pippin, "Recognition and Reconciliation," 140, 142n11.

40. In Brandom's interpretation of the *Phenomenology of Spirit*, trust is an indispensable component of recognitive communities. Indeed, Brandom argues that it is only in the presence of trust that contentful norms can be developed and sustained. He writes: "In confessing, one not only expresses retrospective acknowledgement of the residual disparity in one's beliefs and actions between what things are in themselves and what they are for one, between norm and subjective attitude, one also expresses prospective trust in others to find ways of forgiving that disparity, forging/finding a unity of referent behind the disparity of sense, healing the wound. Such trust is an acknowledgement of dependence on others for recognition in the form of forgiveness" ("From Irony to Trust," in *A Spirit of Trust*, 216).

Chapter Five: Religion, Philosophy, and the Absolute

1. In this passage, Hegel makes good on a promissory note issued in Chapter IV of the *Phenomenology of Spirit*: "What will later come to be for consciousness will be the

experience of what spirit is, that is, this absolute substance which constitutes the unity of its oppositions in their complete freedom and self-sufficiency, namely, in the oppositions of the various self-consciousnesses existing for themselves: The *I* that is *we* and the *we* that is *I*" (§177/145). I argue in this chapter that these passages should not be read as evidence of any commitment to spirit monism but rather read in light of Hegel's grappling with the Kantian conception of the self-conscious subject in ways that overcome givenness, subject-object dualism, and resulting skepticism about what we can know about others and the world.

2. Hodgson, *Hegel and Christian Theology*, 33.

3. While it is likely that Hegel read Spinoza's *Tractatus Theologico-Politicus* shortly after leaving the Tübingen seminary, his discussions of Spinozistic philosophy are more concerned with the popular Spinozism of his contemporaries than with the details of Spinoza's own philosophy. Hegel and his seminary friends, Hölderlin and Schelling, were deeply influenced by the popular Spinozism stirred up by the "pantheism controversy" surrounding F. H. Jacobi's 1785 book, *Über die Lehre des Spinoza in Briefen an den Herrn Moses Mendelssohn*. In the book, Jacobi published a series of letters that he had written to Mendelssohn, in which Jacobi claimed that Lessing, shortly before his death, had confided his "Spinozism" to Jacobi. While the controversy initially involved a dispute between Jacobi and Mendelssohn, it became a major public debate over reason, rational faith, pantheism, and, to use the term that Jacobi himself coined, nihilism. This debate eventually encircled many of the German intellectuals of the period, including Kant, Goethe, and Herder. One effect of the debate was to make Spinoza's philosophy—or at least a Spinozistic pantheism—respectable and popular after a long period of disrepute. Among the new "Spinoza enthusiasts," according to Beiser, were "nearly all of the major figures of the classical *Goethezeit*—Goethe, Novalis, Hölderlin, Herder, F. Schlegel, Hegel, Schleiermacher, and Schelling" (*The Fate of Reason*, 44). For two detailed, but quite different, accounts of the underlying causes of the controversy as well as its effects on German intellectual life in the late eighteenth century, see Beiser, *The Fate of Reason*, 44ff., and Gottlieb, *Faith and Freedom*. While Beiser argues that the pantheism controversy was fundamentally a debate about metaphysical and epistemological questions—particularly "the authority of reason"—Gottlieb contends that the debate was less about metaphysical and epistemological problems than "about ethical and political issues concerning the best means of promoting human dignity and freedom in modern society" (113). For an account of Spinozism in late eighteenth-century Germany, see Bell, *Spinoza in Germany*. Meanwhile, throughout this period, Hegel's own relationship to Spinozism was complex and evolving. Hegel, Hölderlin, and Schelling *were* enthusiastic about Spinozism while in seminary, particularly its rejection of mind-body dualism and of orthodox theism. Yet Hegel comes to reject Spinozism (as well as the other precritical positions to which he was drawn as a young man, such as Greek *Sittlichkeit*), contending that, as Pinkard summarizes the argument of Hegel's later review of Jacobi's work, "the Spinozistic conception of substance cannot account for how it is that itself, this substance, can come to *be aware of* itself and *give an account* of itself, and how this insufficiency in Spinozism requires a move not back to pre-Spinozistic metaphysics but forward to idealist doctrines of self-consciousness" (Pinkard, *Hegel*, 385). Of course, the extent to which Hegel actually moved beyond Spinozism is a matter of debate. See Pinkard, *Hegel*, esp. 30–32, 384–88 and Pippin, *Hegel's Idealism*. Cf. Beiser, *Hegel*, 57ff., and Westphal, "Hegel and Onto-Theology."

4. Stephen Crites nicely frames Hegel's concern about the Spinozistic conception of substance in terms of William James's pluralism: "If the whole were Spinozistic substance, a changeless truth the spatiotemporal appearances of which are merely the illusions of perception, it would be a good example of what William James called a 'block universe' against which James protested on behalf of the validity of experience with its contingency and open-endedness" (*Dialectic and Gospel*, 448).

5. See, especially, Pippin, *Hegel's Idealism* and "Concept and Intuition: On Distinguishability and Separability." Also excellent on this point is Sedgwick, *Hegel's Critique of Kant*.

6. Pippin, "Concept and Intuition," 32.

7. Lewis, *Religion, Modernity, and Politics in Hegel*, 73.

8. As on other points, my reading of this transition follows the post-Kantian line of interpretation. Lewis characterizes the transition in similar terms. He writes: "Previous chapters traced the development of the 'absolute essence,' showing the way in which what was taken to be authoritative or of absolute value for a particular formation of consciousness could not satisfy its own criteria for success. . . . These previous stages had the absolute essence as an object, but Chapter VII is the first to focus on our practices of reflecting on this essence" ("Religion and Demythologization in Hegel's *Phenomenology of Spirit*," 193). This reading of the transition differs from that of many scholars who interpret Hegel's philosophy of religion as, primarily, a metaphysics. Peter Hodgson, for instance, argues that the previous chapters of the *Phenomenology of Spirit* consider religion "from the point of view of consciousness that is conscious *of* absolute being; absolute being in and for itself, the *self*-consciousness of spirit, has not appeared in these forms. This signals a transition from an anthropological to an ontotheological perspective" (*Hegel and Christian Theology*, 36). See also Westphal, *History and Truth*, 187–207.

9. I follow Pinkard's translation of *Vorstellung* as "representation" or "representational thought"; nevertheless, I appreciate Miller's rather poetic translation of *Vorstellung* as "picture thinking" for the way it captures the imagistic quality of this form of reflection and knowledge.

10. In this respect, the presentation of religions in the *Phenomenology of Spirit* differs from that in Hegel's *Lectures on the Philosophy of Religion*, in which he claims to present both a history of religions and a story of the increasing conceptual adequacy of religions. I discuss the *Phenomenology of Spirit*'s chapter on religion in more detail, and address the problems that this conflation of historical and conceptual progression causes for Hegel's philosophy of religion, in Farneth, "G. W. F. Hegel."

11. As he does throughout the book, however, Hegel draws on various historical and literary examples to fill out these conceptual possibilities. On this point, see Jaeschke, *Reason in Religion*, 189–90.

12. O'Regan, "The Trinity in Kant, Hegel, and Schelling," 257. In *The Heterodox Hegel*, O'Regan argues that Hegel's theology has a Lutheran frame but that it departs from Luther and orthodox Lutheranism in several respects. Key among these is his conception of the Trinity. On O'Regan's interpretation, Hegel sees the Trinity not as a tri-personal divinity but as a three-part movement. In this, Hegel's antecedent is less Luther than Jacob Boehme, whose heterodox Lutheranism involved a view of the triune God as a triadic *dynamic* rather than as three persons with a single nature. I am largely convinced by O'Regan's argument, although I suspect that Hegel sees an ongoing tension between these two conceptions of the Trinity in revealed religion.

13. Miller translates *Entäußerung* as "externalization." Baillie translates it as "relinquishment." In the secondary literature, it is sometimes translated as "alienation," although this runs the risk of conflating it with *Entfremdung*, another important term for Hegel, which he uses to rather different ends. In *A Hegel Dictionary*, for instance, Michael Inwood includes both *Entäußerung* and *Entfremdung* in his entry on "alienation and estrangement." See Inwood, *A Hegel Dictionary*, 35–38.

14. I have translated this verse freely from Luther's German. Thanks to Shira Billet for thoughts on this translation.

15. For a more detailed account of self-emptying in Hegel's philosophy, see Farneth, "'The Power to Empty Oneself.'" There, I argue that, for Hegel, self-emptying involves

the subject's refusal to claim certain forms of power over others in epistemic and practical matters. See also Bubbio, "Sacrifice in Hegel's *Phenomenology of Spirit*" and *Sacrifice in the Post-Kantian Tradition*, 61–85. Georges Bataille's well-known essay on Hegel's concept of sacrifice is deeply indebted to Kojève's interpretation of the *Phenomenology*, with its emphasis on human beings' violent transformation of the given. Bataille himself states that his essay is an "excerpt from a study on the—fundamentally Hegelian—thought of Alexander [*sic*] Kojève" ("Hegel, Death and Sacrifice," 9n1). As I argue at the beginning of chapter 4, Kojève's interpretation suffers from an overreliance on the master-slave section. Moreover, Bataille does not discuss sacrifice as it appears in Chapter VII, which he claims "strays from the essential" (18). As my interpretation shows, I strongly disagree with that assessment. For discussions of Hegel's concept of sacrifice in the Kojève-Bataille interpretive tradition, see Forshay, "Tarrying with the Negative" and Keenan, *The Question of Sacrifice*, 160–73.

16. Hegel discusses sacrifice throughout his corpus. In the "Tübingen Essay," as discussed in chapter 3, he claims that sacraments and sacrifices are "essential customs" that express the true content of *Volksreligion*. He also connects sacraments and sacrifices in Part I of his *Lectures on the Philosophy of Religion*, in which he states that these rituals are "external forms through which the feeling of reconciliation is brought forth in an external and sensible manner." In terms of the classificatory scheme that he presents there, these practices belong to the second form of the cultus. The first form is characterized by inward *devotion*, the second by outward practices of *sacrament* and *sacrifice*, and the third by *repentance* (§334, 193–94). This third form echoes both the practices of confession and forgiveness and the practices of self-emptying that he describes in the *Phenomenology of Spirit*.

17. Stephen Crites has a nice discussion of the various doctrines of revealed religion. See Crites, *Dialectic and Gospel*, 497–517.

18. While Hegel's criticism is directed toward revealed religion's account of reconciliation, it also applies to other religious standpoints. This is due to Hegel's very conception of religion. Because religion is spirit's reflection on the absolute, without philosophy's recognition that the movement of thought is itself the movement of spirit reflecting on itself, religion must be alienated from its object. As Walter Jaeschke notes, "What Hegel says about the Christian community is true for religion as a whole: 'it is the spiritual self-consciousness that is not an object to itself as this self-consciousness, or that does not unfold itself to a consciousness of itself'" (*Reason in Religion*, 192).

19. In addition to the social and political context mentioned in chapter 1, personal factors included Hegel's increasing financial distress along with pressure from the publisher to complete the manuscript. Pinkard, *Hegel*, 221–30.

20. Merold Westphal makes a similar point about what I am calling the intrinsic reason for the brevity of the final chapter of the *Phenomenology of Spirit*. He writes, "So far as 'we' are concerned, nothing remains to be done, for 'we' are supposed to have seen throughout the preceding chapter that the truth of Religion lies in correcting its misleading form by recognizing the divine to be nothing beyond us but the social whole of which we are parts" (*History and Truth*, 211).

21. Beiser, *Hegel*, 55. For Beiser's criticism of nonmetaphysical interpretations of Hegel, see Beiser, "Hegel, A Non-Metaphysician! A Polemic," 1–13.

22. Beiser, *Hegel*, 55.

23. For these reasons, contemporary scholarship on Hegel seems to me difficult to parse along metaphysical/nonmetaphysical lines, polemics notwithstanding. Robert Stern, to take one example, provides an account of Hegel's metaphysics that "avoids the kind of extravagant metaphysical views that were suggested by his subsequent critics" and casts Hegelian philosophy as conversant with pragmatism and other metaphysically minimalist philosophical standpoints. See Stern, *Hegelian Metaphysics*, 34.

24. Pippin, "Recognition and Reconciliation," 140.

25. The second part of Pippin's claim is that Hegel does not specify the practices and institutions that accompany absolute spirit. As I suggested at the end of chapter 4, Pippin is largely right about the lack of institutions in Hegel's account of absolute spirit. Hegel discusses such institutions primarily in the *Philosophy of Right*. Yet it is also the case that these institutions are part of the contestable content of absolute spirit. This interpretation raises questions about what a Hegelian social ethics would look like in political terms, questions whose answers need not be tied to the legal and political terms laid out in the *Philosophy of Right*. Indeed, Hegel's optimism about the rationality of bureaucratic elites, as laid out in the *Philosophy of Right*, ought to appear unjustified from our present vantage point. In chapter 7, I suggest what democratic thought and practice might entail if we consider Hegel's insights about absolute spirit in a quite different social and political context from the one in which he wrote the *Phenomenology of Spirit* and *Philosophy of Right*.

26. Crites, *Dialectic and Gospel*, 445. I am not certain whether Crites was self-consciously alluding to Richard Rorty's 1994 essay "Religion as Conversation-Stopper." Whether or not the allusion was self-conscious, the connection is apt. In that essay, Rorty contends that religion is best kept out of the public square, for religion is a conversation-stopper; it causes vital political discussions to break down. Crites's comment suggests that Hegel's "absolute spirit" is not to be understood as a form of life in which claims to a priori knowledge of the absolute serve as trump cards that end discussion, deliberation, or debate.

27. Of course, even if these individuals recognize human beings as the authors of those social roles and norms, and even if they take responsibility for them, there are questions to be asked about the extent to which individuals can rationally revise the roles and norms that have been bequeathed to and inculcated in them.

28. As Hegel writes in the preface, "the spirit of life is not a life that is fearing death and austerely saving itself from ruin; rather, it bears death calmly and in death, it sustains itself. Spirit only wins its truth by finding its feet within its absolute disruption" (§32/36).

29. This distinction is roughly parallel to Brandom's distinction between *de dicto* and *de re* modes of ascribing commitments. In *de dicto* ascription, the interpreter employs only those commitments that the interpretee herself endorses. In *de re* ascription, the interpreter draws on those commitments and employs substitutional commitments and inferences to reach conclusions that the interpretee may or may not herself endorse. Brandom, *Making It Explicit*, 503ff. This distinction has been used in the methodological debates of intellectual historians. See Marshall, "The Implications of Robert Brandom's Inferentialism for Intellectual History."

Chapter Six: Commitment, Conversation, and Contestation

1. Although the second part of the chapter focuses on affinities between basic features of Hegel's social ethics and recent Christian theology, the broader argument of this and the following chapter is that this social ethics is compatible with any number of different religious traditions. Worth noting, in particular, are affinities between the social ethics outlined here and certain strands of modern Jewish thought. Although Kant, rather than Hegel, has long been considered the touchstone of modern Jewish thought, recent work has reconsidered the extent to which late nineteenth- and twentieth-century Jewish philosophy and ethics was grappling with either Hegel's philosophy or concerns about Kant's philosophy that echoed those motivating Hegel. Panels at the American Academy of Religion and the Society of Jewish Ethics, for instance, have considered this Hegelian legacy in the work of Hermann Cohen, Nachman Krochmal, Franz Rosenzweig, and others. Also

instructive is Mordecai Kaplan's view of Judaism as a civilization in which shared social practices generate the ground of authority that governs Jewish life. To my mind, one of the most poignant accounts of the relationship between Hegel and Jewish thought is Martin Kavka's essay "Saying Kaddish for Gillian Rose, or on Levinas and *Geltungsphilosophie*."

2. In some cases, that may well be okay, insofar as people find ways of coping with or enduring those disagreements. I do not mean to suggest that every disagreement or ethical conflict can, or should, be overcome.

3. MacIntyre, "Epistemological Crises, Dramatic Narrative, and the Philosophy of Science," 461.

4. For a detailed account of truth and justification along Hegelian lines, see Stout, *Democracy and Tradition*, 238–40, 248, 276–77, 279 and *Ethics after Babel*, chaps. 1, 11.

5. Pippin, "Back to Hegel?" 18.

6. Hector, *Theology without Metaphysics*, 234.

7. Hector's discussion of the struggle for emancipation is especially helpful on these points. See chap. 6 of *Theology without Metaphysics*.

8. Lindbeck, *The Nature of Doctrine*, 18.

9. Ibid., 74.

10. Ibid., 131.

11. Placher, *Unapologetic Theology*, especially chap. 7; Werpehowski, "Ad Hoc Apologetics," 287.

12. Werpehowski, "Ad Hoc Apologetics," 287. See also p. 292.

13. Marshall, "Absorbing the World," 75.

14. Ibid., 76.

15. Ibid., 82.

16. See Jeffrey Stout's contribution to Springs, "Pragmatism and Democracy," 413–48.

17. See Rorty, "Religion as Conversation-Stopper." Although Rorty later changed the target of his criticism to religious organizations rather than religious individuals, and he began to refer to his position as "anti-clericalism" rather than "atheism," he continued to express the hope that religious organizations would eventually disappear and that religion would be thoroughly privatized. At the American Academy of Religion Annual Meeting in 2003, after he had supposedly revised his view of religion, he reiterated his concern about the deleterious effects of religion in American public life and he asserted that "nontheists make better citizens of democratic societies than theists" (see Rorty's contribution to Springs, "Pragmatism and Democracy"). I consider these issues, along with the philosophical shortcomings of Rorty's view of religion and democracy, in Farneth, "Rorty and Religion."

18. MacIntyre, *Whose Justice? Which Rationality?* especially chap. 1. For a more detailed discussion of this problem in MacIntyre, see Stout, *Ethics after Babel*, esp. 345.

Chapter Seven: Democratic Authority through Conflict and Reconciliation

1. Arendt, "What Is Authority?" 100.

2. Her distinction between authority and power, and her identification of power with violence, in "What Is Authority?" is somewhat different from her distinctions among those terms in her later essay *On Violence*. Cf. Arendt, *On Violence*, 44–45.

3. Arendt, "What Is Authority?" 141.

4. Honig, *Democracy and the Foreigner*, 104.

5. Quoted in Stout, *Blessed Are the Organized*, xv (emphasis added).

6. Taylor, "The Politics of Recognition," 24.

7. See, for instance, Fraser, "Recognition without Ethics?" and Oliver, *Witnessing*, esp. chap. 1.

8. See Markell, *Bound by Recognition*, esp. 1–38.

9. Oliver, for example, suggests that witnessing is an encounter with *subjectivity*, which, she writes, "is experienced as *the sense of agency and response-ability* that are constituted in the infinite encounter with otherness, which is fundamentally ethical" ("Witnessing and Testimony," 82, emphasis added).

10. Borowiak, *Accountability and Democracy*, 101.

11. Waldron, "Accountability," 2.

12. This form of accountability is also relevant to the problem of democratic citizens' moral responsibility for actions undertaken by their governments raised, for instance, by Eric Beerbohm in *In Our Name: The Ethics of Democracy*. Part of Beerbohm's argument is that democratically organized societies need institutions and other mechanisms by which citizens can "officially record their moral opposition to a particular policy or executive action" as a way of limiting their complicity in such policies and actions (*In Our Name*, 253). Beerbohm's proposal is focused on this issue of complicity and does not obviate the need for other forms of democratic accountability.

13. This is an issue raised by Pettit, *Republicanism*, 186ff. What I suggest here, however, is that formal and institutional mechanisms of accountability-holding depend on a broader context of reciprocal recognition among citizens in democratically organized communities.

14. Žižek's reading of Hegel appears similar on many points to the one for which I have argued. Žižek rejects the "end of history" reading of Hegel, and he stresses the impossibility, on Hegel's account, of overcoming conflict once and for all. Conflict is central to Žižek's Hegelianism, as it is to mine. Yet we come to dramatically different conclusions about what *sort* of conflict this should be and what forms of authority and accountability underlie it. Pippin argues that Žižek's political prescriptions depend upon a misreading of Hegel, particularly with respect to the relationship between reason and sociality. See Žižek, *Less than Nothing*, especially 193–240 and 455–504; and Pippin, "Back to Hegel?" 19.

15. Žižek, *Less than Nothing*, 429.

16. Ibid., 963.

17. Grattan, *Populism's Power*, 166. In spite of these criticisms, Grattan is sympathetic to the populist energy and imagination that motivated the Occupy movement. Her broader study offers a theory of "aspirational democratic populism," a category that can include, with caveats, a populist uprising like Occupy as well as local, broad-based democratic organizations such as those operating under the umbrella of the Industrial Areas Foundation or the PICO National Network. It seems to me that to be *democratic*, a populist uprising like Occupy would need to clarify the forms of leadership and structure that make authority and accountability possible and commensurate.

18. Grattan, *Populism's Power*, 166–67.

19. Freeman's "The Tyranny of Structurelessness" was originally written for a conference at the Southern Female Rights Union (1970). Several versions were subsequently published, including Freeman, "The Tyranny of Structurelessness," *Berkeley Journal of Sociology* 17 (1972–73): 151–64.

20. Morris, *The Origins of the Civil Rights Movement*, 4.

21. Payne, *I've Got the Light of Freedom*, 70.

22. Coles, in Hauerwas and Coles, *Christianity, Democracy, and the Radical Ordinary*, 57.

23. Quoted in Payne, *I've Got the Light of Freedom*, 68.

24. We might think of their work as an expression and embodiment of what Martin Luther King Jr. called "beloved community." King himself fell short of embodying that

ideal, particularly when it came to recognizing his own accountability in the face of women's authority and leadership in the movement.

25. Several recent studies of the IAF highlight the centrality of this relationship-building work to its organizing model. See, for instance, Bretherton, *Resurrecting Democracy*, esp. 122–30; Warren, *Dry Bones Rattling*, esp. 31–35; and Stout, *Blessed Are the Organized*, esp. 148–64. For an excellent discussion of broad-based organizing as an exercise of political voice, which draws on Stout's *Blessed Are the Organized*, see Wolterstorff, "Exercising One's Political Voice as a Moral Engagement."

26. Stout, *Blessed Are the Organized*, 149.

27. Connolly, *Identity/Difference*, 178.

28. Connolly, "Agonism, Pluralism, and Contemporary Capitalism," 210. Connolly is more committed to a Nietzschean sense of the contingency of our epistemic foundations than I am (or than Hegel would be). He insists, however, that his vision of pluralism does not require everyone to "accept the fundamental 'contingency' of things. That would make it less pluralistic. . . . The appreciation of contestability, not universal acceptance of contingency, sets a key condition of pluralism and pluralization" (ibid.).

29. For a discussion of the relationship between this account of authority and Brandom's Hegelian pragmatism, see Fossen, "Politicizing Brandom's Pragmatism."

30. There are affinities between the account of democratic authority that I am offering here and the theory of democratic change that Christopher Meckstroth offers in *The Struggle for Democracy*. We both draw on Hegel to develop a nonfoundationalist account of how the commitments and actions of democratic actors might provide the grounds of political authority. See Meckstroth, *The Struggle for Democracy*, esp. 139–69, 242–47.

31. Honig, *Political Theory and the Displacement of Politics*, 210.

32. Recall Brandom's claim that, for Hegel, conflict is perpetual: "The inexhaustibility of concrete, sensuous immediacy guarantees that we will never achieve a set of conceptual contents articulated by relations of material inferential consequence and incompatibility that will not . . . at some point lead to commitments that are incompatible, according to those same standards. No integration or recollection is final at the ground level" (*Reason in Philosophy*, 104).

33. I have found the work of Margaret Urban Walker particularly helpful in constructing the view of forgiveness presented here (not least in her insistence that "forgiveness is a variable human practice and a practice with culturally distinctive versions" [*Moral Repair*, 152]). Like Walker's, my view of forgiveness is connected to a right-order account of justice. Although I disagree with Nicholas Wolterstorff on this and several other questions about what forgiveness is and entails, I have benefited immensely from engagement with his thoughtful and thorough account of forgiveness, particularly in *Justice in Love*. For an overview of the secondary literature and major debates about the concept of forgiveness, see Biggar, "Forgiveness in the Twentieth Century."

34. Melissa Orlie considers the forward-looking aspect of forgiveness in her Arendtian account of ethical and political life. Like Hegel's confession and forgiveness, which transforms the wicked and judging consciousnesses and creates a new relationship between them, Orlie's Arendtian forgiveness is a site of natality: "When we become responsive to other's claims about our effects and when we show a willingness to transpose them, we may disrupt what we are predicted to be and redirect the social necessities that flow from given subjectivity" (*Living Ethically, Acting Politically*, 184). This comparison—between Hegel's forgiveness and Orlie's Arendtian forgiveness—brings Hegel and Arendt closer than many democratic theorists would place them.

35. Walker, *Moral Repair*, 15.

36. Robinson, *When I Was a Child I Read Books*, xiv.

Adams, Nicholas. *Eclipse of Grace: Divine and Human Action in Hegel.* Chichester: Wiley-Blackwell, 2013.

Anscombe, G. E. M. *Intention.* Oxford: Blackwell, 1957.

Arendt, Hannah. *On Violence.* Orlando, FL: Harcourt Books, 1970.

———. "What Is Authority?" In *Between Past and Future: Eight Exercises in Political Thought.* New York: Penguin, 1993.

Asad, Talal. *Genealogies of Religion: Discipline and Reasons of Power in Christianity and Islam.* Baltimore: Johns Hopkins University Press, 1993.

Asendorf, Ulrich. *Luther und Hegel: Untersuchungen zur Grundlegung einer Neuen Systematischen Theologie.* Wiesbaden: Franz Steiner Verlag, 1982.

Bataille, Georges. "Hegel, Death and Sacrifice." *Yale French Studies* 78 (1990): 9–28.

Beerbohm, Eric. *In Our Name: The Ethics of Democracy.* Princeton: Princeton University Press, 2012.

Beiser, Frederick C., ed. *The Cambridge Companion to Hegel.* Cambridge: Cambridge University Press, 1993.

———. *The Fate of Reason: German Philosophy from Kant to Fichte.* Cambridge, MA: Harvard University Press, 1987.

———. *Hegel.* New York: Routledge, 2005.

———. "Hegel, A Non-Metaphysician! A Polemic." *Bulletin of the Hegel Society of Great Britain* 32 (1995): 1–13.

———. "'Morality' in Hegel's *Phenomenology of Spirit*." In K. Westphal, 209–25.

Bell, Catherine. *Ritual Theory, Ritual Practice.* Oxford: Oxford University Press, 1992.

Bell, David. *Spinoza in Germany from 1670 to the Age of Goethe.* London: Institute for Germanic Studies, 1984.

Bellah, Robert N. *Beyond Belief: Essays on Religion in a Post-Traditionalist World.* Berkeley: University of California Press, 1970.

Benhabib, Seyla. *Situating the Self: Gender, Community, and Postmodernism in Contemporary Ethics.* New York: Routledge, 1992.

Bernstein, J. M. "Confession and Forgiveness: Hegel's Poetics of Action." In *Beyond Representation: Philosophy and Poetic Imagination,* ed. Richard Eldridge, 34–65. Cambridge: Cambridge University Press, 1996.

Bernstein, Richard J. *The Pragmatic Turn.* Cambridge: Polity Press, 2010.

Biggar, Nigel. "Forgiveness in the Twentieth Century: A Review of the Literature, 1901–2001." In *Forgiveness and Truth: Explorations in Contemporary Theology,* ed. Alistair McFadyen and Marcel Sarot, 181–217. Edinburgh: T&T Clark, 2001.

Borowiak, Craig T. *Accountability and Democracy: The Pitfalls and Promise of Popular Control.* Oxford: Oxford University Press, 2011.

Bradley, A. C. "Hegel's Theory of Tragedy." In *Hegel on Tragedy,* ed. Anne Paolucci and Henry Paolucci. New York: Harper and Row, 1975.

Brandom, Robert B. *Making It Explicit: Reasoning, Representing, and Discursive Commitment.* Cambridge, MA: Harvard University Press, 1994.

———. *Reason in Philosophy: Animating Ideas.* Cambridge, MA: Harvard University Press, 2009.

———. *A Spirit of Trust: A Semantic Reading of Hegel's "Phenomenology."* Draft available at http://www.pitt.edu/~brandom/hegel/index.html. n.d.

———. *Tales of the Mighty Dead: Historical Essays in the Metaphysics of Intentionality*. Cambridge, MA: Harvard University Press, 2002.

Bretherton, Luke. *Resurrecting Democracy: Faith, Citizenship, and the Politics of a Common Life*. Cambridge: Cambridge University Press, 2015.

Bubbio, Paolo Diego. "Sacrifice in Hegel's *Phenomenology of Spirit*." *British Journal of the History of Philosophy* 20:4 (2012): 797–815.

———. *Sacrifice in the Post-Kantian Tradition: Perspectivism, Intersubjectivity, and Recognition*. Albany: State University of New York Press, 2014.

Burbidge, John W. "Hegel's Open Future." In *Hegel and the Tradition: Essays in Honor of H. S. Harris*, ed. Michael Baur and John Russon, 176–89. Toronto: University of Toronto Press, 1997.

Butler, Judith. *Antigone's Claim: Kinship between Life and Death*. New York: Columbia University Press, 2000.

———. *Subjects of Desire: Hegelian Reflections in Twentieth-Century France*. New York: Columbia University Press, 1987.

Connolly, William E. "Agonism, Pluralism, and Contemporary Capitalism: An Interview." Interview by Mark Anthony Wenman. *Contemporary Political Theory* 7 (2008): 200–219.

———. *Identity/Difference: Democratic Negotiations of Political Paradox*. Expanded ed. Minneapolis: University of Minnesota Press, 2002.

———. *The Terms of Political Discourse*. 3rd ed. Princeton: Princeton University Press, 1993.

Crites, Stephen. *Dialectic and Gospel in the Development of Hegel's Thinking*. University Park: Pennsylvania State University Press, 1998.

———. *In the Twilight of Christendom: Hegel vs. Kierkegaard on Faith and History*. Chambersburg, PA: American Academy of Religion, 1972.

de Boer, Karin. "Beyond Tragedy: Tracing the Aristophanian Subtext of Hegel's *Phenomenology of Spirit*." In Hutchings and Pulkkinen, 133–51.

Deligiorgi, Katerina, ed. *Hegel: New Directions*. Montreal: McGill-Queen's University Press, 2006.

Denker, Alfred, and Michael Vater, eds. *Hegel's Phenomenology of Spirit: New Critical Essays*. Amherst, NY: Humanity Books, 2003.

Desmond, William. *Hegel's God: A Counterfeit Double?* Burlington, VT: Ashgate, 2003.

Dickey, Laurence. *Hegel: Religion, Economics, and the Politics of Spirit, 1770–1807*. Cambridge: Cambridge University Press, 1987.

Fackenheim, Emil L. *The Religious Dimension in Hegel's Thought*. Chicago: University of Chicago Press, 1967.

Farneth, Molly. "G. W. F. Hegel" In *Religion and European Philosophy: Key Thinkers from Kant to Žižek*, ed. Philip Goodchild and Hollis Phelps, 31–43. London: Routledge, 2017.

———. " 'The Power to Empty Oneself': Hegel, Kenosis, and Intellectual Virtue." *Political Theology* 18:2 (2017): 157–171.

———. "Rorty and Religion: Beyond the Culture Wars?" In *A Companion to Rorty*, ed. Alan Malachowski. Oxford: Wiley-Blackwell, forthcoming.

Finlayson, J. G. "Conflict and Reconciliation in Hegel's Theory of the Tragic." *Journal of the History of Philosophy* 37:3 (July 1999): 493–520.

Forshay, Raphael. "Tarrying with the Negative: Bataille and Derrida's Reading of Negation in Hegel's *Phenomenology*." *Heythrop Journal* 43:3 (2002): 295–310.

Förster, Eckart. *The Twenty-Five Years of Philosophy: A Systematic Reconstruction*. Trans. Brady Bowman. Cambridge, MA: Harvard University Press, 2012.

Forster, Michael N. *Hegel's Idea of a Phenomenology of Spirit*. Chicago: University of Chicago Press, 1998.

Fossen, Thomas. "Politicizing Brandom's Pragmatism: Normativity and the Agonal Character of Social Practice." *European Journal of Philosophy* 22:3 (2014): 371–95.

Fraser, Nancy. "Recognition without Ethics?" *Theory, Culture & Society* 18:2–3 (2001): 21–42.

Freeman, Jo. "The Tyranny of Structurelessness." *Berkeley Journal of Sociology* 17 (1972–73): 151–64.

Godlove, Terry F., Jr. "Saving Belief: On the New Materialism in Religious Studies." In *Radical Interpretation in Religion*, ed. Nancy K. Frankenberry, 10–24. Cambridge: Cambridge University Press, 2002.

Gottlieb, Michah. *Faith and Freedom: Moses Mendelssohn's Theological-Political Thought.* Oxford: Oxford University Press, 2011.

Grattan, Laura. *Populism's Power: Radical Grassroots Democracy in America*. Oxford: Oxford University Press, 2016.

Harris, H. S. *Hegel's Ladder I: The Pilgrimage of Reason*. Indianapolis: Hackett Publishing, 1997.

———. *Hegel's Ladder II: The Odyssey of Spirit*. Indianapolis: Hackett Publishing, 1997.

Hauerwas, Stanley, and Romand Coles. *Christianity, Democracy, and the Radical Ordinary: Conversations between a Radical Democrat and a Christian*. Eugene, OR: Cascade Books, 2008.

Hector, Kevin W. *Theology without Metaphysics: God, Language, and the Spirit of Recognition*. Cambridge: Cambridge University Press, 2011.

Hegel, G. W. F. *Aesthetics: Lectures on Fine Art.* 2 vols. Trans. T. M. Knox. Oxford: Clarendon Press, 1975.

———. *Early Theological Writings*. Trans. T. M. Knox. With an introduction and fragments translated by Richard Kroner. Philadelphia: University of Pennsylvania Press, 1975.

———. *Elements of the Philosophy of Right*. Ed. Allen W. Wood. Trans. H. B. Nisbit. Cambridge: Cambridge University Press, 1991.

———. *Frühe Schriften*. Werke 1. Ed. Eva Moldenhauer and Karl Markus Michel. Frankfurt am Main: Suhrkamp Verlag, 1971.

———. *Grundlinien der Philosophie des Rechts*. Werke 7. Ed. Eva Moldenhauer and Karl Markus Michel. Frankfurt am Main: Suhrkamp Verlag, 1970.

———. *Hegel: The Letters*. Trans. Clark Butler and Christiane Seiler. Bloomington: Indiana University Press, 1984.

———. *Lectures on the Philosophy of Religion: One-Volume Edition, The Lectures of 1827*. Ed. Peter C. Hodgson. Trans. R. F. Brown, P. C. Hodgson, and J. M. Stewart. Oxford: Clarendon, 2006.

———. *Phänomenologie des Geistes*. Werke 3. Ed. Eva Moldenhauer and Karl Markus Michel. Frankfurt am Main: Suhrkamp Verlag, 1970.

———. *Phenomenology of Spirit*. Trans. A. V. Miller. Oxford: Oxford University Press, 1977.

———. *Phenomenology of Spirit*. With facing-page German and English. Trans. Terry Pinkard. https://www.academia.edu/16699140/Translation_of_Phenomenology_of_Spirit.

———. *Three Essays, 1793–1795*. Ed. and trans. Peter Fuss and John Dobbins. Notre Dame, IN: University of Notre Dame Press, 1984.

Hinchman, Lewis P. *Hegel's Critique of the Enlightenment*. Gainesville: University Presses of Florida, 1984.

Hodgson, Peter C. *Hegel and Christian Theology: A Reading of the Lectures on the Philosophy of Religion*. Oxford: Oxford University Press, 2005.

Hollywood, Amy. "Performativity, Citationality, Ritualization." *History of Religions* 42:2 (2002): 93–115.

———. "Practice, Belief and Feminist Philosophy of Religion." In *Feminist Philosophy of Religion: Critical Readings*, ed. Pamela Sue Anderson and Beverly Clack, 225–40. London: Routledge, 2004.

Honig, Bonnie. *Antigone, Interrupted.* Cambridge: Cambridge University Press, 2013.

———. *Democracy and the Foreigner.* Princeton: Princeton University Press, 2001.

———. *Political Theory and the Displacement of Politics.* Ithaca: Cornell University Press, 1993.

Honneth, Axel. *The Struggle for Recognition: The Moral Grammar of Social Conflicts.* Trans. J. Anderson. Cambridge, MA: MIT Press, 1995.

Houlgate, Stephen. *Freedom, Truth, and History: An Introduction to Hegel's Philosophy.* London: Routledge, 1991.

———. *Hegel's "Phenomenology of Spirit": A Reader's Guide.* London: Bloomsbury, 2003.

Hoy, Jocelyn B. "Hegel, *Antigone*, and Feminist Critique: The Spirit of Ancient Greece." In K. Westphal, 172–89.

Hutchings, Kimberly. *Hegel and Feminist Philosophy.* Cambridge: Polity Press, 2003.

Hutchings, Kimberly, and Tuija Pulkkinen, eds. *Hegel's Philosophy and Feminist Thought: Beyond Antigone?* New York: Palgrave Macmillan, 2010.

Hyppolite, Jean. *Genesis and Structure of Hegel's "Phenomenology of Spirit."* Trans. Samuel Cherniak and John Heckman. Evanston, IL: Northwestern University Press, 1974.

Inwood, Michael. *A Hegel Dictionary.* Oxford: Blackwell, 1992.

Jaeschke, Walter. *Reason in Religion: The Foundations of Hegel's Philosophy of Religion.* Trans. Michael J. Stewart and Peter C. Hodgson. Berkeley: University of California Press, 1990.

Jameson, Fredric. *The Hegel Variations: On the "Phenomenology of Spirit."* London: Verso, 2010.

Kant, Immanuel. *Critique of Pure Reason.* Trans. and ed. Paul Guyer and Allen W. Wood. Cambridge: Cambridge University Press, 1998.

———. *Religion within the Boundaries of Bare Reason.* Trans. Werner S. Pluhar. Indianapolis: Hackett Publishing, 2009.

Kaufmann, Walter. *Tragedy and Philosophy.* Princeton: Princeton University Press, 1968.

Kavka, Martin. "Saying Kaddish for Gillian Rose, or on Levinas and *Geltungsphilosophie.*" In *Secular Theology: American Radical Theological Thought*, ed. Clayton Crockett, 104–29. London: Routledge, 2001.

Keenan, Dennis King. *The Question of Sacrifice.* Bloomington: Indiana University Press, 2005.

Kelly, George Armstrong. "Notes on Hegel's 'Lordship and Bondage.'" In MacIntyre, 189–218.

Kojève, Alexandre. *Introduction to the Reading of Hegel: Lectures on the "Phenomenology of Spirit."* Assembled by Raymond Queneau. Ed. Allan Bloom. Trans. James H. Nichols Jr. Ithaca: Cornell University Press, 1980.

Kolb, David. "What Is Open and What Is Closed in the Philosophy of Hegel." *Philosophical Topics* 19:2 (1991): 29–50.

Lewis, Thomas A. "Beyond the Totalitarian: Ethics and the Philosophy of Religion in Recent Hegel Scholarship." *Religion Compass* 2:4 (2008): 556–74.

———. *Freedom and Tradition in Hegel: Reconsidering Anthropology, Ethics, and Religion.* Notre Dame, IN: University of Notre Dame Press, 2005.

———. "Religion and Demythologization in Hegel's *Phenomenology of Spirit*." In Moyar and Quante, 192–209.

———. "Religion, Reconciliation, and Modern Society: The Shifting Conclusions of Hegel's *Lectures on the Philosophy of Religion.*" *Harvard Theological Review* 106 (2013): 37–60.

———. *Religion, Modernity, and Politics in Hegel.* Oxford: Oxford University Press, 2011.

Lindbeck, George. *The Nature of Doctrine.* Louisville, KY: Westminster John Knox Press, 1984.

Luther, Martin. "The Babylonian Captivity of the Church." In *Luther's Works.* Vol. 36. Philadelphia: Fortress Press, 1959.

———. "Exhortation to Confession." http://bookofconcord.org/exhortationConfession.php.

———. "The Sacrament of Penance." In *Luther's Works.* Vol. 35. Philadelphia: Fortress Press, 1961.

MacIntyre, Alasdair. *After Virtue: A Study in Moral Theory.* Notre Dame, IN: University of Notre Dame Press, 1981.

———. "Epistemological Crises, Dramatic Narrative, and the Philosophy of Science." *The Monist* 60:4 (1977): 453–72.

———, ed. *Hegel: A Collection of Critical Essays.* Notre Dame, IN: University of Notre Dame Press, 1976.

———. *Whose Justice? Which Rationality?* Notre Dame, IN: University of Notre Dame Press, 1988.

Mahmood, Saba. *Politics of Piety: Islamic Revival and the Feminist Subject.* Princeton: Princeton University Press, 2005.

Malabou, Catherine. *The Future of Hegel: Plasticity, Temporality and Dialectic.* Trans. Lisabeth During. New York: Routledge, 2005.

Markell, Patchen. *Bound by Recognition.* Princeton: Princeton University Press, 2003.

———. "The Insufficiency of Non-Domination." *Political Theory* 36:1 (February 2008): 9–36.

Marshall, Bruce D. "Absorbing the World." In *Theology and Dialogue: Essays in Conversation with George Lindbeck.* Notre Dame: University of Notre Dame Press, 1990.

Marshall, David L. "The Implications of Robert Brandom's Inferentialism for Intellectual History." *History and Theory* 52:1 (February 2003): 1–31.

Meckstroth, Christopher. *The Struggle for Democracy: Paradoxes of Progress and the Politics of Change.* Oxford: Oxford University Press, 2015.

Mills, Patricia Jagentowicz, ed. *Feminist Interpretations of G. W. F. Hegel.* University Park: Pennsylvania State University Press, 1996.

Morris, Aldon D. *The Origins of the Civil Rights Movement: Black Communities Organizing for Change.* New York: The Free Press, 1984.

Moyar, Dean. *Hegel's Conscience.* Oxford: Oxford University Press, 2011.

———. "Self-Completing Alienation: Hegel's Argument for Transparent Conditions of Free Agency." In Moyar and Quante, 150–72.

Moyar, Dean, and Michael Quante, eds. *Hegel's "Phenomenology of Spirit": A Critical Guide.* Cambridge: Cambridge University Press, 2008.

Nussbaum, Martha C. *The Fragility of Goodness: Luck and Ethics in Greek Tragedy and Philosophy.* Updated ed. Cambridge: Cambridge University Press, 2001.

Oliver, Kelly. "Antigone's Ghost: Undoing Hegel's *Phenomenology of Spirit.*" *Hypatia* 11:1 (1996): 67–90.

———. *Witnessing.* Minneapolis: University of Minnesota Press, 2001.

———. "Witnessing and Testimony." *Parallax* 10:1 (2004): 79–88.

Olson, Alan M. *Hegel and the Spirit: Philosophy as Pneumatology.* Princeton: Princeton University Press, 1992.

O'Regan, Cyril. *The Heterodox Hegel.* Albany: State University of New York Press, 1994.

———. "The Trinity in Kant, Hegel, and Schelling." In *The Oxford Handbook of the Trinity*, ed. Gilles Emery and Matthew Levering, 254–66. Oxford: Oxford University Press, 2011.

Orlie, Melissa. *Living Ethically, Acting Politically.* Ithaca: Cornell University Press, 1997.

Ostwald, Martin. *Autonomia: Its Early Genesis and History*. Chico, CA: Scholars Press, 1982.

Payne, Charles. *I've Got the Light of Freedom: The Organizing Tradition and the Mississippi Freedom Struggle*. Berkeley: University of California Press, 1997.

Pettit, Philip. *Republicanism: A Theory of Freedom and Government*. Oxford: Oxford University Press, 1997.

Pinkard, Terry. *Hegel: A Biography*. Cambridge: Cambridge University Press, 2000.

———. *Hegel's Phenomenology: The Sociality of Reason*. Cambridge: Cambridge University Press, 1996.

———. "Was Pragmatism the Successor to Idealism?" In *New Pragmatists*, ed. Cheryl Misak, 142–68. Oxford: Oxford University Press, 2007.

———. "What Is a 'Shape of Spirit'?" In Moyar and Quante, 112–29.

Pippin, Robert B. "Back to Hegel?" *Mediations* 26:1 (Fall 2012–Spring 2013): 7–28.

———. "Brandom's Hegel." *European Journal of Philosophy* 13:3 (December 2005): 381–408.

———. "Concept and Intuition: On Distinguishability and Separability." *Hegel-Studien* 40 (2004): 25–39.

———. *Hegel on Self-Consciousness: Desire and Death in the "Phenomenology of Spirit."* Princeton: Princeton University Press, 2011.

———. *Hegel's Idealism: The Satisfactions of Self-Consciousness*. Cambridge: Cambridge University Press, 1989.

———. *Hegel's Practical Philosophy: Rational Agency as Ethical Life*. Cambridge: Cambridge University Press, 2008.

———. "Recognition and Reconciliation: Actualized Agency in Hegel's Jena Phenomenology." In Deligiorgi, 125–42.

Placher, William C. *Unapologetic Theology: A Christian Voice in a Pluralistic Conversation*. Louisville, KY: Westminster/John Knox Press, 1989.

Quante, Michael. *Hegel's Concept of Action*. Trans. Dean Moyar. Cambridge: Cambridge University Press, 2004.

Redding, Paul. *Hegel's Hermeneutics*. Ithaca: Cornell University Press, 1996.

Richardson, Henry S. "Beyond Good and Right: Toward a Constructive Ethical Pragmatism." *Philosophy and Public Affairs* 24:2 (Spring 1995): 108–41.

———. "Institutionally Divided Moral Responsibility." *Social Philosophy and Policy* 16:2 (Summer 1999): 218–49.

Robinson, Marilynne. *When I Was a Child I Read Books*. New York: Farrar, Straus and Giroux, 2012.

Rorty, Richard. "Religion as Conversation-Stopper." In *Philosophy and Social Hope*, 168–74. London: Penguin, 1999.

Rose, Gillian. *Hegel Contra Sociology*. London: Verso, 2009.

Sedgwick, Sally. *Hegel's Critique of Kant: From Dichotomy to Identity*. Oxford: Oxford University Press, 2012.

Solomon, Robert C. *In the Spirit of Hegel*. Oxford: Oxford University Press, 1983.

Sophocles. *Antigone*. Trans. Paul Woodruff. Indianapolis: Hackett Publishing, 2001.

Speight, C. Allen. "Butler and Hegel on Forgiveness and Agency." *Southern Journal of Philosophy* 43 (2005): 299–316.

Springs, Jason, ed. "Pragmatism and Democracy: Assessing Jeffrey Stout's *Democracy and Tradition*." *Journal of the American Academy of Religion* 78:2 (June 2010): 413–48.

Stern, Robert. *Hegelian Metaphysics*. Oxford: Oxford University Press, 2009.

———. *The Routledge Guidebook to Hegel's "Phenomenology of Spirit."* London: Routledge, 2013.

Stewart, Jon. *The Unity of Hegel's "Phenomenology of Spirit": A Systematic Interpretation.* Evanston, IL: Northwestern University Press, 2000.

Stolzenberg, Jürgen. "Hegel's Critique of the Enlightenment in 'The Struggle of the Enlightenment with Superstition.'" In K. Westphal, 190–208.

Stout, Jeffrey. *Blessed Are the Organized: Grassroots Democracy in America.* Princeton: Princeton University Press, 2010.

———. *Democracy and Tradition.* Princeton: Princeton University Press, 2004.

———. *Ethics after Babel: The Languages of Morals and Their Discontents.* Princeton: Princeton University Press, 1988.

———. "Rorty on Religion and Politics." In *The Philosophy of Richard Rorty*, ed. Randall E. Auxier and Lewis Edward Hahn. Chicago: Open Court, 2010.

———. "The Spirit of Pragmatism: Bernstein's Variations on Hegelian Themes." *Graduate Faculty Philosophy Journal* 33:1 (2012): 185–246.

———. "What Is It That Absolute Knowing Knows?" *Journal of Religion* 95:2 (April 2015): 163–82.

Taylor, Charles. *Hegel.* Cambridge: Cambridge University Press, 1975.

———. *Hegel and Modern Society.* 1979. Reprint, Cambridge: Cambridge University Press, 2015.

———. "The Politics of Recognition." In *Multiculturalism: Examining the Politics of Recognition*, ed. Amy Gutmann. Princeton: Princeton University Press, 1994.

Waldron, Jeremy. "Accountability: Fundamental to Democracy." Public Law Research Paper No. 14-13, New York University School of Law. Available at SSRN: http://dx.doi.org/10.2139/ssrn.2410812.

Walker, Margaret Urban. *Moral Repair: Reconstructing Moral Relations after Wrongdoing.* Cambridge: Cambridge University Press, 2006.

Warren, Mark R. *Dry Bones Rattling: Community Building to Revitalize American Democracy.* Princeton: Princeton University Press, 2001.

Wendte, Martin. *Gottmenschliche Einheit bei Hegel: Eine Logische und Theologische Untersuchung.* Berlin: Walter de Gruyter, 2007.

Werpehowski, William. "Ad Hoc Apologetics." *Journal of Religion* 66:3 (1986): 282–301.

Westphal, Kenneth R., ed. *The Blackwell Guide to Hegel's "Phenomenology of Spirit."* Chichester: Wiley-Blackwell, 2009.

Westphal, Merold. "Hegel and Onto-Theology." *Bulletin of the Hegel Society of Great Britain* 41/42 (2000): 142–65.

———. *History and Truth in Hegel's "Phenomenology."* 3rd ed. Bloomington: Indiana University Press, 1998.

Williams, Robert R. *Hegel's Ethics of Recognition.* Berkeley: University of California Press, 1997.

———. *Tragedy, Recognition, and the Death of God: Studies in Hegel & Nietzsche.* Oxford: Oxford University Press, 2012.

Wolterstorff, Nicholas. "Exercising One's Political Voice as a Moral Engagement." In *Understanding Liberal Democracy: Essays in Political Philosophy*, 143–73. Oxford: Oxford University Press, 2012.

———. *Justice in Love.* Grand Rapids, MI: Eerdmans, 2011.

Wood, Allen W. *Hegel's Ethical Thought.* Cambridge: Cambridge University Press, 1990.

Žižek, Slavoj. *Less than Nothing: Hegel and the Shadow of Dialectical Materialism.* London: Verso, 2012.

INDEX

abortion debate, 102, 112–13

absolute, the: emergent character of, 96–97; end of conflict not required by, 98; philosophy and spirit as, 92–95; reconciliation of substance and subject in, 83–86; religion, philosophy, and, 81–83; religion and God as, 86–92, 96

absolute knowing, 3, 92–98

absolute spirit: closure and, 11; confession and forgiveness and, 75–76; contemporary interpreters of Hegel on, 6–9; emergence of, 6, 72–73; epistemological and ethical implications of concept of, 81; meaning of, 76, 81; reciprocal recognition as, 82 (*see also* reciprocal recognition); tragic conflict in paradigmatic form of ethical confrontation in, impossibility of, 33–34

accountability: agent, 119; in democratic communities, 119–23, 125, 129, 149n12; domination and absence of, 57; of fellow citizens, 131; normativity and, 48; as ongoing, 118–19; recognition, as aspect of, 81, 97, 118, 130; subject as locus of authority and, 4, 17, 33–34, 58, 76–77, 82, 85, 89, 114, 118, 126, 128

action: the acknowledgment of guilt and, 21–28; conscience and, 61–62, 64; wicked and judging consciousnesses and, 66–70

Adorno, Theodor, 11

Aesthetics (Hegel), 135n5, 138n28

agonism, 99, 102, 105, 107–13, 117, 125, 127–28

alienation: account of, account of intention and, 49–50; of Faith and Enlightenment from actual existence in the world, 45–51; of the judging consciousness, 68; relationship of the legal person and the community as, 38–39; social dimensions of, 50

Allen, Danielle, 136n13

anerkennen/Anerkennung, 26, 57. *See also* recognition

Anscombe, G. E. M., 49

Antigone (Sophocles): action and the acknowledgement of guilt, 21–28; Antigone as representative of "woman" and "kinship," 17–18; character and conflict in, 19–21; confession and forgiveness section and discussion of, similarities between, 72–73; feminist ethics and, development of, 28–32; the law, references to, 135–36n6; one-sided and fixed characters of, 78, 84; the plot of, 18–19; social ethics and, development of, 32–34; tragic conflict in, 32–33. *See also* Greek *Sittlichkeit*

Arendt, Hannah, 115–16, 150n34

authority: Arendt on the disappearance of, 115–16; as aspect of recognition, 81, 97, 118, 130; democratic (*see* democratic authority); in modern life, Hegel's account of what is required for, 116; subject as locus of accountability and, 4, 17, 33–34, 58, 76–77, 82, 85, 89, 114, 118, 126, 128

Baker, Ella, 123–24, 131

Bataille, Georges, 146n15

Battle of Jena, 1

beautiful soul, 65, 70, 77, 142n20

Beerbohm, Eric, 149n12

Beiser, Frederick, 95–96, 134n10, 142n20, 144n3

Bellah, Robert, 138–39n2

Benhabib, Seyla, 31–32

Bernstein, J. M., 77–79

Bernstein, Richard J., 9

Boehme, Jacob, 145n12

Borowiak, Craig, 119

Bourdieu, Pierre, 9

Brandom, Robert: on actions and commitments, 48–49; *de dicto* and *de re* ascriptions, distinction between, 147n29; on Faith and Enlightenment,

A NOTE ON THE TYPE

{⚘⚘⚘}

THIS BOOK has been composed in Miller, a Scotch Roman typeface designed by Matthew Carter and first released by Font Bureau in 1997. It resembles Monticello, the typeface developed for The Papers of Thomas Jefferson in the 1940s by C. H. Griffith and P. J. Conkwright and reinterpreted in digital form by Carter in 2003.

Pleasant Jefferson ("P. J.") Conkwright (1905–1986) was Typographer at Princeton University Press from 1939 to 1970. He was an acclaimed book designer and AIGA Medalist.

The ornament used throughout this book was designed by Pierre Simon Fournier (1712–1768) and was a favorite of Conkwright's, used in his design of the *Princeton University Library Chronicle*.